ISBN 978-0-282-75317-7
PIBN 10125371

1 MONTH OF
FREE
READING

at

www.ForgottenBooks.com

By purchasing this book you are
eligible for one month membership to
ForgottenBooks.com, giving you
unlimited access to our entire
collection of over 1,000,000 titles via
our web site and mobile apps.

To claim your free month visit:

www.forgottenbooks.com/free125371

English
Français
Deutsche
Italiano
Español
Português

www.forgottenbooks.com

Mythology Photography **Fiction**
Fishing Christianity **Art** Cooking
Essays Buddhism Freemasonry
Medicine **Biology** Music **Ancient**
Egypt Evolution Carpentry Physics
Dance Geology **Mathematics** Fitness
Shakespeare **Folklore** Yoga Marketing
Confidence Immortality Biographies
Poetry **Psychology** Witchcraft
Electronics Chemistry History **Law**
Accounting **Philosophy** Anthropology
Alchemy Drama Quantum Mechanics
Atheism Sexual Health **Ancient History**
Entrepreneurship Languages Sport
Paleontology Needlework Islam
Metaphysics Investment Archaeology
Parenting Statistics Criminology
Motivational

THE

ENGLISH AT HOME

BY

ALPHONSE ESQUIROS.

TRANSLATED AND EDITED BY

LASCELLES WRAXALL.

IN TWO VOLUMES.

VOL. II.

LONDON:

CHAPMAN AND HALL, 193, PICCADILLY.

MDCCCLXI.

1868. Aug. 17.

Lane Fund

CONTENTS TO VOL. II.

CHAPTER XIII.

CHAPTER XIV.

CHAPTER XV.

THE ENGLISH AT HOME.

CHAPTER I.

MINOR TRADES—THE STREET WORLD—THE COSTERMONGERS—BIL-
LINGSGATE MARKET — SALES BY AUCTION — OYSTER-STREET—THE
EEL BOATS—RODWAY'S COFFEE-HOUSE—COVENT-GARDEN MARKET—
FRUITS AND VEGETABLES—STALL-MONGERS—ITINERANT DEALERS.

WITH the name of Great Britain is naturally associated the idea of trade and commerce. The wooden walls not only defend the British coasts from any foreign invader, but they also guard on the seas the produce of the most distant countries, and throw over it the ægis of the Union Jack. Docks, to which all the riches of the world know the road; manufactories in which water, iron, and fire rest neither day nor night; mercantile palaces; banks in which the gold streams through the hands of the cashiers—all announces the victory of labour over matter. Still, the natural succession of these essays does not lead me towards this

great trade supported on navigation, the count-
less manufactures, and the mines whose wealth
the English have ransacked. I have in view
another more obscure branch of trade, very extensive, however, and which ramifies through the
humblest classes of English society. If I attach
myself principally to the lower zones of social life,
it is because the originality of the Anglo-Saxon
race is principally found in them. Those who
pass Faubourg Saint Germain or Chausée d'Antin
evenings in the West-end circles, only effect a
change of drawing-rooms. You find there, with
but slight shades, the same habits, and often the
same tongue, for the educated English like to talk
French with Frenchmen : it is no longer the same,
however, when you descend to the deep strata of
society, or, as geologists would say, the primitive rock.

Hitherto history has forgotten to tell us how
peoples live : the annual government reports of
England, though so rich in details as to some
branches of the higher trades, are silent, or nearly
so, on the subject of the minor trades of London.
The only earnest inquiry into the condition of
these humble means of getting a livelihood was
commenced in 1851 by Mr. Henry Mayhew,* and

* It is cheering to hear that the great work, "London Labour
and the London Poor," is now in the course of completion. Such a
monument to human intellect and perseverance Mr. Mayhew owed it
to himself to finish, if only to show how much one earnest thinker
can effect on behalf of suffering humanity.—L. W.

yet the street world, as some English economists call it, has for centuries offered a stage of curious facts, peculiar manners, and more or less nomadic tribes, which deserved something better than silence.

The small trades of London are divisible into three very distinct classes : those who sell, those who seek, and those who clean. The sellers hold the useful trades, such as street sellers; the finders have the solitary trades; while the cleaners represent what may be termed the " social trades."

At the head of the dealers who sell in the public streets stands the costermonger. Originally, the coster or costard-monger was, as his name indicates, an apple-seller, but his trade is now very far from being limited to that winter produce, and he sells every sort of comestibles. It would be difficult for me to follow, through the immensity of London, the movements of a floating army which invades the streets, the squares, the suburbs, and the lanes, if there were no meeting points in existence among them. To study the manners of the costers, we will therefore at once select one of their head-quarters, where they assemble on certain days if only for a few hours, and whence they radiate over the whole extent of the British metropolis. These centres of reunion are the chief London markets, as, for instance, Billingsgate and Covent-garden.

Knowing that Billingsgate market opened at a

very early hour, I rose on the morning of June 30th
before the sun.   London was slumbering, while
the church steeples, answering each others' challenge, like sentries, in the calm and limpid matin
air, proclaimed with their bronze voice the hour
of half-past three.   I crossed London-bridge, and
from this spot the view was majestic; one portion
of the sky was opaline, and the moon was being
effaced in this whiteness, while on the other side
the heavens were already gilded by the first beams
of the rising sun.   The city, enfolded in the morning dawn as in a garment, stood out silently on
the banks of the Thames; the houses border-
ing the river slumbered; on the old wharfs, idle
chains and ropes hung from the huge cranes at
either verge of the horizon.   St. Paul's and the
Tower of London seemed to be dreaming in a
misty light.   The Thames itself, which the English
call the busiest river in the world, was at rest;
not being troubled at this hour by the movement
of the penny boats, those water omnibuses which
traverse and agitate its surface during the day, it
flowed on as it listed, thick but calm.   I had
never seen such a prodigy: London-bridge without a crowd or a stream of carriages!   Morning,
that fresh and embalmed youth of the day, is an
hour unknown to the majority of the denizens of
the great city: the few passers-by stared at each
other in surprise, and on the stone seats raised at
intervals along the bridge, poor girls, who had,

perhaps, passed the night in the open air, were
hiding their heads beneath their rags, as if afraid
to present themselves to the virgin beams of dawn.

When I came opposite the Monument, I discovered a file of carts extending the whole length
of Fish-street-hill, and continued in the adjoining
streets, often even in the most mysterious and narrow passages. This uniform line was only interrupted at intervals by large two-horse vans, of a
different character, and necessarily belonging to
a different branch of the same trade. I entered
Lower Thames-street: the fishmongers' shops,
widely opening on the street by day, windowless
and doorless, were still shut up in their wooden
coverings, or, as an Englishman said to me, in
their nightgowns. These large storehouses were
once on a time only stalls, which have gradually
grown into houses. I at length found myself in
front of Billingsgate. This market, built of brick
with iron arches, is better-looking on the water
than on the land side. A rather neat clock-tower
is there the landmark of the vessels that arrive
from Hartlepool, Whitstable, Great Grimsby, and
other English ports and fisheries. Before becoming a market, Billingsgate was a port, where, according to Stow, vessels unloaded fish, shell-fish,
salt, onions, and fruit; and its name has considerably puzzled the knowledge of English antiquaries. Some assert, that Bilin, king of the Britons,
about 400 years B.C., built here a water-gate, to

which he gave his name, and that, on his death, his ashes were placed over the edifice in a sort of stone obelisk. This origin is now regarded as fabulous, and it is generally believed that the name of Billingsgate is derived from one of the old owners of this quay. I was besides, I confess, more curious to study the present history of the market than venture into the field of London antiquities.

I had chosen a Friday, that day in the week when Billingsgate most merits the attention of the observer, and for this there is a religious and a social motive. In the poorest districts of London a great number of Irish reside, who follow the commandments of the Roman Church; on the other hand, English workmen, being paid every Saturday, generally find themselves very short of money on the penultimate day of the week. Fish is, therefore, bought in the streets on Friday evening, both by those who fast, and by those who are obliged to fast, according to English notions. As the market was not yet opened, I amused myself with examining, along with the crowd, the rich turbots, the salmon with their pearly scales, and the white-mouthed haddocks, which were being unloaded and piled on the wharfs. Maritime nations like fish, not only as food, but also as an object of art, and English poets have given the name of a " mackerel sky" to the blue ether dotted with white cloudlets.

A young fishwife, seeing me observe the contrasts between the lobsters in their natural robe and in their cardinal's gown, said to me, with a laugh: "It is to show us how handsome we become after being boiled in death's caldron." Shell-fish and crustaceans, the fresh morning air laden with a marine smell, the quivering of the vessels' rigging, still damp with salt water,—all reminded me of the shores of ocean. To complete the illusion, from the neighbouring streets and gloomy passages, like Dark-house-lane, could be heard the bellowing of the crowd, which rapidly increased, and resounded like the voice of mighty waters.

The eight auctioneers attached to Billingsgate market had met between three and four o'clock at one of the principal taverns, in order to consult about the quantity and quality of the fish they were going to put up for sale. At five o'clock they went to their official desks, and the sale began. Before each box enormous baskets were piled up, filled with the *frutti di mare*, and known by the name of " doubles," each containing from three to four dozen fish, and the purchasers are not allowed to inspect the wares before bidding. Hitherto the market had only been attended by the great London fish-dealers and a few rich " bummarees"—the crowd of small buyers kept aloof. I do not allude, besides, to the salmon and trout, which are not submitted to

the humiliating trial of being cried; these aristocratic fish are sold at so much the pound by private contract. When the dealers, known as the
" regular fishmongers," had picked the flower of
the market, there was a movement resembling a
high tide—what the English call a rush. It had
just gone six o'clock, and that is the moment
when the costers bravely enter the ring. The
bidding places were soon besieged by a multitude
in coarse velveteen waistcoats and caps—for the
number of costers frequenting Billingsgate is
from three to four thousand in winter, from
two thousand five hundred to two thousand eight
hundred in summer, and they buy one-third of
the fish brought to market. Some branches of
this trade are, indeed, entirely in their hands, and
among them a tall, thin, greasy man, with a red
and yellow handkerchief round his neck, was
pointed out to me, who buys from fifteen to
eighteen doubles every morning. This piscatorial
Rothschild resides in Somers Town. He sells a
great portion of his merchandise to the fried-fish-
shops. Billingsgate market was at this moment a
Babel, in which what I may call a competition
of tongues was going on. Above the tumult of
voices rose the cries of the salesmen, who,
mounted on tables, and wearing white aprons,
looked down on the mob, and yelled the prices.
I was struck by the reflecting air that appeared
on the hard and coarse features of the men,

women, even girls, that followed the biddings, that gravely contrasted with the scene of disorder and confusion offered by the market. Porters in linen jackets bent beneath the weight of monstrous baskets piled on their backs, and opened a passage through the crowd by shouts of "Move on there!"

The covered part of the market is not the only place where the sales go on. The customers have given the name of Oyster-street to a row of fishing-boats tied up along the front of the building. It is situated slightly beneath the level of the market, and you go down by ladders leading to a floating wharf, which rises and falls with the tide. Some twenty boats were anchored here, and on seeing their high decks loaded with a multitude of men and women, I could not help fancying they must sink before me. A man, of whom all that can be seen is a red nightcap appearing and disappearing, brings the oysters out of the hold with a shovel; another measures them in a vessel, while the sailors in their Guernsey frocks sit on the bulwarks carelessly smoking their morning pipe. The buyer cannot carry his oysters ashore himself: he must place them in the hands of the regular shore-men. There are also mussels and other shell-fish brought to market in sacks; and at last I discovered through the haze a number of vessels with polished oak sides, and whose shape indicated a

Dutch origin. These were the eel-boats, and were surrounded by skiffs loaded with buyers. At each order the master of the fishing-boat—a Dutchman—thrust a sort of net into a tank, and brought up a cluster of eels: the buyers examined them carefully, and had to beat down the price. This market on the water is one of the most interesting and lively scenes in London. When I passed through Billingsgate market again the auction was nearly over, and I only saw in obscure nooks parties engaged in dividing the lots of fish. The costers generally club together the money to pay for the fish, and then divide the purchase among them in bags and baskets. It was now half-past nine—the breakfast hour.

Leaving their wealth of the day to the care of Heaven and the policemen, the street-sellers dispersed; and I followed a large body of them to a house well known to the costers, Rodway's coffee-house, where a man can breakfast for twopence. I entered a large room surrounded by tables, and where more than fifteen hundred persons were taking their morning meal; the assembly was silent, and all faces announced the arrival of the solemn hour which precedes the great affair of the street life—namely, the sale. The few words I was enabled to catch were not English: I remarked on this to one of my neighbours—whose face seemed the least repulsive—and asked him if his comrades were foreigners. He began laugh-

ing, and answered, "We talk slang when together; it is understood by neither swells nor policemen, nor Irish, and that is lucky, for those people
have nothing to do with our affairs."

After the breakfast, which was hurried, the
crowd of costers scattered through the various quarters of London. It was interesting to notice their
means of transport: the poorest had trucks which
they dragged themselves, the greater number had
a donkey-cart, while the most favoured by fortune
possessed a pony. The harness of these draught
animals varied according to the social condition
of the costers; some had ornaments of copper, or
wood, or varnished leather, while others were fastened to the carts by wretched cords. The best
possible understanding appeared to prevail between master and animal, and I saw more than
one street-seller sharing with his donkey or pony
the lump of bread he had saved from his breakfast.

While Billingsgate market is the sphere of the
costermongers who sell fish to the working classes,
Covent-garden is the gathering-place of those who
carry fruit and vegetables for sale round London.
At the spot where the market is now built was formerly a large garden belonging to Westminster
Abbey, and the same spot, dear to Pomona, which
once supplied the table of the monks, is now expected to provide for the nourishment of that
ogre called London. The green-market ought to

be visited at six o'clock on Saturday morning, and as the quarter is principally inhabited by artists and the theatrical world, I found the blinds still carefully drawn down over all the windows. All these slumbering people are replaced in the street by the valiant and early rising country folk, and by costers, who have invaded the approaches of the market from Long-acre to the Strand, from Bow-street to Bedford-street. There is opportunity for admiring here, too, that distribution of labour introduced by social life: those who supply the London markets and streets are awake in the morning for those who will be awake at night. As you advance through the waves of the crowd, you see around you nothing but pyramids of baskets filled with fruit, and mountains of vegetables heaped on other mountains. Enormous vans which have travelled the whole night groan beneath the walls of cabbages, over whose erection a skilful hand has presided. It is not without some difficulty that you reach Covent-garden market, properly so called: there are no cries as at Billingsgate, but a lengthened murmur, resembling the buzzing of an immense hive, spreads along. Men in all sorts of costumes, from the coster in his coarse corduroy clothes to the greengrocer in his blue apron, succeed each other in this garden, where Nature lays all her offerings at the feet of civilisation. The market people walk up and down, with their eyes fixed on the produce, and their brow laden with thought and calculation. Through all this movement pass athletic porters with columns of round baskets on their heads, and young flower-girls buried beneath violets; these cut-flowers typify the existence of the seller, fresh and blooming, but with no root in life, and condemned to run about the streets of London, where beauty soon fades. It has been calculated that two thousand men with carts, and three thousand women with "shallows," visit Covent-garden market on a Saturday morning, especially in summer; the costers purchase about one-third of the fruit and vegetables. No credit is given them, for the salesmen regard them as slippery customers, here to-day and gone to-morrow. The market and neighbouring streets were filled on my visit in July with peas, strawberries, raspberries, and aromatic herbs, whose smell reminded me of green fields; all that was wanting was the song of the birds. It must also be mentioned that all the British islands, Belgium, Holland, France, and even the Southern countries, had contributed to the richness of the market by offering their produce to the Queen city, and a great part of these fruits and vegetables had crossed the sea. At the north-west angle of the market, from the corner of King-street to the entrance of the great avenue, ran a parterre of potted flowers; these common flowers, which, however, are worth many more pretentious ones—roses, geraniums, pinks, mignionette—were destined to be carried about London streets on trucks. The costers swap them frequently for old clothes in the poorest quarters of the town, in alleys without air and sun, where these flowers, exposed on the sill of a gloomy window, seem at any rate to recal an idea of nature. The Semiramis of these hanging gardens is generally a needlewoman. English moralists are fond of alluding to the development which the trade in potted flowers has lately taken in the populous quarters, and they support their assertion on the testimony of a beggar who said, " I am never afraid of rapping at the door of a house when I see a flower-pot in the window, for I am sure a good soul lives there, and to find an odour of charity."

Beneath the arcades running round the market another interesting scene was going on: against some of the low and wide pillars coffee-stalls were standing. Monstrous tin cans poured forth for each comer a black and steaming liquid, while enormous piles of bread-and-butter appeased the appetites, sharpened by the morning air. These *cafés* are protected against the breeze, especially in winter, by screens and cloths thrown over them, and in these improvised parlours the customers breakfast on stools and chairs. But London is by this time hungry, for it is nine or ten o'clock. In all the streets adjoining the market the procession of carts sets in motion, and even on the steps of the churches and the theatres you could see little barefooted girls gravely occupied in dividing into penny bundles the vegetables purchased at Covent-garden. They have come a long distance with a few coins knotted in the corner of their shawls; and they have yet to walk many miles through the cruel streets of London, and perambulate the most obscure alleys, only too happy if by the end of the day they make a little profit.

We have seen that the great fish-market took place on Friday at Billingsgate, because that day marked low water in the households of the working classes; but the principal vegetable market is held on Saturday at Covent-garden for a very different reason. On Saturday evening the English workman receives the reward for his week's toil, and it is also the moment to lay in his provisions. It is curious to visit at that time certain wide and populous streets of old London. Such, for instance, as Whitechapel-road: it is rather a fair than a market. Hundreds on hundreds of little stalls are drawn up on either side the street, and each of these shops has at least one light. The candles burning in a paper lantern, the round and dazzling globes of the tea-dealers, the gas-jets pouring forth torrents of fire, and flickering gas over the butchers' shops, and which, from a distance, colour the atmosphere with a ruddy tinge like the aurora borealis; the confusion of cries, the eager movement of the crowd, the number of trucks striving to force a passage through the medley,—all this imparts a strange character to the night scene, before which you would like to see old Hogarth standing, pencil and sketch-book in hand.

It will now be more easy for us to give a general idea of the costermongering class of London, which is estimated at forty thousand persons, men, women, and children. Some are stationary, others nomadic: those who fix themselves at certain localities, go by the name of stall-mongers; those who wander, as itinerant dealers. In the latter family there are legitimate and illegitimate children: the legitimate — of course I do not mean by birth—are the regular costers who sell all kinds of fish, vegetables, and native fruits: the illegitimate carry about London oranges, chesnuts, Spanish nuts, and cocoa nuts: they are also the dealers in water-cresses, sprats, and periwinkles. Nothing can equal the sublime disdain the regular costers entertain for the bastardised branches of street trade: sooner than descend to such indignities, they' would die of hunger. The orange season is called by them ironically " the Irish harvest." Here we find the root of a curious prejudice which prevails among a certain class against exotic and perfumed fruits: the street sale of oranges is almost entirely in the hands of the Irish; that of cocoa-nuts is, in great measure, left to the Jews.

The street world is composed of three elements, which, besides, soon become blended : those born in it, those brought into it by inclination, and lastly, those who had been forced into it by circumstances. The true costermongers mingle but little with the other classes of the population, and the result is, that they adhere closely to their habits and mode of life. This numerous family has a tendency to increase with the hardness of the times; the frequent stoppages in various branches of trade and bad years exercise a marked influence on the development of selling in the streets. During the famine which desolated Ireland fourteen years ago, the floating population of Irish sellers in the streets was nearly doubled.

Another cause—natural and much less afflicting—which helps annually to increase the group of street-dealers, is the great number of children who take to their father's trade at a very early age. The street-sellers form a very ancient social family, in which hereditary descent has been clearly traced. 'Nomadic trade preceded fixed trade, and it is not the itinerant dealers but the shopkeepers who are modern. Comic authors have borrowed from the costermongers of olden times one or two types which they have introduced on the English stage. Socially, this class deserves to fix our attention, for the costers, poor themselves, are the purveyors of the poor; these useful intermediaries add a value to the objects produced, by distributing them and saving the time of the small consumers. For some years, however, the street-dealers of London have considered themselves a persecuted caste: these wandering tribes are harried by the City police much in the same way as the red-skins were followed up by the immigrants in America. The crusade against the apple-sellers, the war on baskets and trucks, is an event which agitates the minds of a numerous populace much more than does a Crimean or Italian campaign. Still, it is this proscribed, wretched, and too often degraded family, which maintains the prosperity of the great London markets: the value of the fish and fruit sold by their obscure hands in the streets of London, is estimated at more than two hundred thousand pounds a year. The precarious and menaced situation of the costers, the importance of their trade dealings, the manly obstinacy with which they endure this combat of life, which ends each night only to begin again with the morrow, and the real services they give the working classes, all combine to render the character and manners of these street-sellers an interesting subject of study.

CHAPTER II.

ENGLISH COSTERS—THEIR RELIGION—REV. W. ROGERS—MAHOGANY
BAR—THE LIFE OF A COSTER—THE POLICE—IRISH STREET-SELLERS
—THE CHOLERA—PEDLARS AND HAWKERS—GENTEEL POVERTY—
THE PATTERERS—CHEAP JACK—THE STREET-BOOKSELLER—HENRY
MAYHEW—SOCIAL IMPROVEMENT OF COSTERS.

THE costermongers of London belong to two
distinct races, the English and Irish. The English
costers reside in courts and alleys in the vicinity
of the various London markets, and those localities
in which a colony of street-sellers is established
are known to themselves by the name of the coster
districts. Their domicile generally consists of a
room in which they boil their shell-fish, smoke
sprats, steam oranges, trim apples, and sleep all
together — men, women, and children. Such a
place offers, as may be supposed, but slight
attractions, and hence their home is the street,
the beer-shop, and the market. It is calculated
that only one-third of the costers have a capital
of their own; some borrow the money to buy
their daily stock, others the stock itself; many,

again, hire their basket shallows, truck, or donkey-cart, while some even hire their weights and scales. The interest of money lent generally amounts to twenty per cent. per week. The most sad thing is, that this iniquitous tax does not fall only on the street-sellers, but also on the poor classes whom the costers supply with provisions: the public food is, therefore, in great measure tributary to the usurers. Taken as a body, the nomadic dealers form an ignorant class, and only one in ten can read. A child is hardly able to walk ere it follows its father's or mother's truck: these children grow old quickly, and by the age of seven are thorough business people. You are amazed to find in them, by the side of the deepest ignorance, great readiness of mind, judgment, and a marvellous trade knowledge in a certain line. The English costers do not avowedly belong to the English Church, or any sect, but it must not be concluded from this that they are utter strangers to religious sentiment. What touches them most in the Gospels—of which they know very little, however—is the history of Our Saviour feeding so many poor people, and giving each of them a barley-loaf and two small fishes. "That proves," they add simply, "that he was a thorough gentle-man." The girls thank Heaven for a fine day and for sprats, which they declare a present sent direct thence to the poor. In 1850, the street-sellers were nearly all Chartists; but the most distinct political opinion I have been able to find among them now, is a hatred of the administrative regulations concerning themselves: with them, the Government is personified in the policeman and the Lord Mayor of London.

The itinerant costers follow in their wanderings through town a regular line, from which they never diverge. Generally they seek dark alleys and poor quarters, for in these places they do most business. In addition to their regular rounds, they make chance visits to the suburbs, where they expect to find customers. Finally, most of them experience from time to time a longing for change of air, and then venture into the country. These country rounds sometimes last weeks and entire months, and some have been known to extend their wanderings one hundred miles from London. Like all the errant classes, the costers are attached to the bitter, painful, and laborious life they lead, by ties which it is impossible to sever. A few years back, a literary gentleman, struck by the heroic struggles a young street-seller daily made in London streets in order to support her mother, took her into his house as servant. The transition was painful for the bird free yesterday, caged to-day: as from her earliest years she had walked barefooted about the streets, shoes were a torture to this poor creature, and at night, when she had finished her work, she would ask leave to take a little recreation—that is, remove her shoes. Kindly attentions, and the advantages of a comfortable life, reconciled her for a while with captivity, but one day she heard it stated that sprats had come to market, and at the news her heart bounded, as if there were in that fish a magic spell, a talisman—she asked her master's leave, while thanking him, to return to the streets.

The costermonger's profits are generally very small, and subject to disastrous chances. The sellers of water-cresses, oranges, onions, and apples, who generally carry their stock in a basket, earn on an average twopence to threepence a day. The sellers of garden plants, flowers, fruits, and fresh fish, gain about tenpence profit, but from this small sum losses entailed by the deterioration of the produce have, in too many cases, to be deducted. There are, however, street-dealers who raise themselves above wretchedness by the exercise of energy and temperance, though, unhappily, the last virtue is by no means one of those that run about London streets. The Rev. W. Rogers, at a lecture I heard two years ago at the Society of Arts, attributed the great distress of the street-dealers much more to their improvidence and dissipation than to the notorious insufficiency of their profits; and he told, in support of his opinion, an anecdote which produced a laugh. One day, while visiting a house in his parish, he heard somebody singing coming up the first-floor stairs. Surprised by his joyous accent, which contrasted with the sinister appearance of the place, he made some excuse to enter the room, where he found a little man with a very contented face, surrounded by baskets of excellent fruit, which he was arranging with some display of taste. "You seem to me happy," said Mr. Rogers. "Yes, sir, I am so," the owner of the room answered, with a light heart; "God has been good to me." "What has happened to you, then?" "I have lost my old woman, and since it pleased God to take her from me, I have always been a happy man." He added, pointing to his riches, "You see those fruits; they are all mine and paid for. I have already saved up 20l., and it is my intention this summer to buy a cart and pony, and carry on in a grand style." "Very good; but what can all that have to do with the death of your wife?" "Everything, sir, for she drank and ruined me. Eighteen months ago, I had not a stick of furniture, not even a bed to lie on; now you see how I am. God bless you, sir, if I go on long in this way, I shall soon become a gentleman."

I was most desirous to obtain from the lips of the costers themselves some information as to their mode of life, and one of them, an intelligent and open-hearted man, gave me the meeting for the next Monday night, at a tavern known by the name of "Mahogany Bar," a rather wicked place, I confess, where the male and female street-sellers collect to hear music. His history, which he told me in the pauses of the concert, was, with a few slight variations, that of all the street-sellers.

"I don't know," he said to me, "when or where I was born; after all, it would do me no good to know it. All I can remember is, that we were three brothers and two sisters, who went about London selling. Don't suppose that it takes much money to set up a child, for a bushel of potatoes is generally sufficient. We brought back at night, to our parents, all we had been able to earn during the day. The most unhappy of us all, and the one I loved the best, was my youngest sister: at the age of seven, she carried about water-cresses in a basket. I don't call that a way of getting a livelihood though, but only a slow death by starvation. More than one night she did not dare return home, because she had not got together the few halfpence expected from her for her board and lodging, though Heaven knows the poor girl was not dainty, and did not cost much to support. One day I found her in an empty yard picking up a piece of bread which the servants had probably thrown out for the birds. 'Nonsense,' she said to me, laughing; 'surely I can eat it, if the birds eat it. It is not stealing, is it, to take a few crumbs from creatures which have wings, and can go and feed in the wheat-fields without fear of the policeman?'

"Being the eldest, I usually accompanied my

father on his rounds, and it was he who instructed
me. I never learned to read and write; my
school was the street and the market, and it is
certain that with eyes and ears you can grow
acquainted with the things of this world. My
life, however, was not a very easy one, for in
summer I had to be up by four in the morning.
As I was nearly thirteen, and felt my wings
sprouting, I began to have a craving for my
liberty, for that is a critical age with the lads of
our class. One day I quarrelled with my father,
and left the nest in which my family brooded.
After all, my father was sorry for it, for in our
rounds my young shrill voice was better heard
than his male and hoarse one. He had been
rather harsh to me, but then the poor fellow was
the same to himself. I borrowed six shillings
and a truck: that was enough to make my way
in the world, for though I had neither gold nor
silver, I had plenty of brass. There is nothing
like having a street-seller's blood in your veins.
Those who are not born to the trade make poor
costers: at market they don't know how to make
a bid, and have no confidence in themselves or
fortune. When about sixteen, I began to grow
tired of a solitary life, and the idea occurred to
me of taking a wife. So I went one evening to a
dancing-room, where I knew that affairs of that
sort were arranged, when I met plenty of girls who
picked up their bread on London pavement by

selling, according to the season, oranges, apples, or violets. It is but right to say that our females are generally stout, healthy, and pleasant-looking, and there was one among them who specially caught my eye. Her petticoats being of the shortest, enabled me to see a neat instep and smart boots; and you know, perhaps, that we costermongers are very particular about the feet. Any one else would have considered that her voice was of the roughest, but as that proved she had cried bravely about the streets, the fault—if it were one—seemed to me a good quality. As for the rest, she was light-haired and rosy-cheeked, and might be two years older than myself. I offered her some refreshments, and presently asked leave to see her home and carry her basket for her. As it was light, she consented. We were married; as much, at any rate, as most young coster-mongers are married. We hired a furnished room for four shillings a week, and during the day I sold my goods, and my wife did the same. At night we often went to the concert-rooms, the penny gaffs, and the theatres, such as the Surrey and Victoria; sometimes even Astley's. We costers are very fond of amusements, for street life is so gloomy, busy, and laborious, that we try to get as much fun as we can. The theatre is a nobby place, but I think there is too much talking there, and too little action. I don't know if you are of my opinion, but I fancy that Shakspere

would be better half the length. Hamlet, for instance, which I have seen played several times,
would be better liked—I mean by our class—if
the actors reduced it to the ghost scene, the
funeral, and the duel that winds it up. I should
also like Macbeth better if only the witches' scene
and the battle were played. For comedy, I adore
Cruikshank.* If you know the managers, you
ought to advise them to introduce more fighting
into their pieces."

Without combating, as may easily be supposed,
the literary notions of the worthy costermonger, I
tried to bring him back gently to the history of
his life. He continued:

"Our little trade prospered. My wife—I say
it not to flatter her, for she is dead—was a model
to the women of her class. She kept our room
clean, and was as industrious as she was courageous. Generally, our females are worth more
than us, for they do not gamble. Gambling ruins
us: it is a vice which we street-children contracted
with our blood. They are more faithful, too, than
the men; and if they display any coquetry in their
dress, it is to please the man they regard as their
husband. Still, I should not have been a true
coster if the fire of jealousy had not burned in
my veins. This feeling sometimes rendered me

---

* I need hardly say that Cruikshank is not a comic writer; but
the street-sellers have seen very amusing caricatures drawn by that
artist, and, through a singular confusion of ideas, attribute to him
everything that makes them laugh.

unjust to her. I always believed that it was
cowardly for a man to beat a woman, but there
were days when it was stronger than I—when I
was not thoroughly sober—and I then lifted my
hand higher than I ought to have done, though
on the next day I felt sorry for it. I tell you the
good and the bad; still, if you write my life, I
must ask you not to speak of that. We had three
children—chance children as they are sometimes
called; but it is a shame, for I have stuck to the
children, and most of my mates do the same. I
brought up my two sons and my daughter to sell
in the streets, as I was brought up myself. They
are now established, so that when I meet them at
market or in the streets I have no cause to
reproach myself. There is nothing that renders
the heart so light as having done one's duty.

"My ambition now is to take a greengrocer's
shop. Some of my mates who have dragged a truck
about London streets have risen to that position
to my knowledge, and now are voters. I must do
them the justice to say that they did not turn
their backs on me in their prosperity, but have
remained friendly with their old mates, the poor
devils of costermongers. I should probably have
been a shopkeeper by this time, was it not for the
severity of the police. You must have heard tell
that we have a fight to wage with the authorities.
A friend of mine, who knows how to read, saw
the other day, in *Reynolds's Newspaper*, that

our extermination was resolved on. The last
Lord Mayor of London, Sir Robert Carden,
bullied us terribly; for you know that the Lord
Mayor is king in the City, and the City is one of
the best pitches in London for street-selling. On
the coming in of the new mayor we all hoped to
be treated with more indulgence, but we were
taken in. Of course you have read in the papers
the case of Mary Ann Donovan? I don't like the
Irish, and I consider those who pursue passers-by
with combs in their hands carry on a wretched
livelihood: but what is to become of a poor girl?
She must either sell or steal. We are accused of
cumbering the streets with our trucks, as if the
carriages and carts standing along the footway did
not hinder the traffic quite as much! And then
see how the authorities contradict each other.
When, through illness or any misfortune we get
into the workhouse, the parish readily gives us a
truck and some stuff to set us up again: but what
good's that, I ask you, if the police prevent us
selling, and often seize with one hand what was
given us by the other hand? That is acting
badly, you will allow, to the poor folk, who are
the life and providence of the great London
markets. I shall never believe that the Lord
Mayor was the first to propose these measures,
for he can't be a bad man, as he likes sprats;
still, I must say, he eats them in the close season.
The true authors of the system by which we

suffer are the City tradesmen, who are jealous because they cannot sell as cheaply as the trucks; and yet we do them no harm: they serve the gentry and we the workmen."

The life of the Irish costers offers several contrasts and some features of resemblance with that of the English: I will only dwell on the former. On nearly all the poor districts of London you will find rookeries of Irish; but I will choose, before all, Rosemary-lane as one of the most curious points at which the population of the sister isle is accumulated. Ramifying courts and lanes form a perfect labyrinth of blind alleys, and the opposite houses are so near each other, that the inhabitants can easily converse from their windows. The dwellers in these Irish colonies are accustomed to assemble with their baskets and gossip together at nightfall: at the entrance of each obscure court stands a group of women and girls carelessly leaning against the walls. Contrary to the English custom, they generally have bare heads, and their flaxen hair falls in disorder on their shoulders: nearly all have a large shawl folded over the chest, under which their hands are concealed. The Irish girls who sell in the streets are generally chaster than the English, and shrink from any union which the Church has not consecrated. An unfortunately too characteristic feature of their race is the absence of dignity: the most of them readily descend from their position of sellers to that of beggars, and then implore charity with an eloquence which only appertains to the daughters of unhappy Erin. The Irish costers, men and women, live aloof: they will not associate with the English costers, who despise and regard them as intruders. Owing to this separate life, they maintain in the heart of London their national habits, manners, and customs, and the isolation has only served to draw closer the ties of fraternity between the members of a family which considers itself as strange on the banks of the Thames as the Hebrews did by the waters of Babylon. The Irish rarely have recourse to money-lenders: if a poor fish street-seller wants five shillings, he borrows that sum of a luckier brother living in the same court, and pays no interest for it. As a rule, the Irish costers aid one another regularly: it is the law of patriotism. In the event of illness, they raffle some article for the benefit of the suffering member of the colony, and if one of them, ruined by any accident, enter the workhouse, his friends do not lose him out of sight. If he dies, they usually claim his body, and bury it at the common expense. All this has led to the report that a family bond existed among the Irish.

The Irish costermongers generally sell poor merchandise at a cheap rate: fish, especially herrings, which are not fit for even the poorest ranks, are good enough to be sold by candlelight in the baskets of the Irish. There is, indeed, a way of freshening up the herring, and restoring it to the silvery hues of health. One night, when I was prowling about a court in Rosemary-lane, I saw an old Irishwoman between two girls with glistening black hair, large grey eyes fringed with long lashes, short-skirted, and barefooted. The Irishwomen readily talk with foreigners, especially with the French, whom they consider good Catholics. She told me that she and her family were drawn from Ireland by the famine. Being then young, she soon grew accustomed to London street-life, for it is one of the characteristics of this hard race to grow habituated at once to all hard conditions. Her two grown-up daughters sold, and so did she, but the money earned was placed in a joint purse. She did not complain much about trade, but she regretted the glorious cholera time. Then, owing to the panic (a word, by the way, she did not understand), the finest fruits, melons, and pine-apples were running about the London streets. "I don't wish anybody any harm," she added, " but if the cholera came back, it would be a great blessing to people of our class."

The costermongers represent the most important class of street-trade: but the hawkers and pedlars must be added to them. The hawkers are those who cry in the public streets every variety of wares: they form a very ancient class, which in olden times, I am bound to say, had a very bad reputation. The name of hawker is derived from "hawk," and some analogy was doubtlessly traced between their wandering life and that of the hawkers who went about hunting up their game. The pedlars are men who travel on foot in the country and suburbs of London: they do not cry their goods aloud, but visit the houses they pass. Among the hawkers are some who cry in the streets the produce of their own labour—at once workmen and traders; they have suppressed what is called the middle-man. Among them are specially the makers of children's toys: while others give accumulative value to the objects made by other hands. They sell everything: almanacks, portfolios, purses, puzzles, spices, shells, more or less rare, birds, and gold fish. This class of street-dealers is better educated than the costers.

The most interesting persons in the large tribe of hawkers and pedlars are undoubtedly the women, Some among them have seen better days, and their history, such as I learned it from their own lips, varies but very slightly. One of them, about twenty-five years of age, went about the suburbs with a basket on her arm, containing ribbons, laces, embroidery, envelopes, and matches, She rapped with a trembling hand at the door of a house where I was staying, and offered her wares with a blush on her forehead. Her face was pleasing, her dress clean and neat, so I asked her what reverse of fortune had reduced her to this state. "I am," she answered, with a modest air, "the wife of a sailor. When he went away, he left me half his wages to draw, fifteen shillings a month. I soon found it was impossible to support myself and my three children on that sum, for I had besides to pay the rent, and buy coals and candles. I worked for some time with my needle, but I did not earn enough to get my little ones bread. So three weeks ago I made up my mind to go from door to door with my scanty stock-in-trade. The profit is not great, but for all that I thank Heaven for the idea it suggested through love of my children." Gratitude glistened in her eyes when the lady of the house bought some trifles of her. Another, of whom I asked several questions, was a widow, dressed with some coquettishness, and who seemed to be above poverty. Her husband had been killed six weeks previously by the fall of a mass of iron, as he was unloading a vessel in the London Docks. "I was left," she added, "with three guineas in the house. At my age (she looked about thirty) I did not like to claim the parish relief, which would only have given me a shilling and two loaves a week. I went to Woolwich, where I had a sister, with whom I am now living; but, as she was too poor to support me, I took up this little trade. I am not making a fortune, but I can live."

A third family, lastly, is connected with the street-trade : it is that of the patterers. The latter try to attract attention either by a pompous harangue, an extravagant costume, or even, at times, by beating a drum, which is advertising in an embryonic state. I sometimes have seen in London streets a man holding an open-air lecture on domestic economy, which he concluded by inviting his hearers, for their own sake, to buy the savealls which lay on a table before him. In a street at Wapping, a medical botanist invented, some time back, a novel mode of increasing his trade. Palmer's trial, which excited immense interest, was going on at the time, and he announced that he would read aloud each evening from the *Times* the progress of the trial. During the Crimean war another patterer displayed a large painted canvas, representing the Emperor of Russia in the form of a bear. This group of street-dealers offers some analogy with the showmen: they play a little farce to stop the passers, but a sale is what they aim at. According to their notions they form the aristocracy of the street-sellers, and nothing can surpass their contempt for the low herd of costers, whom they regard as an ignorant class, while they live by their wits. Some of the patterers have received education, and among them may be found members of the universities, surgeons, and lawyers' clerks. One of them was the son of a captain, who was appointed sub-director of Bute Docks. This young man received an excellent education, but not having been brought up to any profession, he came to London after his father's death, hoping to gain a livelihood by his classical acquirements. He was soon undeceived, however: after earning for a time two guineas a week by copying for the House of Commons, he lost that employment, and drifted into the family of street-patterers. Another had held thirty-eight situations in the course of twelve years; he told his history to the audience that assembled round his table, and defined himself as a "reed borne away by the current of life." If the patterers are generally better educated than the costers and pedlars, on the other hand their morals are much less regular. Most of them have been dragged down to their present condition by a liking for a vagabond life : generally, they have no residence, and sleep at night in the common lodging-houses. Improper language, habits of intoxication, and unbounded self-esteem, are the principal traits of their character. These street orators and actors form a fraternity, whose brothers are initiated in the art and mystery of patterism, and they speak a sort of slang among themselves different from that of the costers. A violent desire to excite admiration often drives them to the tap-room, less, perhaps, through the love of drink than for the society met there. In this disorderly life they usually lose even the desire for an amelioration of their moral situation.

Among the crowd of patterers, I will choose

an original figure—the street bookseller, who is also called Cheap Jack. On Saturday evenings, in the vicinity of Whitechapel, a grey-haired man, standing on a flat cart, cries, by the flickering light of a gas-jet, second-hand books. His system of selling is to stop the crowd by an harangue, and I have met the same itinerant bookseller at Woolwich and other towns near London. He begins his address by most humbly accusing himself with being unable to read, but as he gives rather clever explanations about each book and its author, it is easy to see that this feigned ignorance is an oratorical pretext by which to enhance the advantages of reading. Having introduced myself into his good graces by purchasing a few books, I obtained from him some information about his trade, and the style of literature best suited to the working classes of Great Britain. "I was," he told me, "clerk to a bookseller, but dependence and imprisonment did not agree with my character. I like the air, the street, the crowd; I like to speak and be heard. So soon as I had saved a few shillings, I bought some volumes, which I sold again on my own account. From that moment I had tried my wings, and the cage was not strong enough to hold me, and I began visiting markets and fairs with very slight baggage, but it soon grew larger. The great art in my trade is to know the tastes of the public I address. Some years back, I sold a large quantity of ser-

mons; now, that branch of literature is decaying.
The best selling books are English classics; you
can't believe the number of Goldsmith's History
of England I have disposed of in the last sixteen
years. The lives of sailors are a hit in some
quarters like Wapping, and military annals in
others such as Woolwich. The magazines are
eagerly bought up, for the people find in them a
source of instruction which the pictures render
more attractive. I read, or at least run through
most books that come into my hands, for I love
books as my children. Good authors, also, have
my sympathies ; as for the bad ones, I do not
care a bit about them; they do us more harm
than good, for we are obliged to drag these books
about from place to place for months. One day,
among my hearers I noticed Southey, whom I
knew from his coming to my old master's shop.
You know my way of selling, which consists in
asking for each volume a large price, which I
reduce shilling by shilling, or penny by penny, to
just one-sixth of the price first asked, for experience has proved to me that this is better than
selling by auction. I read in Southey's eyes that
he wanted one of my books—a rare old edition—
and quickly ran down even below the price the
book had cost me—eighteenpence. I would have
offered it him for nothing if I had not feared a re-
fusal, but what was my grief when he placed in

my hand a crown, and went away just as I was giving him the change. I called him back, but he said, with a shake of the head, 'Keep it, the book's worth that to me.'"

There are two other types of Cheap Jack; the one more or less serious, the other a thorough mountebank. The first selling everything, from a needle to an anchor, as he himself says in a famous harangue intended to arrest the passers-by. This is about his usual beginning: "You see in me the real, the only Sheffield Cheap Jack. I have not come here to gain money; oh, no! but for the benefit of the public solely. I wish you to learn how you have been robbed up to this day by a band of pompous shopkeepers, who gain more than a hundred per cent. on their goods. Here is a letter—I wish I had time to read it to you—in which I am offered a large sum of money if I will consent to go away: but no; I am too much your friend not to put you up to the scandalous tricks of trade." The second Cheap Jack is much more unceremonious: "Distrust my words," he says, "for I am the biggest impostor in the world. For each falsehood I forgot to tell when I was little, my mother gave me a box on the ears, my father a kick. Still, you shall judge for yourselves whether anybody can sell more cheaply than I do; for I buy all my goods on credit, and haven't the least intention of paying for them." Most of the

Cheap Jacks are Irish, though there are many English among them; they live in covered carts in summer, and in some shop through the winter.

In fine, the street-dealers have formed for centuries an abandoned, neglected, and proscribed race, which lacks before all a feeling of ideality and beauty. Two moralists—they are very few—have, however, attempted to raise this fallen family. About ten years back, Mr. Henry Mayhew had the idea of calling a meeting and founding a Friendly Association of London Costermongers; proposing in this way to redeem the misfortunes attaching to street-life. The meeting took place on June 12, 1850, and offered a truly interesting spectacle, in spite of some confusion; but as for the association, it is still waiting for funds, and hence Mr. Mayhew's good intentions have, in this respect, remained sterile. Another friend of the small dealers, the Rev. W. Rogers, has founded in his parish a school for the children of street-hawkers, and of eighty pupils who attended the classes, fifty gained the pecuniary reward with which the English Government rewards the assiduity of poor scholars. The same clergyman also opened a room for religious meetings, which was attended by one hundred and fifty women and eighty men. We may consider this a very feeble dyke raised against the overflow of ignorance and demoralisation, which stifle in this unfortunate class even the germs of social progress; but such honourable efforts cannot be regarded without hearty sympathy. What has been effected in one district of London may be done elsewhere, and it is permitted us to hope that a regenerating beam will at length shine on the heads of this gloomy and dispersed family. I build more, I confess, on the agency of these moralists than on the repressive efforts of the City magistrates to restore sap to a withered branch, and cover it at length with the tardy fruits of civilisation.

CHAPTER III.

THE FINDERS—THE MUD-LARK—THE SEWER-HUNTER—A HORRIBLE
DEATH—UNDERGROUND LONDON—FOUND DEAD!—LIFE IN THE
SEWERS—RATS—CURIOUS LEGENDS.

WE must now talk about another industrial
family, perhaps even stranger than that of the
costermongers to the delicate habits of society and
the conquests of the human mind, for it is incessantly looking at its feet, in order to pick up in
the dust or mud, frequently even in the subterraneous passages, aptly christened the realms of
horror, all that human neglect and accident have
thrown away, all that the dirty waters of the City
have swallowed up.

The family of finders is not nearly so numerous
as that of the itinerant dealers; and one type is
wanting in London which is found in Paris and
other large continental cities—the rag-picker.
There are, certainly, men, women, and children
who pick up in the streets mites of small value;
but various causes oppose the development of
that minor trade. Then the dust and sweepings

of London houses are collected every morning by
the dustman, who carries them off in his cart;
while a man, bearing a bag, is constantly going
about the streets uttering the well-known cry,
"Rags and bones!" Lastly, there are, in the obscure
parts of the town principally, shops where the
outscourings of wardrobes and kitchens are bought
up: the windows of these shops are often covered
with grotesque images and inscriptions in prose
or verse, appealing to the domestic economy of
housekeepers and servants—some of them even
display art. "Here," says an inscription, "bones
and rags are bought, and poetry is sold." Where
will Apollo hide himself? These trades injure
the street-finders, who complain bitterly about
them. Still, there is one branch kept up in spite
of all obstacles: it is that of the cigar-ends finder.
The latter is generally an Irish boy; he proceeds
at night to the aristocratic quarters, the vicinity
of the theatres and casinos and public walks. I
do not assert that in the best case he can live by
what he gleans by the wayside, but it is a useful
and rather profitable amusement. Somebody has
had the patience to estimate the number of cigar-
ends thrown away in a single day on the London
pavement, and the result of the calculation is, that
such a search is by no means a bad speculation.

Without stopping with those little trades which
exist elsewhere, we will choose in the family two
thoroughly English types, and which are not re-

presented on the Continent—the mud-lark and the sewer-hunter.

I had one day taken the boat to go from Chelsea to Gravesend: it was a fine April morning, and the tide was rapidly running down. Groups of children spread over the banks were waiting till the river, exposed to its bed of sand, left bare on its banks tongues of damp mud, sullen promontories, which at regular distances ran at low water down into the stream. When the tide was perfectly low, these bands of boys, among whom I noticed girls, a few men, and many old women, scattered on both sides of the Thames over the exposed mud and among the vessels the tide had left high and dry. I there saw them waded up to their knees in the viscous mud covering the sand: they were mud-larks. It may be asked what these swarms of finders expect to find on these sterile spots: they collect in baskets pieces of coal, wood, nails, and, by extreme good luck, a few coppers. They are seen along the whole distance from Vauxhall to Woolwich: some of the children are not above six years of age: nearly all the old women have decrepid features, rendered even more hideous by their wretched rags; the boys all look rather wild and savage; their clothing generally consists of an old straw hat, a coloured shirt, and trousers tucked up to the knees, though some of them do not possess what can be called a garment, but only rags scarce covering them. The mud-larks mostly perch in the vicinity of the river, at the bottom of some gloomy court or alley black as the wood: like the field-larks, a bed of straw suffices them. I saw in one of the poorer streets of Blackwall a house kept by a woman in which fifteen children, all mud-larks, were lodged. The landlady, a species of virago, caused her authority to be respected by the undeniable weight of her fists. Possessing a stern, taciturn, and concentrated character, these sons of the Thames do not readily speak to strangers about their affairs; they seem to have exhausted their vocabulary when they have asked for charity. This reserve is probably the simple result of the limited extent of their knowledge, which does not extend beyond the tides or the practice of their small livelihood. Some English moralists consider the mud-larks as children lost to society, but their opinion must not be accepted hap-hazard. Mr. Mayhew noticed one day among a group of mud-larks a lad of fifteen with a very interesting face: he spoke about him to one of his friends, who procured him a place in a printing-office. Thanks to the exertions and good conduct of the ex-mud-lark, his mother kept a shop in London a few years back. Still, I am bound to allow that the majority of the mud-larks spread over the sandy plains of the Thames have a fatal attachment for their sorrowful and ungrateful condition; and a vague feeling for nature is not

absent from this professional love. Another mud-
lark was placed by his father at a forge a long
distance from London; but, like the caged lark,
he pined for space and liberty. His dreams were
a perpetual image representing to him vessels
entering the Thames with all sail set, and the
grand horizon of houses, wharfs, steeples, plains,
and wooded hills, extending as far as the eye could
reach along the banks of the river. The blowing
of the forge bellows reminded him of the wind
howling over the waters in a tempestuous day.
He left his apprenticeship and returned to the
river, drawn by an irresistible attraction, and
after being a mud-lark for some time longer, he
afterwards turned sewer-hunter.

People may have visited the Strand and the
great arteries of London, have lived for years in
the British metropolis, and not suspect the architectural works which they walk over on the pavement or macadamised roads. There are streets
beneath streets, passages under passages, a city
below a city. This subterranean London figures
in no map or guide: very few historians or antiquaries have even spoken of it, for it is the accursed,
polluted, desolate, and badly-known city. There
all the impure waters incessantly flow away from
the houses: there falls everything that has no
longer a form in nature or a name in human
language. The London sewers, though in several
respects defective, present in their entirety an im-

posing system of constructions, which has caused
them to be compared to the sewers of ancient
Rome. Some of their works date back to unknown times: others, whose age is known, do not
the less enjoy a respectable antiquity. From the
quarters most remote from the Thames, small
drains disembogue into larger ones, and the latter,
after numerous windings, open out into the river.
If there were a map of these complicated subterranean currents, which branch from each other,
however, like the veins and arteries of the human
body, with a regularity more or less perfect, such
a chart would probably furnish as grand an idea
of English civilisation as the most magnificent
London streets. Most of these conduits are made
of brick; they are of every shape, but most frequently vaulted, and are generally at various
depths underground. This mass of works represents a buried capital, which has been estimated
at the enormous sum of two millions. When one
of the main sewers of London is exposed for
repair, it is curious to see how deep the excavation is, and how many lines of gas-pipes and
water-pipes the workmen must pass ere they reach
the vault of the subterranean canal. Several main
sewers were streams or small rivers which mean-
dered through the fields before London had grown
the giant we now know. Among these old swal-
lowed-up rivers we may mention the Fleet—now
the London Styx—which formerly flowed in the

open air from Islington, through Bagnigge Wells, Clerkenwell, Holborn, and Farringdon-street, into the Thames: it appears to have been once deep enough for merchant vessels, which came up to Holborn. Two others of these departed streams were the Wall Brook and the Lang (or Long) Bourne, which, in disappearing, at any rate left its name to one of the London wards.

Engineers attached to the Metropolitan Commission of Sewers have indicated the ruinous state of some of these sewers; the accumulations of mud formed there; the repulsive and at times deadly smell that exhales from such deposits; the terrible explosions of certain gases coming in contact with a torch, and which may destroy living beings. It is in these fields of horror, night, and silence, that the sewer-hunter proceeds to seek his booty. Beneath the city which men and vehicles cross in the blessed sunshine, the hunter walks, or more often crawls, sad, restless, and bent, seeking in this tomb—which begins and ends no knowing where—what has fallen from the city of the living. I hasten to add that this trade is dying out; formerly, the entrance to the sewers was free: the ancient architects doubtless supposing that the repulsive character of these subterranean spots sufficiently protected them against human curiosity and the love of gain. At any rate, any one who liked could venture, at his own risk and peril, into these gloomy defiles, where all presents the image of death, and desolation even more hideous than death. For the last few years this has been changed; the entrance of the sewers debouching on the Thames has been closed by a brick wall, and in this wall is an opening defended by an iron grating. When the tide is low, the force of the muddy waters, moved by the current in the interior of the sewer, lifts this trap, and allows the outpourings to be discharged into the bed of the Thames. If, on the contrary, the tide rises, the pressure exercised by the mass of river-water, increasing every moment, closes tightly the inexorable gate. In spite of this ingenious mechanism in spite of written prohibitions and severe penalties, some men, urged by a desire of gain, still find ways to enter the gloomy London sewers. There is generally a link between the mud-larks and sewer-hunters in the community of their labours in the mud, and thus, as they grow older, the larks readily become the bats of these unclean and gloomy crypts.

Public rumour not long back spread frightful stories about the dangers that surround the traveller amid these regions of night, solitude, and horror. About fifteen years ago, an old man who, without the knowledge of any one, was accustomed to visit the London sewers, all at once disappeared from society. The few people who had known him, but chiefly his wife and children, made anxious inquiries at the police-offices, but

obtained no information. Months elapsed, and
his name was almost effaced from the memory of
man, when a young sewer-hunter, passing under
ground with a torch, started back at seeing a man
standing before him in the darkness. It was in
the angle formed by a drain with the principal
stream of the Fleet, at about a mile from the
spot where this subterranean river falls into the
Thames. The young adventurer shouted and
called; but the only reply he received was the
sound of the turbid water as it rolled along, and
he was plashed by an army of startled rats, which
at once plunged into the black river. He advanced bravely, placed his torch in the face of
the silent figure, and perceived that he was standing before a skeleton. Struck with terror, he lost
his senses, tottered against the gloomy object, and
fell. His torch went out. The living man's situation was fearful, but his strength of mind returned
instead of being crushed in the cold horrors of the
darkness. He knew his way by the number of
gratings which interrupted the crushing monotony
of the vault at regular distances, and allowed a
little light to filter through. He groped along
dumb and subterranean passages, shouting with
all his strength to give himself courage, and to
keep the rats at a respectful distance. He thus
passed from grating to grating; each time he approached one of them he could hear the rolling of
vehicles; at times, also, the conversation of men

and women. For a moment he stood beneath one near which an apple-woman kept her stall: he was even tempted to give an alarm and ask to be drawn out; then he reflected that such an operation would take time, and determined to continue his journey. After a long walk he at length reached the banks of the Thames safe and sound, and his first care was to tell his mates of the strange discovery he had made. It was at once presumed that the skeleton might be that of the man who had so long been missing: the police were informed, and a constable was sent to the spot to verify the fact. He did not, however, dare to enter the drain, and remained on the river bank, while three men went in with torches and a basket to collect the remains of the dead man. On reaching the spot, they saw that the first sewer-hunter, in falling, had pulled down the skeleton with him: a skull, a shapeless mass of bones, a few buttons, and part of a shoe were all that remained of the old man. His flesh and clothes had been entirely devoured by the rats. The coroner held an inquest the next day, and the identity of the dead person was established by the buttons. The circumstances under which the old man lost his life remained a mystery; but the doctors supposed that he had either been suffocated by the mephitic air, or attacked by an apoplectic stroke as he went along. The jury returned a verdict of " Found dead."

This tragic end, and other accidents far too numerous, have, during the last few years, thrown a sinister light on a gloomy branch of trade hitherto but little known. Life in the sewers is a separate life, and one that demands our close attention; for venturing along these gloomy and solitary roads without any map but that engraved on memory, braving vapours often mortal, and dangerous tides, is not a slight undertaking. Many men have grown illustrious by less perilous achievements, and yet, Heaven knows that the respect in which the sewer-hunters are held cannot be worth envying, though they are, for the most part, courageous and intelligent men, at least in a certain class of facts. Some of them prowl about the Surrey side of the Thames: with old shoes on their feet, a bag on their back, a canvas apron fastened round their waist, and a long staff in their hand, they enter, no one knowing exactly how, these horrible and forbidden places. This pole, armed with an iron hook, serves to secure their footing and sound the ground, while they have a dark lantern fastened on their chests, which throws a light some distance before them. It is rare for the sewer-hunters to work alone, and they generally go in parties of three or four, to help one another. Most of these bands are led by an old and experienced hand, and, whenever they pass under the street gratings, they close the lantern and glide furtively along in the shade, fearful lest their light should attract the attention of people walking over their heads. For the same reason they avoid taking dogs with them, which would be of great help in these dangerous regions, but the dogs might bark and the noise reach the ears of passers overhead, who would put the police on the alert.

We have already seen that the sewer-hunter has a special enemy in the animal kingdom—the rat. This rodent has the black and ferocious temper of the spots where it lives: most usually it flies, but, when driven into a corner, it will turn on the man who is bold enough to pursue it in its lair. Stories are told of sewer-hunters being besieged by myriads of enormous rats, and that after fighting with all their strength, they succumbed to the numbers of their ferocious enemies. Another legend attaches to the London sewers. The hunters declare that several years back a breeding sow fell by chance through one of the openings of the subterranean city; it farrowed in the darkness and brought up its young there, which increased and multiplied. There was no want of food; and, if we may believe the stories current, the race of these animals, as numerous as they are furious, now goes about the drains near Hampstead. Still I am bound to say that the hunters who talk about these fearful wild boars of the night never met any of them.

On the road, the sewer-hunter picks up bones,

nails, pieces of iron and copper, and dead animals, whose skins he sells. It is a very meagre result for so much fatigue and danger, you will say, but chance is sometimes kinder. The sewer-hunters very often find copper coins and sixpences, even half-sovereigns and sovereigns. They also discover below, spoons, forks, and cups, at times watches and jewellery. We now see what nature of attraction can overcome the repugnance connected with hunting the sewers, for hope opens the door of these gloomy abodes. Clever people at the trade do not stop at sewers whose current is rapid like that of the Fleet, for they find nothing in them; they sound the black streams whose slow and idle course does not carry away objects of value. If we may believe the statement of experienced hunters, in certain places, nails, coins, and fragments of iron and copper have become amalgamated into a compact mass, and form a species of rock; and these metallic conglomerates daily increase by the new elements they receive. To remove these masses is the dream of the hunter, but they are too heavy, and defy all human strength. The time they pass underground is, moreover, limited, for they can only remain in the sewer between two tides. The result is, that the most daring and skilful hunters have never penetrated beyond a few miles in the London sewers: the rest is unknown to them. The dangers the tide brings with it are, perhaps, the most serious of all: the traps then open, the water intended to clean the sewers rush in, and the black streams are suddenly changed into rivers. If the wretch, surprised by this inundation, cannot take refuge at once in one of the branches of the sewer, he is inevitably lost. A fact will be sufficient to give an idea of the violence of these unchained currents. Some years ago, one of the underground streets of London was opened for repairs: a long ladder reached to the bottom of the sewer, and a journeyman bricklayer went down loaded with a certain quantity of bricks, when suddenly the water rushing from a sewer swept away the ladder, man and all. The poor fellow's body was found a few hours later horribly disfigured.

When the sewer-hunters have finished work, they proceed to the house of one of them, count the money picked up, and share the booty. Formerly each member of the band received from thirty shillings to two pounds after each trip: that was the glorious time. The present hunters speak of it enthusiastically, and complain bitterly of the obstacles that have been raised during the last two years against their trade. They will not admit that these restrictions are based on a feeling of humanity. "The sewers," they say, "are black and not very agreeable; but hunger is a den far more gloomy and terrible. Of what use to keep the dangers of death from poor people, if,

on the other side, they are robbed of the means
of getting a livelihood?" In spite of the prohibitions which impede and thwart these mysterious
journeys, the earnings of the sewer-hunters are
still above those of most workmen, and they un-
deniably form the aristocracy of the finders,
through their intelligence, courage, and the importance of their profits. At the same time, they
live from hand to mouth, and what comes by
hazard goes again by hazard. Foresight and
saving are not their characteristic virtues. They
have scarce had a good hunt ere they proceed
to some low pot-house, where they eat and
drink until their pockets are empty. Hunger,
which drives the wolf out of the forests, makes
the sewer-hunters go again into the gloomy
haunts, whence they emerge to indulge in fresh
excesses. Perhaps this taste for dissipation is
dependent on the nature of their calling, for
gloomy and repugnant toil needs violent distrac-
tions. And then, again, if there be really a link,
as is generally believed, between physical un-
cleanliness and certain moral habits, we must not
expect to find very delicate inclinations among
men who live with mud, and night, and solitude.
Owing to this dissipation, they are poor and badly
housed, amid the elements of a certain degree of
welfare. Their frightful dens are situated in the
very lowest parts of London; and though they
may be found in a few obscure and foetid haunts

of the Borough, their chief home is the valley of wretchedness stretching between the docks and Rosemary-lane. In Holborn there are also five families living by what they can glean in the fields of corruption and death.

We might be tempted to believe that men who spend a part of their time amid nauseous vapours would bear on their faces the livid imprint of the medium through which they move; but such is not generally the condition of the sewer-hunters, who are powerful men, with jolly faces and rosy cheeks. They form a secret brotherhood, and will not allow intruders to poach on their manor, and they are known to each other by a nickname, which completely effaces their patronymic. Gloomy though it be, their calling possesses charms for them. In addition to the gain, the sewer-hunters are attracted by the pleasures of independence. " I like this kind of life," said one of them; " I work when it is my pleasure, I rest when I like, and no one has a right to order me about."

CHAPTER IV.

THE SHOE-BLACK BRIGADE—THE MEETING AT ST. MARTIN'S HALL—MR.
MACGREGOR—THE RAGGED SCHOOLS—THE CROSSING-SWEEPER—
THE BLACK SWEEPER—THE CHIMNEY-SWEEPS—CLIMBING-BOYS—
KNULLERS—LADY MONTAGUE—INFLUENCE OF THE MINOR TRADES.

THE third category of minor trades, those who
sweep, brings us back, as it were, to light, to
London street-life, to the movement of society.

On the evening of February 9, 1858, I entered
the porch of St. Martin's Hall, an establishment
celebrated for its concerts, singing classes, and
liberal meetings, when I saw an army of boys
with flags and banners debouching from the
street. They were arranged in brigades of many
colours—red, blue, green, purple, and some half-
brown, half-red. Their costume, or uniform, consisted of a cap, a woollen blouse, blue trousers,
and shoes cleaned with irreproachable care. All
these young faces expressed joy, under an air of
attentive and military discipline. They were the
shoe-blacks, and February 9th was their holiday. I

obtained leave to enter the vast concert-room, where their meeting was to be held, whose imposing character rivals the old mediæval churches.* This hall was decorated with Chinese lanterns and banners, and at six o'clock the children were given tea and coffee; a band, the members of which were drawn from the yellow shoe-black brigade, playing at intervals appropriate airs. The meeting was brilliant: a crowd of ladies and gentlemen, the ornaments of English society, were present at the festival. A young barrister of great talent and most polished manners, Mr. T. Mac Gregor, explained, in a brilliant and lucid speech, the condition of the different shoe-black societies; after which the lads, fifty in number, who had received medals during the year for their good conduct, and for having earned the most money, advanced to the platform opposite the president, the Earl of Shaftesbury. The emotion was at its height, when this white-haired man, who honours the English aristocracy by the support he gives the labouring classes, made a touching and paternal speech to the boys of all colours. The words he uttered, all, perhaps, felt in their hearts, but the age and kindly intonation gave them an invincible charm. The party broke up at an early hour, each bearing

* On consideration, I have left this passage as it stood, as it may cause our readers more fully to appreciate the loss Mr. Hullah has sustained, and all London with him.—L. W.

away from the meeting mingled feelings of joy and tenderness.

A few years back, the shoe-black trade was a forgotten one in London. The last had been seen about 1820, in one of the numerous courts leading out of Fleet-street. Nature seemed to have pre-destined him to this profession, for he was of the black race. This man had the spirit and colour of his calling, for at daybreak he stepped from his lodging and placed his stool on the silent pave-ment, by which he stood patiently till the after-noon. He had a wife and child, and the last re-presentatives of an expiring trade, two or three woolly-headed lads, grouped round this son of Africa and helped him to clean the shoes of his customers. Firm at his post, he contemplated with a melancholy eye the improvements intro-duced daily into the London streets in the shape of pavement, and the granite flags drew a sigh from him. Another nightmare that troubled his nights, was the development of the crossing-sweepers, for this preventive system to his eyes increased the repressive system. After a long struggle, the negro shoe-black, seeing that all cir-cumstances conspired against him, went into the workhouse, and his children profited by their parents' absence to join the enemy's ranks: they embraced the profession the negro detested most, and, ingrates as they were, began sweeping cross-ings. The last of the shoe-blacks belonged to history, and he passed into English literature as a type and characteristic memorial of old London.

We know the Horatian proverb *multa renascentur*, and shoe-blacking is now a reformed trade in London. In 1851, before the opening of the great Exhibition, a meeting was held in Fieldlane, the object being to procure work for the poor boys idling about the streets. Everybody was agreed in the object, but they were still seeking the best sort of work suited to these young hands softened by idleness, when Mr. Mac Gregor proposed to regenerate a branch of labour, as circumstances appeared to favour its development. The French, who were then expected over by swarms, would doubtless like to find in London streets an advantage they enjoyed in Paris, of having the outrage done their boots by the mud of great cities effaced. The plan was carried out, and four little shoe-blacks in red frocks appeared on April 1, 1851, in the great metropolis. It was an event: our young pioneers invaded the Strand, seized on Piccadilly, and haughtily established themselves at the posts conceded to them by the London police. This was only the vanguard of a reserve it was proposed to launch successively on the pavement of the great city, if the experiment was successful. Some of the poor children received by the Shoe-black Society were orphans; others, since their birth, had been starving about the streets; most of them had not a roof to shelter

their heads; they slept at night in carts or on door-
steps; all were wretched, desolate, and covered with
rags. At the end of a few days success was ensured;
the flow of strangers to London extended, as was
hoped, this rising trade. During the Exhibition the
young shoe-blacks cleaned one hundred thousand
pairs of boots, and received for their trouble five
hundred pounds. The new trade—and that was
better still—was grafted on a generally recognised
want, and would therefore survive a temporary
occasion. The Crystal Palace vanished, but the
Society of London Shoe-blacks remained: shopkeepers looked with a friendly eye on the boys,
and gave them food; ladies called them to their
carriage-doors and made them presents; artists
drew their portraits, and paid them to be models.
To form an idea of the mechanism of this institution, and the life of the lads, we must now visit
an humble house in Ship-yard, which serves as
head-quarters to the red brigade.

I was taken to this house by Mr. Mac Gregor: it
was five o'clock on a winter's evening: that is the
moment when the young shoe-blacks return from
work, with black faces and hands, but with the roses
of youth on their cheeks. They wash themselves,
put by their boxes, and faithfully pay over to the
cashier the day's earnings. Each lad receives in the
first place sixpence as his wages; the remainder is
then divided into three parts, one of which goes
to him, the second belongs to the society, and the

third is placed in a savings bank for him. It is interesting to see their young heads grouped with a confident air round the members of the committee, from whom they seek words of encouragement, and whom they regard as benefactors. The shoe-blacks do not sleep in the house, for such a barrack system would be repugnant to English habits, but at their own lodgings or in the houses of refuge. In the house there is only a refreshment-room, kept by a matron, and where the boys can get tea and coffee at their own charges. At night they go to the Ragged Schools, or, if it be a Wednesday, hear an interesting lecture from one of the committee. At daybreak, joyous and light as larks, they return to the house; some of them live a great distance off, and frequently arrive by the halfpenny boats. After prayers, read at seven o'clock, each boy dons his black apron, puts his box on his shoulder, and proceeds to his allotted spot. A penny is the price paid for cleaning each *pair* of boots: I underline the word pair, because one day an old wooden-legged gentleman refused to pay the ordinary price, and only gave a halfpenny for cleaning his solitary boot. The shoe-black's earnings vary according to the season, and they clean more boots in summer than winter, for in fine weather dirty boots are ashamed to appear in the sunshine. On holidays (I except Sundays, when the boys do not work), the greatest amount of coppers is harvested, and one date has

remained fixed on the memory of the London
shoe-blacks—the one on which M. Kossuth entered
the City. "On that day," they say, "the mob was
so eager, that folk walked on one another's feet."
Three English citizens are exempted from the
common tax—viz. Mr. Judge Payne, who recites
verses at the shoe-blacks' meetings; Mr. Alderman
Finnis, who gives them plum-puddings; and the
Earl of Shaftesbury, their patron. As a general
rule, the conduct of these boys is exemplary: they
have, however, a great deal to endure from other
independent shoe-blacks, who steal their places,
and offer them unfair competition. It was a sight
that often rejoiced my heart to see the young
shoe-blacks, between the intervals of labour, reading a book or newspaper lying open on their box.

I was, before all, anxious to know the moral
fruits the institution had borne, and Mr. MacGregor
was kind enough to facilitate my inquiries.
"Among the lads we had to guide," he told me,
"one had been thrice brought before a magistrate,
and several had been in prison. The life of these
young wretches was marked by poignant scenes.
Our task—and it offers difficulties—consists in
reforming the character of these youths, making
the boy-thief into an honest man, fixing the vagabond, grafting habits of saving on a taste for dissipation, and changing the idler into a useful and
industrious member of society. But we have succeeded beyond our hopes: at a meeting where

I was present, I noticed a boy who was fearfully pale, and I asked him if he would like to enter the society. 'Oh yes, sir,' he answered. I afterwards learned that he had nothing to eat for three days. I enlisted him among the shoe-blacks: he got on, and after a while left the institution with a small sum of money. I met him later, but he was so well dressed that I did not recognise him; his mother, of whom he had taken care, expressed her gratitude to me by saying, proudly, 'You see I am quite a lady now; my son and I are rich.' He had a place as footman in a good house where he was respected. Another came to his parents' help at a moment when they were in great distress, and their furniture had been seized to pay the rent of their room. A third sent money to his father to come up to London, and the father was thus enabled to see his son, from whom he had been separated for years.

"Among the benefits offered by the establishment, I must place in the first rank the instruction the shoe-blacks receive in the ragged schools. In St. Pancras, a boy did not know how to write or read when we received him into the society in 1851: he is now a clerk in the Tower. The teacher of a ragged school was about to retire, and one of the pupils made him an eloquent speech, and offered him a silver inkstand bought by subscription: the speaker was a shoe-black.

"The morality of these boys has been raised

by education and discipline. A customer by mistake gave a shoe-black a sovereign between two halfpennies; the boy was honest, and after several hours' search, succeeded in finding the gentleman. He had, I regret to say, no other reward than the words, 'I thank you.'

" Although the earnings of the shoe-blacks are not insignificant, we do not regard shoe-blacking as a permanent trade. It is a temporary measure, saving the poor boys from hunger and vice, a step which enables them to reach better situations. As soon as they are old enough, and have saved sufficient to buy clothes, they leave us. Most of them enter service, and we keep their portraits in the establishment. Several of them have means to emigrate, and we have sent them to all parts of the world: China, Australia, India, the Crimea, and Canada. It was affecting to see, at the moment these lads were about to leave London, the other shoe-blacks give them a small box full of pence, shillings, and half-crowns. During my late journey in Canada, I visited some thirty of the young emigrants, and they were all doing well. Only one of the seven hundred who have crossed the Atlantic has found his way into prison. Our success has been contagious, and there are now in London nine other shoe-black societies, sharing the various parts of town; but ours, the Red Brigade, is the only one that is self-supporting; the others live, more or less, by help and voluntary gifts. We like these boys for their age, their misery, their good will, and the dangers from which we have withdrawn them. Once a year we take them to the Zoological Gardens, and another time for a country trip, where they drink tea under the shade of nature. To keep their minds happy, and give them a certain feeling for art, we let some of them practise music. You must have heard at night in the London streets their merry band, passing with a sound of drums and wind instruments. They give concerts once a week in the open air, and their warlike marches, and their melodies, whose execution is satisfactory, must inspire a feeling of gratitude to Providence at the sight of these children who were lost to society, and whom society has regained."

The shoe-black has an antagonist in the street-crossing-sweeper. I do not speak here of the street-orderlies who are attached to the Public Works Department, but of the volunteers who offer to sweep the pavement in front of shops, or form a practicable path between two oceans of mud. For a season the shoe-black society tried to take in hand and regulate this branch of trade, but gave it up again. There is certainly another company of "broomers," the boys of which wear blue trousers, a blue blouse fastened by a black belt, and a leathern hat, on which the words are inscribed, "Ragged Schools." Still, the profession of the street-sweeper is most frequently independent. The sweepers are recruited among the boys out of work, injured mechanics, and old women. Their earnings are precarious, depending on the generosity of the passers-by; but the English consider that every service deserves payment, and their purse readily opens to those who ask charity in the name of labour. Still, it is too true that the crossing-sweepers receive more promises than pence. "I have no change about me," said a gentleman to a sweeper, who held out his hand to him; but I will give you something as I come back." "Thankye," the boy answered, "but if your honour knew how many pence I have lost in that way!" The street-sweeper has also seen his importance diminish since the era of the shoe-blacks: the black brushman had a correct glance—one trade must kill the other. Sweeping the streets and public squares of London was formerly a profitable little trade, and there was a time when the sweepers of the old city picked up considerable sums of money. In more than one case, some of them left a portion of their savings to benevolent persons, who had been accustomed to speak kindly to them, and give them alms as they passed. Alderman Waithman's daughter received in this way a considerable legacy: an old negro swept the crossing before her father's house, and on his death-bed he did not forget the lady he had loved during life as an angel of charity.

The shoe-black and street-crossing sweeper, though often changing their stations, may be regarded as working at fixed posts; but we find among the group of cleaners a wandering trade, that of the chimney-sweeper. On May 1, 1856, I was in one of the streets of Wapping, when I saw a grotesque procession pass me. Men disguised in an extravagant manner, covered with rags of tinsel-paper ornaments and other frippery, were dancing to the sound of drum and fifes, while clattering shovels and brooms in their hands. The principal personages in this masquerade were Columbine, My Lord, the Clown, the drummer, " Jack in the Green," and a band of small vagabonds. A man standing on a door-step regarded this procession pass with jaundiced eye, and I recognised in him a chimney-sweep who had come at the beginning of the winter to sweep my landlord's chimneys. He was a tall thin man, on whose forehead smoky wrinkles engraved a precocious old age, and whose harsh features announced a persevering struggle with adversity. I addressed him, expressing my surprise at not seeing him mingled with his comrades in the games and dances of May 1st.

"Pooh!" he answered me, tossing his head sadly, " I don't call that games and dancing. Our traditions are going; but in my time it was a real holiday: we went all about town, greeted by bursts of laughter and the delight of the crowd;

but now-a-days the show is confined to a few
paltry East-end streets. The trade has been
spoiled by putting down the old system: it took
place in 1829, a fatal date, fixed in my memory
like a nail: the parliament forbad, under fine and
imprisonment, boys being sent up chimneys. The
law allowed the masters three years to make a
change, so that in 1832 the odious machine you
now know made its appearance in London streets.
I allow that the fate of the children employed to
climb up the chimneys was not the pleasantest:
badly clothed, badly fed, and badly lodged, compelled to climb at all hours up narrow and stifling
funnels—running a risk of breaking their necks—
they underwent a severe apprenticeship to life.
Nearly all detested their master as a tyrant, and
their condition as the harshest slavery: I have
known them become thieves to escape the ill-
treatment of their employer, for in their eyes the
prison was a refuge. I, who am speaking to you,
went through it all, and am one of the last London sweeps. Well! I declare that, in spite of all
that, the invention introduced by the law has been
ruinous. In the first place, the machine does not
work so well as the climbing-boys did: this is so
certain, that in old houses young hands are usually
employed to sweep the chimneys where nooks
and twists defy the new process. And then, is
it not sad to see boys idling about the streets, who
in the fine time of sweeping would have been

worth their pound a week each? But what I most reproach the machine with, is having thrown open the trade to everybody: any one who has not, like myself, passed through the horrors of the chimney, knows nothing of the tricks of these black tribes, which often branch one from the other. More than half the fires in London result from the bad state of the chimneys, and the carelessness with which they are swept. No, I don't like innovations; they always take the trade from the skilful to give it to intruders and idlers. Now-a-days, in our trades, it is no longer the man who works, but the machine."

Doubtless enchanted at having found some one to listen to his wrongs, he roughly invited me to enter his house, and I was too curious to inspect a chimney-sweeper's life to decline the invitation. A passage, in which a strong smell of soot was visible, led to a parlour level with the street: the furniture of this room consisted of a round table covered with a red cloth, some chairs, a carpet, chimney ornaments, and an engraving under glass representing an old London climbing-boy. The artist had chosen a snowy day; no doubt to heighten the contrast between the boy's black garments and the white flakes attaching to it. After sitting down and lighting his pipe, the chimney-sweeper asked no better than to tell me the struggles of his life.

"There are some," he said to me, "who are

born with silver spoons in their mouths; but I
was born with a wooden one, or an iron ladle
between my teeth. I knew my father and mother
very slightly. By the age of twelve, I had tried
several trades without sticking to one, when I met
one day in the street a black man, who proposed
to introduce me into chimneys; 'that will be
better,' he added, 'than running about with scamps,
and being pulled up by the police.' The apprenticeship was not long, for I was bold, and had
been used to climbing trees in my boyhood.
There were six boys of nearly the same age in
my master's house: before daybreak, we rose
fresh and active from our straw pallet, and began
our rounds through London streets; then, the only
things to be heard were our cries, the notes of
the milk-woman, and the *peep, peep* of the spar-
rows. The other children ridiculed us and called
us little white niggers, but we pretended not to
hear them. I had grown up in the trade, and
under the storm of soot that fell on me, when I
all at once thought of setting up for myself. I was
thoroughly acquainted with the chimneys, and
liked by my customers, whom I always contrived
to make laugh. Master in my turn of two climbing-boys, I was beginning to feel my feet, when
the fatal machine arrived introduced by act of
parliament. It did me a great deal of harm, as
well as the old-established hands, who had legal
and acquired rights: before 1831, there were in

London only twenty master sweepers, or great gentlemen, as they were called; now, there are more than one hundred and twenty. These usurpers, whom we know by the name of 'leeches,' have invaded the ground: I know one who is rich as Crœsus, who buys houses, land, and rides in his carriage, and is as much a stranger to the secrets of the chimney as you are. The leeches, sir, the leeches devour us: only those who were apprenticed to the trade should have been allowed to set up in it.

"We have another enemy, the 'knuller.' He goes about looking for work in the suburbs, and knocks at doors. Sooner than lower myself to that extent, I would tie a bag of soot round my neck and throw myself over Blackfriars-bridge. They play us, besides, all sorts of tricks; they often go to houses, saying impudently that they are sent by one of us to sweep the chimney; they do it badly, and we are blamed if it catch fire. Stealing a man's reputation is worse than stealing his trade, for it deprives him of the means of gaining it. I tell you, for you own sake, never employ knullers.

"Since the introduction of the new system, I work with two journeymen and a boy, who carries the machine. Their day begins at dawn and ends at about twelve, sometimes later. The trade would be good enough for them and me, if we had no slack time. During the bad season (summer, I mean), more than a hundred men are

thrown out of work; some become costers, others
tinkers or knife-grinders, while the rest spread
over the country hay-making. I must say besides,
for I must tell you everything, that we chimney-
sweepers are fond of a drop of drink; the trade
produces that. A good pull of ale or porter produces precisely the same effect on our throats as
the machine does in the chimney; it sweeps down
the soot, and the doctors themselves recommend
us to smoke and drink. And then, some public-
houses, especially in Whitechapel, are used by some
of our men as houses of call to find work. What
I do not like in our trade is, that we are isolated,
despised, regarded as a set of savages by the other
mechanics, who are not a bit better than us after
all. When I go past, the mothers point me out to
their children to frighten them with the black
beast. I allow that we are not a body of learned
men—very few of us can sign our names—but this
ignorance is the fault of the evil star under which
we are born. The species of disfavour which
pursues us has had the effect—which is, perhaps,
an evil—of keeping us aloof, and making us come
together like the black sheep of a flock. After
all, I have no reason to complain, for there are
many worse off than I am. I have not, like some
of the high masters—who don't know either how
to read or write — horses to my carriage with
livery servants on the box, but I have a small

pony which drags my soot along capitally in a cart. I also hope to escape the gloomy charity of the workhouse, as chimney-sweepers do not generally make old bones. The trade kills us before our time; and that is very lucky, for few of us save enough in the winter to be able to rest in the dog-days."

Before we separated, he presented to me his companion—generally, the chimney-sweepers are not married—a blonde with black eyes, much younger than himself, and who had been a street doll-seller. She told me that she had played the part of Columbine in one of the shows of May last. A tradition, or rather an episode, sheds a ray of poesy over the humble festival of the chimney-sweepers. A noble widow, Lady Montague, had a son in the pride of youth who suddenly disappeared. All London learnt the news; but the search to find traces of the lost boy remained fruitless. A long time after this mysterious disappearance, a climbing-boy was sent by his master to sweep the chimneys in the luxurious abode of Lady Montague, near Portman-square. The lad lost his way in the black passages running through the houses; instead of returning by the right chimney, he descended by another into one of the bedrooms, where he saw a sumptuous bed. Exhausted by fatigue, and yielding, perhaps, to the influence of vague memories, the young sweep, all black as he was, stepped between the white and dainty sheets.* The softness of the couch plunged him into deep sleep, and he was still slumbering when the housekeeper accidentally entered the room. Struck by the delicate features and interesting appearance of the little sweeper, she proceeded to inform the family, and the idea of the lost child at once occurred to the mother's heart. The young sweep was cross-questioned, and blushed beneath his innocent blackness. Either the harsh treatment he had endured had effaced the impressions of infancy from his memory, or he was troubled and confused, but he could give no information about himself: but his age, his voice, and a certain air of ease, showed that he was no stranger to the spot whither the greatest accident had conducted him. The identity having been established, Lady Montague recognised the little sweep as her son, and restored him his name, his rank, and his fortune. Wishing, besides, to consecrate by a festival the remembrance of this strange adventure, she instituted an annual dinner, which came off on May 1st, at White Conduit House, and to which all the climbing-boys of London were bidden. As no other certificate was requested of the lads beyond the soot on their faces, several street boys, it is asserted, blackened their faces for the occasion, and thus slipped among the chimney-sweeps in the banquet-hall. This festival was

---

* This bed was long kept as a curiosity at Arundel Castle.

continued during Lady Montague's life; her son
kept it up for two or three years, but then quitted
England; but the tradition was so well engraved
on the manners of the age, that the master
sweepers and other London citizens clubbed together to perpetuate the amusement of May 1st.
A great number of persons proceeded on that
day to White Conduit House, and in return for
their contributions witnessed the sweepers' feast.
This lasted up to the act of parliament; but after
1831 the dinner passed, with the rest, into the
legendary era.

We see, then, that the minor trades of London
are allied to the history of labour in England.
Each of these modest callings provides a great
number of people with a livelihood, and con-
tributes in a certain degree to the development of
civilisation. " Great things," as an English economist says, "are accomplished by the aid of little
ones." It is, in fact, in this obscure mass of
services that the prosperity of trade, manufactures, and the liberal arts is elevated: the edifice
of British society resembles St. Paul's Cathedral,
gloomy and smoky at the base, but whose summit
is white and gilded in proportion as it reaches the
regions of air and sun.

CHAPTER V.

GEOLOGICAL FORMATION OF SALT—UPPER RED SANDSTONE—CHESTER
—THE CHEIROTHERIUM—THE CITY WALL AND ROWS—THE ANTI-
QUARY—THE ROODEE—MIRACLE PLAYS—DELAMERE FOREST.

SALT is employed in all civilised countries: but
nowhere on the Continent is the use of that
mineralogical product so spread as in Great
Britain. That rich nation owes a branch of its
important commerce to the salt mines and springs.
Certain English counties live doubly from the
earth: not satisfied with collecting the crops and
fruit that grow on the surface, they have laid the
subsoil under contribution to provide them with
a condiment that heightens the savour of the
alimentary substances.

Salt must be regarded from three points of view:
the formation of the soil in which it is met; the
mode of extraction; and, lastly, the applications
of that mineral to domestic economy, the arts,
trade, and agriculture. The natural history of
salt will carry us back to the geological terrain, for
how, in fact, is this substance to be separated from
the mighty rocks that envelop it in nature? We

shall have to change the field of our operations several times: the saliferous rocks demand study in the vicinity of Chester; the salt-
mines and springs at Northwich; and the application of salt to trade on all points of British territory, but principally at Sheffield. It is interesting to see the influence so common a mineralogical
product has exercised over the manners and prosperity of a great nation.

A railway trip is a pleasan tlesson in 'geology,
brought within reach of everybody. To profit by
this study, all that is needed is to examine the
colour and texture of the rocks which the railway
cuts through and lays bare on each side of the
road. I was coming from Manchester, when, on
emerging from a tunnel, I found myself, for the
first time, between two masses of red sandstone,
which rose like peaked walls, and bounded on
either side the horizon of the railway. The same
rock, more or less divided by earth-slips, accompanied me with intervals to Chester station, where
I stopped. In England the subterraneous strata of
salt repose on that series of rocks which has
received the name of the "upper new red sandstone," which forms a geological province of considerable extent, occupying all Cheshire, a large
portion of Lancashire, and some districts of
Shropshire, Warwickshire, and other counties.
With very few exceptions, coal-fields border the
limits of this formation. The new red sandstone

is not merely a soil, but almost an era of nature: through the age of the rock, the external features which the events of the globe have engraved on it, and the extinct animals met with, we can without any difficulty form an idea of what England was at the period when those vast magazines of salt were deposited, from which man now abundantly draws an element of trade and prosperity.

Life had already changed its character several times on the surface of what is now called Great Britain. The *débris* of extinct worlds rose from the bottom of an abyss and marked the first earths, which, connected together by successive formations, would eventually constitute an important island. The gloomy group of Cambrian and Silurian mountains sketched out in this night of ages the region of Shropshire and Wales: the old red sandstone, in which masses of marble and calcareous slabs were embedded, threw its cyclopean limbs over the provinces known now as Devonshire, Cornwall, and Herefordshire; while, mingled with granitic and gneiss rocks, it upheaved the great Grampian chain in Scotland. The mountains of magnesian limestone, the old bed of an ocean which had seen the carboniferous flora born and die out, formed the gigantic scaffolding of Derbyshire and a part of Ireland; and some weak strips of permian rocks designed the future counties of Nottingham and York. Although the physiognomy of England, since the end of the epoch called primary, had been altered, changed, and overthrown by the accessions of new rocks, by the movement of the sea, and especially by the action of time, we can, to a certain point, form an idea of the principal features of this oceanic chaos. Still nature was about to take a step forward: between the new red sandstone and Permian age, which the trias succeed in the series of geological facts, there is a separating abyss more marked than between the worlds belonging to the primary division. We are here on the edge of a change of system: the first-born races have disappeared, and their place is taken, partly at least, by a new creation, which will be continued from epoch to epoch during the whole of the secondary formation. With the Permian era ends a long and grand period, antiquity; with the triassic soil begins the mediæval age of extinct beings. If we were permitted to compare the study of these rocks to that of monuments, the new red sandstone would mark something like the passage from Roman to Gothic architecture.

Before becoming solid ground the new red sandstone was a sea, but no longer one of those deep and raging oceans like those at the bottom of which the Silurian and Devonian rocks had reposed. This has been proved by the nature of the univalve molluscs found in a fossil state in the rocks of this epoch, and which indicate that the

sea grew shallower as it approached the coasts.
There was a beach over whose soft and damp
sand strange animals passed. Footprints have
ever played a great part in judicial investigations,
travelling adventures, and romances: we call to
mind Zadig and Robinson Crusoe. If the sight
of such vestiges marked on the sand is of a nature
to astonish the traveller in desert countries, the
geologist, who also travels in the gloomy regions
of the past, has certainly the right to halt with
profound interest and curiosity before these mysterious traces. Engraved on the rock, they show
him that at that period—that is to say, an epoch of
which no other written history remains—the earth
was inhabited. The fossil imprints of paws,
though not limited to any formation, are yet found
principally in the new red sandstone: in the quarries of Cheshire several rock plates have been discovered on which the footprints of the tortoise were
incrusted, with drops of rain hollowed out. Geologists asked themselves if this rain fell after or
before the passage of the animal, and the answer
to the question was deposited on the stone: the
rain fell afterwards, for the small hollows are
printed in the traces of the footprint, though more
lightly than in the rest of the surface. Near
Shrewsbury, the traces of another species of reptile
were laid bare, a Saurian which offers remarkable
characteristics, and to which the name of the *Rynchosaurus* has been given. As far as can be judged

from some fragments of the animal, it seems to have had a toothless mouth, a head resembling that of a bird, and which was enclosed in a horny sheath. But among the denizens of this ancient world there is one which has specially occupied the science and conjectures of the geologist.

All that was found of this lost being were, at the quarries near Lymm (Cheshire), or Storeton Hill, near Birkenhead, footprints of a strange form, as if man had wished to take possession of these remote ages by marking them with his hand. This left, shapeless, rudimentary limb was, however, not a hand, but a foot. Somebody had passed that way—but who was this mysterious walker? It was a long time a puzzle for naturalists, and at all hazards they named this sphynx-footed animal the *cheirotherium*. On the same plates of stone were found the ripple marks. of the waves engraved on the stone. The opinions of the learned were divided: some referred the animal which had hidden its bones so well to the kangaroo family, some believed it was a crocodile, while others finally declared it a batrachian. While the doctors were deliberating, some teeth were discovered in the heart of the same formation in Warwickshire. They were of a curious structure, for on cutting them irregular and undulating bands were found, intertwined with one another, like the winding paths of a labyrinth. The animal to which these fossil teeth had belonged was consequently named the *labyrinth-odon*. At length, some bones were found, still in the same series of rocks; and, by putting this and that together, Professor Owen established that the *labyrinthodon* and the *cheirotherium* were one and the same animal. It inhaled the free air, and belonged to the toad or frog family; but compared to the modern batrachians it was a gigantic creature. The fable of the frog wishing to make itself as big as the ox is only a myth with reference to the present state of nature. Numerous tortoises, the *rynchosaurus*, the *labyrinthodon*, with other animals, doubtless, whose remains have not yet been found—such were the strange inhabitants this ancient Red Sea saw wandering on its shores at a time when man did not exist, and his place was occupied on the surface of the earth by reptiles.

That which was a sea has become, with the progress of time, a pile of rocks. In order to explain this metamorphosis of oceans into dry land, geologists have imagined all sorts of violent and marvellous forces, by the help of which the primitive bed of the waters was uplifted; but at the present day everything leads to the belief that the natural causes which under our eyes are altering the physical features of the globe were sufficient to produce these grand transformations. Rivers are continually destroying the mountains in which they have their source: they wear away the earth they water, and bear all these materials to the sea. Tides fill up the arms of Ocean, cross currents excavate the bed of the waves, while they carry to other points enormous accumulations of sand. A traveller tells us that he saw in the Highlands and certain Scottish isles the seas that bathe the western coasts obscured by a multitude of small living spirals—a mud of scarce visible animals. These glistening and organised grains of sand were workmen employed in constructing land. Their task lasts but a short while: they are born on Monday morning to die on Friday evening; but their number is so considerable that the traveller compares them to the hair of all the men, women, and children who have seen daylight since the commencement of the world. These architects, besides, are born again from generation to generation, and their work is con-, tinued. Such natural action necessarily presupposes the aid of time; but everything also proves that the rocks, daughters of ancient seas, have been hardening with the dust of ages. The thickness of the entire series of new red sandstone in England is estimated at eighteen hundred. feet. If we reflect on the grains of sand buried in this mass, and admit that such a stratification is the work of natural causes, we grow in a manner terrified at the antiquity of a rock to which the human language has given the title of *new*, in opposition to another and even older deposit.

Though the new red sandstone is not peculiarly a mountainous formation, it here and there imparts marked and pleasant features to the landscape. The winding-sheet of an ancient sea, this ground was in its turn troubled by the tempest of geological events. This upheaving of rocks, which may be followed from hill to hill, like the movement of an agitated ocean, casts over the green plains of Cheshire a character of stern grandeur and beauty. From time to time these hills, covered with gorse, are rent asunder, and display on their exposed flanks red ochreous deposits, over which the blood of the Titans seems to have flowed.

This formation is not the only one in the world in which salt is found in a solid state, and, as it were, prepared by the hands of Nature. In other countries there are plains covered with sand, extending for enormous distances. There are even mountains of this mineral which rise ten thousand feet above the present level of the sea. In other countries, again, this condiment is found buried at varying depths in the different strata of the secondary formation, while in England the rocks of salt are only met with in the new red sandstone. Such a fact gives this soil a great economic value, and supplies a further reason for us to inquire whence comes this mineral wealth, and how was it formed? The origin of these immense subterranean deposits is as gloomy as the working of salt mines in England is important. Some naturalists have attributed the masses of rock salt found in the new red sandstone to old lakes evaporated by the action of the sun, or ancient seas which have long died out. A more probable opinion is that these salt-fields were deposited in the lagunes then communicating with the ocean as it was at that epoch. This origin is, at any rate, based on natural facts going on in our day on the surface of the globe. There are in South America patches of salt water, according to travellers, neither land nor sea; that is to say, the ocean covers them during one part of the year, and abandons them during the other part to the torrifying beams of the sun. The same thing, then, takes place in these lagunes as happens in the artificial *salines*—wide and flat expanses of lánd, or sand, surrounded by dykes, like the Dutch polders, into which man introduces, at certain seasons of the year, the sea. The sun imbibes the water, and the salt is precipitated in the dried-up bed of these reservoirs. It doubtless required ages on ages to pile up by such mechanism, strata upon strata, the enormous salt rocks now buried in the depths of the earth. The mass of new red sandstone, the extinct reptiles which imprinted their footsteps on sands now hardened and petrified, the changes that have occurred in the distribution of land and sea—everything, in a word, proclaims the antiquity of these rocks and the duration of the triassic age. But, however long this age may appear, it is but an episode itself in the history of the terrestrial globe, and the seas of that day changed into salt, like Lot's wife, because they looked behind them into the past, were followed by the movement of the creation on the surface of Great Britain.

To the ancient history of nature, we must oppose the features of the living landscape, the meadows cropped by the cattle, the fields shorn by the scythes, the rivers covered with sails, the hamlets and the towns. The triassic soil is interesting not only geologically and commercially, but it offers the arts, especially architecture, materials possessing a certain value. I visited in Cheshire the red sandstone quarries which had been worked for centuries: the stone is easily extracted, by the way; one or two workmen mark on the rock with a pick the parallelopiped shape of the block they propose to detach. When the form of the stone is thus disengaged, the base of the block, still adhering to the mother rock, is broken by means of a lever on which two men throw their weight. These masses then obey the hand, and are raised from the bottom of the mine by powerful cranes, which deposit them on a platform. These rocks of red sandstone are extremely abundant, and are at times met with on the surface of the ground: on the road from Chester to Northwich I passed through a village the streets of which are paved with this natural flooring. The rock serves as a foundation to brick houses, and the steps have here and there been cut out of the strata exposed to the air. The new red sandstone has contributed, to a great extent, in certain parts of England to mediæval building—churches and castles: one of the finest specimens of this stone as applied to architecture is Hereford cathedral: but I will select among the cities which owe their existence and monuments to the new red sandstone, the ancient city of Chester.

Chester resembles no other town in England, and I have seen nothing like it on the Continent. Its history is very ancient: the Romans gave it the name of Deva, doubtless, because it was situated on the river Dee, in Latin *Dea*. The present shape of the city, and the division of the streets into four quarters, are what we may term a Roman imprint. Before becoming a city, Chester was a camp, and this military station, formerly occupied by the masters of the world, left its principal features to the city that took its place. Various traces of the residence of the Romans have been found: such as altars with Greek and Latin inscriptions, mosaics, medals, leaden pigs, curious memorials of the metallurgic trade, then in its infancy, but to which Great Britain now owes a part of its wealth. This city is a museum: the Celtic era, the Nor-

man period, the middle ages, the religious reform,
and the renaissance, engraved reminiscences on
this new red sandstone, where extinct animals had
already left traces of their passage.   With its
buildings of soft and friable stone crumbling in
the wind, with its old bending houses—its chronicles of another age—Chester speaks at each
footstep to the traveller of the fragility of human
things and the ravages of time: but it speaks of
them philosophically.   This language of the stones
has nothing in it sad and despairing; on the contrary, it bears to the most perturbed hearts a
feeling of peace and soft melancholy.   There is
so much repose in these streets, which are not
agitated by the buzz of business; so much grave
quietude in the old building; so much calmness
and pleasant affability in the faces!   The dress
of the ladies, though elegant, has even a quiet
character; their summer dresses may be fresh
and cheerful, but they are simple.   Chester is the
metropolis of the district in which agriculture
flourishes, and the two portions of the city which,
before all, demand the visitor's attention, are the
city wall and the Rows.

The ramparts of Chester constitute the sole
model still existing in England of the old mode
of fortification.   It is a high wall, wide enough
for two persons to walk abreast, and runs round
the whole town.   Built during the middle ages,
this wall rests on the foundations of an older one

constructed by the Romans. You may still see, at more than one spot, the base of the Roman erection which served as the root of the modern works. Thus enclosed in a corset of red sandstone, the city could neither extend nor grow larger. The ramparts of Chester form an agreeable promenade, probably unique in the world: these fortifications, cut in the rock and raised to destroy the life of man, now serve to prolong it, for convalescents, old persons, and delicate ladies, come here to breathe the pure air and enjoy the freshness of the scenery. In Eastgate-street I went up a flight of steps that led to a bridge and thence to the city wall: it was curious to look down at the houses leaning at the base of the old wall, into yards, gardens full of grass and verdure, where frail creepers threw their delicate shoots and flowers over the age-worn masonry; but you must advance a little for the view to expand. Here the eye follows for a long distance the windings of the Dee, proceeding to its mouth: there is the deep bed of a canal cut through the solid bed of red sandstone; and, indeed, nothing is more beautiful than the ocean of valleys and meadows surrounding Chester, save the savage pride of the Welsh mountains, visible in the distance. These mountains, standing erect in their tranquil majesty, display another system, or, to speak more correctly, another age of nature, from the rock of which Chester wall was built,

and the gloomy masses of slate seem to despise
the red sandstone as an upstart, for the nobility
of rocks, like that of men, lies in the antiquity of
their origin.   Seen from Chester wall, the Welsh
mountains are blended with the farthest sky line,
and in truth might, themselves, be taken for clouds
hardened into stone.   This comparison may, perhaps, appear insulting to the monuments of nature
which represent strength and stability; but, geologically regarded, mountains are not protected
from vicissitudes, and pass with ages from one
shape into another.   The wind disperses the
cloud which changes, and time alters the mountain.

On this city wall I met a man of about fifty, who
was contemplating with thoughtful eye the so-
lemnities of nature and the past.   He was an ex-
parish -clerk, compelled to resign his office owing
to a disease which had weakened his eyesight; he
was not a professional antiquarian, and yet it was
easy to recognise in his language a sincere and
assiduous admirer of the venerable relics of history.   According to him, there was only Chester
in the world, and I confess that momentarily I
shared his enthusiasm.   Though poor and meanly
clad, he was an optimist: at the sight of the old
memorials which recalled recollections of feu-
dalism, the bloody wars of religion, and the times
of ignorance, he burst into ecstasies at the happiness of living in an enlightened age.   I have no

liking for ciceroni, but this man was not a professional one.

"I am," he told me, "a native of the city.
Formerly I spent my leisure hours in studying
old histories of Chester, but now I have bad eyesight, and this walk is my book, and I find here,
written in legible characters, the happy changes
which time has introduced into human institutions. That old tower you see down there is
Water Tower, an old fortress erected to repulse
maritime foes, for at that period an arm of the
river flowed under this portion of the walls, and
vessels could sail up to the foot of the tower.
Now-a-days, thank Heaven, there is no enemy
and no water; our age has no need of the military
works which make the mind revert to scenes of
carnage. That other square tower, which received the name of Bonwaldesthorne's Tower, and
which stands there blood-hued beneath its mantle
of ivy, is now the museum of the Mechanics' Institution. The contrast between the murderous
intention of that edifice and the use made of it in
modern times, victoriously opposes the gentle and
practical manners of our age to the gloomy genius
of the thirteenth century. This again is Phœnix
Tower; from the top of that ruin Charles I. saw
the defeat of his army on September 24, 1645, by
the Parliamentary troops 'on Bowton Moor. I am
only a poor man, and have a hard matter to gain
a living, but when I look with a light heart at the

splendid scenery surrounding us, and think of the
painful impressions the same beauties of nature
must have produced on the downcast monarch, I
thank Heaven for not having made me a king in
those sad times. And then to think of the calmness which has succeeded such ravages! The destructive elements have themselves abandoned
the field to the useful arts and the amusements of
man. This splendid meadow, undulating to such
a distance, and on which oxen are tranquilly
grazing, is called the Roodee: formerly it was a
lake, now it is devoted to gymnastics, cricket, and
races.

" Still," the old antiquary added, " we must be
just; we must allow that if the neighbourhood
has gained much agriculturally, the city itself
has lost commercially. There was a time when
Chester was a flourishing port; but rivers change,
and, owing to the fickleness of the Dee, navigation
has withdrawn. Liverpool has reaped this rich
harvest. The Dee consoles itself, as you can
see, by keeping its girdle of pretty cottages and
villas, its old romantic bridge, its fresh and leafy
groves, its pleasure-boats, and, above all, its mills,
which are great antiquities. It has also had the
honour of being sung in verse by Drayton, Browne,
Spenser, and Milton, who gave it the epithets
of ' divine,' ' enchanting,' and ' wizard.'

" I was certain that something pleasant would
happen to me to-day, for my wife threw a shoe

after me as I went out. You cannot, in fact, credit the pleasure I feel in speaking of the history of Chester with any one who takes an interest in it. Being a very ancient city, my home has retained many customs and traditions of the past, and is rich in chronicles. At Newgate, where we now stand, there was formerly a postern called Wolfsgate, or Peppergate. In the sixteenth century, the Mayor of Chester had a daughter, who was playing at ball in Pepperstreet with some other young girls: one day she was carried off by her lover, and the father, clever too late, ordered the gate of the city to be closed through which the escape took place. Hence the proverb existing in Chester: 'Shut the postern when the girl is carried off.'

"Formerly the inhabitants of Chester were distinguished for a very lively taste for dramatic representations: it may even be said that our city was the cradle of the English stage. Another source of amusement that attracted a great many strangers was the fair, and it was a custom during this fair that a glove should be hung up in the town-hall and afterwards on the roof of St. Peter's church. To understand the meaning of this emblem, you must know that Chester was celebrated for centuries for its manufacture of gloves, and that in the time I speak of trade was not free; the right of carrying on any traffic was a privilege reserved solely for citizens born within

the city. During the fair, on the contrary, everybody might set up as a trader, and the glove hung
up was the signal that proclaimed the temporary liberty. The custom had lasted for centuries,
when the Reform Bill, that just and obstinate
foe of ancient monopolies, extended the rights
throughout the whole year to all—strangers and
townsmen. The authorities of the city still continued for some time to hang up the old banner
outside the wall. I have myself seen this public
ceremony—a reminiscence of another age—and
it is only during the last twenty years that the
custom has been abolished."

Before leaving me, this amiable enthusiast recommended me, before all, to visit the Rows; and
they are, in fact, one of the curiosities of Chester,
nothing like them, probably, existing in the known
world. Each side of the street has two rows of
shops, one on the ground the other on the first
floor, and there is a communication by upper
galleries with those above. These galleries,
reached by stone steps standing at regular distances, are what are called the Rows: the roofs
of the bottom shops form the platform on which
you walk, and which runs regularly from house to
house all along the street. On one side, the roof
of the gallery is supported by wooden pillars, more
or less carved; on the other, it rests upon the front
of the shops. The first floor shops are let at a
higher rent than those below, and are also more

ornamented. These cloisters render thus more than one service; thanks to them, the inhabitants can go from one end to the other of the street without exposing themselves to rain or mud. These sheltered and hanging streets suit the humour of the lounging traveller; he can walk about, stop before the shop windows, or, leaning over the wooden balustrade, watch what goes on in the street. For the artist, such passages, imprinted with a character at once elegant and cenobitic, possess the charm of novelty.

Externally, this first floor, open to the street, and along which people walk, gives a strange appearance to the architecture of the houses; inside, the old arcades, in which the light is discreetly tempered, are equally characteristic. The general style of the Rows is enhanced by the very old wooden houses which set it in; and they have suffered very slightly from works of repair. The origin of the Rows has been a hard nut for antiquaries to crack. According to some, they were means of defence at a time when Chester was necessarily exposed to the sudden invasions of the Welsh, and especially to cavalry charges. Others insinuate, no doubt in jest, that these galleries were built to protect sensitive females from meeting horned animals. It is Pennant's opinion that the prototype of this style of architecture will be found in the Roman vestibules or porticos, but, however this may be, it is certain that the city of

Chester has best of all understood the English climate. After that, you are amazed to find um-brella sellers there.

Though the majority of the houses is built of brick or wood, the relations of geology with the architecture of towns may be specially studied at Chester. All the old edifices are built of new red sandstone, and the most admirable of all are the cathedral and St. John's church, which offers a few remains of Norman architecture. It is, be-sides, curious to see how art has been brought to agree with the character of the stone; the red sandstone being a tender material which crumbles under the hand of time, the architects have paid no attention to details or ornaments : they are rather painters than sculptors. The mediæval buildings, in truth, assume an august appearance through the mass, the colour, and the effects of light and shade. Nothing is more majestic than the cathedral tower seen from a distance, and which, even under a cloudy sky, seems floating in a perpetual sunset. Age gives this stone, coloured by oxide of iron, a ruinous appearance, which does not injure the effect. You find at Chester old ruins of chapels, towers, keeps, which have re-tained no other shape than that of the rock, but which, enlaced by the creeping ivy, bear a haughty and noble air even in their decadence. These red spectres of the past add an interesting character to the city, which has fallen asleep in the tranquillity of a happy old age.

I was obliged to tear myself from Chester not without a pang, for after studying the new red sandstone at the different spots where the history of this rock is written, the natural order of events made me proceed through the splendid royal forest of Delamere to Northwich, where I should find the salt mines and springs. Salt is extracted from the sea, springs, and mines, and Great Britain has, then, these resources ready to hand. The sea surrounds it; in the interior, the salt water springs bubble up; and the mines of rock are hollowed beneath the verdurous soil of Cheshire and Worcestershire.

CHAPTER VI.

SALT-PRODUCING—NORTHWICH—THE SALT SPRINGS—THE MINES—
THE BOILING-HOUSE—THE STORE-HOUSE—ACCIDENTS—A HAUNTED
MINE.

ALTHOUGH the ocean was in all probability the first workshop, this source of saline wealth is now abandoned by England: it is only in Scotland that salt is still obtained from the sea. The Scotch manufactories where the process is carried on are situated on the sea-shore, at spots more or less picturesque; they are long and low buildings divided into two parts : one, called the "fire-house," is intended to shelter the workmen and receive the combustibles; the other, the "boiling-house," contains the caldron, in which the evaporation is effected, and the furnace that heats the water. In warm countries the sunbeams are employed to separate the water from the salt: this is the method practised in France, Spain, and Portugal. At Ruthwell, on the shores of the Solway Frith, salt was formerly made by the same process. The people of the place picked up, during the summer, a saline crust mixed with earth, which they presently purified in reservoirs. At the present day, it has been recognised that the sun did not work well enough in these cold countries, and that fire must be substituted for it. The boiler, consequently, plays, throughout the whole of Scotland, the same part performed in Southern Europe by sands heated by a more generous luminary. The Scotch factories form a tolerably profitable branch of trade: from a boiler containing 1300 gallons of sea water, fifteen or sixteen bushels of salt are obtained in twenty-four hours.

These salt works are very old. In 1128 they were presented to the abbeys. At a later date the French, who were at Queen Mary's court, improved the Scotch works, we are told, and consequently obtained an exclusive privilege for the kingdom of England, which lasted till the reign of Charles the Second. It is a curious fact, that up to 1776 the workers in salt, as well as the men employed in coal mines, were slaves, and it even appears that they liked their servitude. When even their emancipation was obtained by act of parliament, they revolted against this liberty, and said it was a trick on the part of their masters, who wanted to get off paying a small tribute consecrated by custom. It was, in fact, the usage, that when the slave took a wife the master should make him a present. At the present day, the Scotch salt workers form a free and rough population, almost as black as the miners, but I will not dwell on these works, which have retained but slight importance in the face of the English salt pits and springs.

These are found isolated from each other at various points of Cheshire and Worcestershire, but they are only found combined at Northwich. This little town, surrounded by thoroughly English scenery, stands on the banks of the Weaver, a pretty river running over a bed of marl, and uniting with the Daw a little distance further on. There are two churches, one of which, perched on a mound and built of red sandstone, salutes the visitor from a distance. The town itself has nothing remarkable about it; the only thing that struck me on arrival was the ruinous state of the houses. At the *Angel*, where I lodged—and which, I believe, is the only inn in the town—the staircase staggered like a drunken man, and the walls of my room, half disjointed, seemed to be on bad terms with the floor. The innkeeper told me, however, with a very serious face, that it was one of the most substantial houses in Northwich, and I was soon forced to share his opinion, for, on walking through certain streets, I saw roofs no longer resting on the houses, brick walls rent, windows that had assumed the quaintest forms, and chimneys that allowed the smoke to emerge half way up through yawning crevices. I entered,

through curiosity, a public-house situated much
lower than the level of the street, and whose
architectural lines offered the strangest confusion.
The landlady, an aged woman, who brought my
beer, told me that for some years past the house
had been gradually settling; formerly you went
down into the yard by three steps, now you ascend
to it. "Our house will fall," she added, calmly;
" I only hope my son will not be in it at the moment, for I feel sure I shall finish with it." The
inhabitants of Northwich have the recklessness
of sailors at sea in a leaky ship; not only do
masonry works daily lose their balance on this
mined ground, but within the memory of man
remarkable changes have occurred in the level of
the land and river, and I was shown valleys which
were formerly almost hills. The bed of the
Weaver itself has sunk: a few years back, a boat
could hardly make its way in one of the bends of
the river; now, at the same spot, a man-of-war
might tack, so considerable is the depth. The
cause of these changes may be easily discovered.
The town and the neighbourhood rest on a soil
internally traversed by abundant springs, and these
subterranean water-courses, formed by the rains,
become saline at the expense of the solid masses of
salt over which they run. The result is, that
they disintegrate the rock, and the crust of super-
ficial earth settles with the houses, the fields, and
the streams. It is no longer astonishing, then, to

meet at each step the precursive signs of a great ruin. It is salt which made Northwich, and it is salt, I fear, that will destroy it. The town is, in fact, menaced by the progress of a slow and silent earthquake.

If the salt springs ravage the subsoil, they, on the other hand, give rise to a branch of flourishing trade. This natural wealth, by the way, is extremely limited, for the springs of saline water only exist in two English counties, and are almost entirely absent in Scotland and Ireland. At Northwich they are met with almost on leaving the town: in the midst of an open landscape, studded with fields, trees, and isolated houses, round which horses and cattle graze, rise at regular distances buildings of a gloomy hue and black aspect, surmounted by one or two brick chimneys, from which smoke pours, casting a cloud over the verdure. In these buildings a steam-pump is at work, superintended by an overseer; it fetches the water from a depth of ninety to one hundred and twenty feet below the surface. This water is strongly impregnated with salt, as I was able to convince myself, for a bucket of brine being offered me, I drank some out of the hollow of my hand, and found it much more bitter than sea-water. This bitterness constitutes the excellence of the English springs, which contain twice as much salt as those existing in France. They say at Northwich, that strangers visiting the salt works pass the water from hand to hand with many a wry face. This water runs subterraneously over a salt rock from twenty-four to thirty feet in thickness; under this rock is a layer of stone, and beneath that again another salt rock. When pumped up, the water is conveyed by pipes to a reservoir: it is a long journey, and it crosses fields, meadows, and fresh-water pools in which ducks swim and quack. These pipes, placed some distance above the ground, are usually trunks of trees hollowed out and fitted to each other. The reservoir or cistern is an immense wooden erection, to which you mount by a ladder, and where a tranquil salt lake stretches out between earth and sky. This water is eventually conveyed to the factory as required, where, after boiling a day and night in a boiling-pan, the saline matter is deposited by evaporation, and is then collected and dried. Some of the Cheshire springs furnish as much as twenty-two, in some cases twenty-five per cent. of salt. The workmen in these establishments are five in number: two men manage the boiler, one watching by day, the other by night. They earn thirty shillings a week each.

The salt-springs of Cheshire have only been extensively worked since the reign of Charles the Second. What most astonishes the traveller, is to find in the heart of the land, in a thoroughly agricultural country, works he might reasonably expect to see only on the coast. This bitter water, which bubbles and meanders in every direction, allowing salt to filter and crystallise in the sun between the pores of the troughs—this marine odour of the factories, these dismantled houses bowing to the ground like wind-beaten ships—all produces a strange contrast with the ploughed fields, the sheep browsing on the plain, and the pleasing pictures of rural life. The image of the ocean becomes still more lively, when we remember that the Cheshire springs owe their mineral wealth to old seas petrified into salt rocks: at such a moment the visitor does not fancy himself separated from the stormy waves by districts of land, but only by the shores of time.

Though the salt springs are very productive, the mines offer the stranger a scene of facts and works even more interesting. A vague tradition tells us that the salt mines, like the brine springs, were formerly worked by the Romans: it is more certain, however, that the salt rocks were discovered, if not found again, about a mile from Northwich, in 1670, by English miners who were looking for coal. Before this period, the salt supply of Great Britain was obtained from the Droitwich springs, in Worcestershire. The opening of the Cheshire mines—for the precious mineral was successively found at Wilton, Marston, Wincham, Sevenington, and Nantwich—increased the internal and external trade to a very considerable extent. At the present day, the nature of the

subsoil is known, and the English, by a wise feeling of foresight, have measured the depths of the
treasure buried by terrestrial revolutions. At
Northwich, a first bed of rock salt is found separated from a second and deeper one by a bed of
hard and stony clay. These two saline masses,
nearly free from earthy matter, have the astonishing thickness of ninety to one hundred feet; from
this fact we may form an idea of the richness of
this formation, but in order to read the secret of
the British race, which incessantly renews its force
and means of supply by industrious contact with
the interior of the earth, we must go down into a
salt mine.

I was led along a path by the side of a field,
on which a black flock of rooks had settled: and
beneath this field the mine extended. High chimneys and buildings of clumsy construction denoted
the mouth of the pit; beneath a shed, covered
with tiles, and in which lay, pell-mell, enormous
fragments of rock salt, was the shaft, or, as the
English have it, the eye of the mine, on the edge
of which I found a man, who asked me if I wished
to go down. On my affirmative reply, a large
barrel, three or four feet in circumference, suspended in the air by a powerful chain, was
lowered. I mounted the platform and jumped
into the tub, which covered me nearly to the neck.
As there were three of us, we were advised to
keep close together, because the mouth of the pit

was narrow, and lined with iron to a certain depth, and we ran a risk of coming into a rude contact with the sides of the shaft. The barrel, lifted by the chain, oscillated for a second over the pit's mouth, and then rapidly descended in the growing night. Already all was silent; nothing was to be heard save the filtering of the salt water through the rock: though the depth of the shaft was not more than three hundred and thirty feet, and the descent only lasted a few minutes, this journey even seemed to me long and monotonous. It is natural enough, in such a case, to raise the eyes to the pit's mouth in order to seek the light, the circle of which grew momentarily narrower. At about the middle of the shaft, this light appeared like a moon: when the barrel reached the earth, it was only a star.

We were received by a man of about fifty, with grey hair and a venerable face, who had worked in the mine since the age of twelve. He gave us long and thin candles; he had in his own hands a miner's candlestick; that is to say, a lump of soft clay, which allowed the light to be fixed against the sides of the rock, and easily assumes any shape. These torches only seemed to render the darkness more visible, which, at the first glance especially, seemed to cover the cavern like a black veil. The salt mines, however, have nothing of that solemn horror which reigns in the entrance of coal mines, and you do not feel those drops of muddy

water fall on your head, which trickle through
the damp and low roof, like the tears of the night.
A salted but dry air, a pleasant and uniform tem-
perature, penetrate these gloomy places, and the
roof of the mine, supported by side walls or by
pillars cut in the solid rock, is of considerable elevation. For the rest, the works and system of
excavation are nearly the same as in collieries:
man forces a way through the thickness of the
solid and crystallised masses by the aid of pick
and wedge or gunpowder. As you advance in
the salt mine, the scene widens, and the internal
space is revealed to you: it is, then, difficult not
to admire this simple but grand architecture, these
empty spaces extending in the darkness like the
nave of an immense subterranean church; these
works, which have the shape, colour, and trans-
parency of sugar-candy; these massive pillars
whose fronts shine in the reflexion of the light
you carry in your hand; and, more than all this,
the religious character which silence and night
shed over these labours of human industry. From
time to time, you see one or more lights flashing
in the black extremity of the mine: they are the
workmen. When they move, their lights vaguely
design human forms, like those we fancy to ourselves inhabiting a wizard's cave. From time to
time, too, the habitual silence of these vaults is
violently disturbed by explosions that sound like
thunder: it is the powder dislocating the limbs of

the rock. You walk over a pile of ruins: the uneven floor is covered with gigantic fragments of crystal, which have principally a yellow or reddish colour, though some are white and transparent as glass. At the sight of these rent rocks, this mineral wealth, which seems to grow again beneath the strokes of the pick or the train of gunpowder—for the mass is so inexhaustible—you cannot but believe in a wise Providence of nature. Man likes to imagine that for him, and in view of his wants, these enormous magazines of salt were swallowed in the earth, these works of departed seas, which laboured for him and built these rocks at an infinitely remote period, when none of the animal forms now living on the surface of the British Isles had as yet left the mould of creation. If, when performing this task, the elements of that age did not think of human societies, some one must have done so for them.

The salt miners have their festivals. At Christmas and Whitsuntide, as many as six hundred candles are lighted, and I leave my readers to guess the effect thus produced in the subterranean crystal palace by the reflexion of these lights on so many glistening surfaces. Bands of music play suitable airs, and dancing sometimes goes on, the wives of the miners being on those days substituted for the somewhat coarse divinities with whom the ancients loved to people these deep

grottos. During the rest of the year, however, the
salt mines have that serious character best suited
to labour and night. My guide knew this vault
as well as his bedroom, but I fancied that every
pillar must be the last, for the rays of the candle
I carried in my hand did not extend beyond that,
but it was followed by another, then by another,
and between these two points ran wide vaults,
appearing suspended over an abyss. At intervals,
the eye lost itself amid an endless obscurity, where
all had the immobility of the tomb. At length
we reached the end of the mine: a party of workmen were engaged here in extracting blocks of
salt, which were piled up nearly to the roof.
Among these workmen, some were performing a
very hard task: with their heads bowed under
the arch like antique Caryatides, they were
digging out large pieces of crystal in the thickness of the wall, or forming the channel, which,
when filled with powder, would blow up the
masses of rock. The number of workmen and
mode of transport vary according to the importance of the mine; in the one I was visiting,
fifty men extract weekly fifteen hundred tons of
raw salt, and receive a daily wage of three shillings
and sixpence; and the men themselves remove
the rock. In other mines, horses, ponies, and
donkeys are employed to drag the blocks of salt
on a tramway. These animals were taken down

the mine when very young, and only leave it to be killed: during the hours of rest, they lie in a stable cut out of the rock-salt.

We returned to the entrance of the mine by a different road from that by which we had reached the end. Though the time spent in these underground passages is not very long, and despite the very real interest aroused by the great features of human industry, the soul feels oppressed by the darkness as by a cloak of lead. My guide felt nothing of the sort, for he was attached to the mine as to an old acquaintance. He was proud of the admiration expressed on all faces by the sight of this rough crystal edifice, which seemed built by fairies in the interior of the earth. "The only misfortune is," he told me, "that the salt mines cost a deal to work, and their duration is uncertain. They may be destroyed by divers accidents, but chiefly by the springs that run over the roof, and continually wear it away. At times these springs force their way into the works, dissolve the pillars on which the various parts of the edifice rest, and produce the downfal of the whole mass, which leaves vast craters on the surface of the soil, as if after an earthquake. The miners then at work are lost! Of course you saw, close by, the spot where a salt mine fell in a few years back, bearing with it a steam-engine, six horses, nine men, and several houses." The idea that the water ran over our heads, and that the roof of the mine might burst, had nothing very reassuring about it; but this imaginary danger added the charm of emotion to the gloomy beauty of the scene. By this time we had reached, through a vast gallery, the ventilating shaft, which English engineers compare with the trachean artery, for the miner breathes through it. Through the circles of gloom which rose whirling to the sky, the light of day could be seen of the shape and whiteness of a shilling. Our guide made us presents—a few curious pieces of rock-salt—and then bade us good day. The vehicle which had carried us to the bottom of the mine drew us up again silently: in our ascent, we saw the candles and men gradually disappear; and after traversing the night, we found ourselves again in the shed, in the midst of the blocks landed by the barrel.

This mineral is employed in certain countries to sculpture works of art: in Spain, near Cordova, in Catalonia, there is a mountain of salt rising to a height of four to five hundred feet. The Cordova salt is often variously coloured, but generally white and transparent as crystal, and lies for a long time in water ere dissolving; it is made into vases, urns, and chandeliers. The rock-salt found in England is much more sensible of the effects of damp, and hence it is speedily converted into an article of trade. From the mouth of the mine it is first conveyed to the boiling-house, where it is puri-fied, and assumes the whiteness of snow. These

boiling-houses are clumsy buildings, with a furnace and tall chimneys, which at night flare in
the sky like torches: you ascend by a wooden
ladder to a platform, in the centre of which
steams a caldron, open and of but slight depth,
about twenty feet long by twelve feet wide. Into
this the salt is thrown, more or less loaded with
earthy matter, and just as it emerges from the
bowels of the earth. When it has boiled for six or
seven hours, it is collected in barrows, which are
nearly the shape of a sugar-loaf, and conveyed
to a hot room, where it is left to dry for some
days. From this moment the salt is made,
and it only remains is to place it in the store-
house, in which it is curious to see these snowy
mountains, more or less covered with a slight
crust of dust. The whiteness of the manufactured
salt, in truth, contrasts strikingly with the gloomy
and smoke-stained walls of the factory, the heaps
of coals, and all sorts of black things. When
brought into trade, the salt is moved with a spade,
and loaded on carts or boats. The sight of such
works arouses more than one thought as to the
care and sacrifices required for the preparation of
the most ordinary matters. The Cheshire furnaces have roared, the engine wheels have turned,
the lives of workmen have even been destroyed
in more than one instance by various accidents,
before man can enjoy on his table a thing so
trifling as a pinch of salt.

With reference to the salt trade, the position of Northwich is excellent: nearly all the salt intended for export is made in the valley of the Weaver, and is sent down that river in barges. The Weaver communicates with the Mersey. Among the other mines of Cheshire, I may mention those of Wilton and Nantwich. At the former place I visited the finest and most gigantic works of this nature, I believe, which exist in England. Imagine a circular building, one hundred and twenty yards in circumference, whose roof is supported by twenty-five pillars of enormous dimensions, and when lighted with candles these masses of solid salt produce a grand and entrancing effect. The stupified visitor knows not which to admire most —the subterranean wealth of nature, or the titanic character of the constructions. Nor must we forget Droitwich, which produces the whitest salt known in the world. This place was known to the Romans; it now sends, by canal, immense quantities of salt, which, not having been tossed by the waves, reach London in the best condition, that is to say, in the shape of snow-white bricks of a fine and sparkling grain. At London, the great *entrepôt* of this article is in the City-road, where, from the bridge crossing the canal, you can see the wharfs and salt stores, and there are other establishments of the same nature at Wapping, and near Billingsgate Market. We are in this way enabled to form an idea of the bond existing between the geology of the British Isles and the commercial prosperity of the English nation. The inexhaustible springs and mines of Cheshire supply salt to several European and American states, and the English especially export this merchandise to Holland, Prussia, and Russia. The annual production of salt in England is estimated at 500,000 tons : the capital embarked in the manufactories is said to be a million, and the number of workmen they provide with a livelihood is calculated at from 10,000 to 12,000.

The working of the salt mines leads us to speak of the life of the miners, who form a very distinct corporation, and must not be confounded with the colliers. In the first place, the constant presence in the salt mines is much less unpleasant and dangerous than in the other underground workshops of Great Britain. The air there is dry and salubrious, and the men even complain that it is too good, for the saline air produces the effect of a sea breeze, by exciting thirst and appetite. The Cheshire miners who commit no excesses attain the ordinary average of mortality, but, unfortunately, the temptation is great : these men have, as they say themselves, a devil in their throats, and, as their wages are rather high for the country, they too frequently exorcise the evil spirit by a glass of ale or porter. In the coach that carried me from Northwich to the station was a girl, who, having come a long distance to see her brother at work in the mines, was returning with tears in her eyes, for she had only seen the walls of the prison in which that brother, otherwise respectable, had been locked up owing to excesses provoked by drink. I should not like the morals of all the salt miners to be judged by this isolated fact; but I have it from a Protestant clergyman in those parts—Mr. Waller—that providence and sobriety are the virtues least practised by these men, who come up from the mine very thirsty souls. Though more civilised than the colliers, the salt miners still leave much to be desired under the head of education : they have hitherto but slightly benefited by the sources of moral development opened up in Northwich and other towns by public benevolence.

The Saxon race has in its veins a drop of the blood of the Titans : nothing checks it, nothing terrifies it in the conquest of the physical world: it hurls haughty defiance at nature, hollows mountains, levels rocks, and casts in the face of heaven the riches dragged from the bosom of the earth; but this strong-armed race all at once becomes timid, so soon as an attempt is made to tamper with its hereditary customs. Perhaps we ought to see in this circumstance a wise economy of nature, who has thus placed limits and counterpoises to the audacity of certain human families. The group of miners is distinguished even more than the other branches of English society by a tenacious attachment to the customs and traditions of the past : it is rare for them to take the initiative of any measure tending to ameliorate their condition. Their time, I might almost say their affection, is divided between the mine, to which they are affianced at an early age, and family life.

A few years back, a great many women were employed in the Worcestershire salt works, but the laborious nature of the work, and the state of semi-nudity they require, were altogether incompatible with feelings of delicacy. A reform introduced by Mr. Corbett, the contractor, and seconded by the clergy, has now limited the number of females employed in the salt works, and nothing of the sort exists in Cheshire, where the women content themselves with looking after their household affairs.

Groups of houses, scattered over fields and situated in the vicinity of the mines or springs, shelter an industrious population. Built of brick, they have a family look about them, announcing the presence of equal social conditions: while a garden, frequently cultivated by the women, a few chickens, and that indispensable friend of the family, an honest porker, add an air of ease and rustic comfort to the miner's abode. These quiet roofs amid a tranquil scene often conceal, however, more than one painful scene: when the husband is late home, the wife trembles;

she fears lest the chain has broken, or a mass
of rock has fallen and wounded her husband.
Such catastrophes are, in truth, too common
to all the miners. At the door of a cottage,
I noticed a woman of about thirty, dressed in a
plain black gown, and a widow's cap surrounding
a pleasant but thin face. A bunch of wooden
grapes hanging over the door told me that this
widow kept a beer-shop and I could go in; and
after sitting down, I asked her by what accident
she had lost her husband. "It is," she answered,
" a story known to all the miners round. My husband—Heaven rest his soul!—had worked from
infancy in a salt-pit, the chimneys of which you
can see from here. The first time he paid me his
attentions was at a feast held at Christmas-tide
in the mine, where more than a thousand candles
were lit. I was then seventeen, and considered
good-looking: he was twenty-two, and admired
by all the girls round, and I believe that our
growing love aroused the jealousy of one of the
spirits living in the interior of the earth. I must
tell you that it is a haunted mine, and that fact
was well known to my grandmother. Indeed, I
heard through the mine strange voices murmuring in my ear, and my heart beat loudly: hence I
left the mine in a state of sad trouble. A few
days later, I was taking my kid out for a country
stroll, when I met William (that was his name)
returning from work. He addressed me, and as

I was confused, I raised my eyes to heaven, where I saw the new moon. 'William,' I said to him, 'make haste and give me some money;' for I had none in my apron-pocket. He offered me his leathern purse, adding, it was mine if I liked to accept it. 'It is not that,' I replied, 'but I want to make a wish.' I turned a piece of money in my hand and wished: I don't know whether I was red at the moment, but he understood the wish I had whispered to myself, for he said, 'It will be: my word is as good as the moon's.' In fact, six months later we were married. William was a good workman, who did not spend his money with his mates: hence, our little house prospered, and our marriage was blessed by the birth of two children. Still, I was not free from anxiety, for I knew too well the spite of the spirits, and whenever he was late in coming home, I lost my head. One night (it is just eighteen months ago), I had uselessly counted hour after hour, and, suffering from extreme agitation, I ran to the pit's mouth: I read at once in the faces of the men that an accident had happened down in the mine; though they tried to hold me back, I leaped into the bucket in spite of them; and, when they saw I was resolute, they consented to let loose the chain. The mine was silent and gloomy, for the works were stopped; and, at any other moment I should have been frightened, but the fear of a real danger and some terrible event gave me courage. I staggered from pillar to pillar to the end of the mine, where a quantity of candles were burning; and you can judge of my despair, when, amid a circle of miners, I perceived my husband lying almost insensible on piles of salt, and a comrade holding his head. The other workmen had thrown their coats over him to cover him. He recognised me and tried to smile, but the pallor of death was on his face: they had sent for a doctor, who arrived a few moments later. He examined him; then shaking his head with a look that froze the blood in my veins, he asked an explanation of the accident. 'This block fell on him,' said one of the workmen, pointing to an enormous mass of salt that lay on the ground. By the doctor's directions, two of the men carried my poor husband carefully, and laid him on a sledge which was dragged to the shaft. During the journey I held his right hand, which was pendent and cold; but when we reached the shaft he expired. The miners are good to each other, and take compassion on poor widows; they helped me into this little trade, and now come to drink at my beer-shop in preference to any other in the neighbourhood."

Such are the dangerous works extracting salt demands. In order to know the application of that mineral, I was compelled to proceed to other industrial or agricultural districts.

CHAPTER VII.

MUNGO PARK—THE SALT-CELLAR—SALT STREET-DEALERS—TRADE
USES OF SALT—SHEFFIELD—THE SHEAF WORKS—STEEL—TRADE
SOCIETIES—THE SCOTCHMAN—SOWING SALT—AGRICULTURAL USE
OF SALT.

To form an idea of the value of any natural produce we must suppose it absent from the surface of the globe, and this hypothesis is not devoid of all foundation if we look at it from a certain geographical point of view. There are countries in which salt has not yet been discovered, and where, as the commercial relations are extremely limited, the inhabitants can only procure that object of luxury by chance. I will quote, as an instance, the interior of Africa, where the European traveller is surprised to see the children sucking with delight a piece of rock-salt, just as if it were a lump of sugar. This dainty is interdicted to the poor, and hence, in the language of the country, to say that a man eats salt with his meals is a manner of declaring that he is rich. A celebrated English traveller, Mungo Park, who

visited these barbarous regions, himself confesses
that he suffered severely by the privation of this
condiment, and he says that a lengthened course
of vegetable food, without a salt seasoning, produces a feeling of discomfort such as human language cannot describe.

Salt is not only an aliment in itself, but it im-
proves the taste of nearly all other alimentary
substances. The use of this condiment is extremely old, and is lost in the night of ages: and
a kitchen article of such daily use was mingled
with domestic manners and customs. In Scotland
the floor of a new house, or of one that changed
its tenant, was always strewn with salt—good
luck, it was supposed, was thus introduced. A
plate of salt was also placed on the body of the
dead after the completion of the funeral toilet,
the object of this custom being to avert evil influences. Salt was, in addition, connected with the
relations of social life. The master offered it to
his servants, and the head of the house presented it
to his guests as a pledge of the fidelity that must
prevail among them. It even served to mark the
distinction of ranks. Formerly, in Scotland, persons of rank dined with their subordinates and
servants: the head of the house occupied, like the
members of the family, the head of the table, and
the flooring of the hall was raised at that spot, as
if to do them honour. The most distinguished
guests sat by the side of their host, the others fol-

lowed, the rank of the persons declining in this way to the end of the table, where the servants were. Thus was offered a perfect image of the society of the day, with the differences of rank, assembled beneath the authority of the pater-familias. At a certain spot on the table was a large salt-cellar, serving as the line of demarcation between the superiors and inferiors: sitting above the salt was the privilege of a gentleman, or man of good family, while "sitting below the salt" was a general expression indicating an humble position in society. There was also a corresponding re-duction in the quality of the liquors: a generous wine flowed at the head of the table in horns, then the beverage became more ordinary, and finished at the end of the table in small beer.

At the present day salt, if we regard the cheap-ness of that product, is in Great Britain rather a symbol of equality than inequality between the classes. We must, in the first place, point out the causes which have lately reduced so low the value of this ware; namely, first, the richness of the salt mines and springs; and next, the abolition of the tax. This tax was imposed by William the Third, in 1798: it was five shillings a bushel, or about a penny on each pound of salt; but during the Napoleonic wars it was raised to fifteen shillings a bushel. Public opinion was roused, and the tax on salt was abolished, in 1823, by the House of Commons. It is curious to notice with what ease the English parliament suppresses suddenly and without reservation any of the important branches of the public revenue, so soon as the general feeling is pronounced against such contributions. The consequences of the measure passed in 1823 were excellent; the abolition of the tax put an end to salt smuggling, which was formerly carried on upon a considerable scale. The smugglers practised their frauds with extreme boldness, at times passing through villages on Sundays, when everybody was at church. The noise of their heavy waggons rolling on the road, we are told, reached the ears of the pious congregation, scandalised, but motionless, and restrained by the austerity of the Protestant ritual. Another service, no less considerable, rendered by the suppression of the tax, was to increase the use of an article of primary necessity, for salt is a product whose consequences extend to everything—to domestic comfort, the arts, trade, and agriculture.

Before 1823, and even for some years after the abolition of the salt tax, the trade was in the hands of shopkeepers, who were obliged to take out special licenses, but the cheapness of the article and freedom of selling have given rise, during the last thirty years, to the trade of street salt-dealers. The latter go about London, and even the country, with a small flat-surfaced vehicle, on which are laid the salt bricks in their unspotted whiteness. The most conscientious of these petty dealers, those who are anxious to keep their reputation white as their salt, buy it at Moore's Wharf, Paddington, where the dearest and best refined is sold. They pay at the rate of two shillings a hundred-weight, and sell it retail at a penny per pound; for in trade salt is not measured but weighed. A man can set up as itinerant salt-merchant with a very small capital. What costs most is the horse, donkey, or pony; and hence several of them do without it, and bravely drag their own truck. One of these dealers, whom, having once known possessed of a donkey and a cart, I afterwards met in Plumstead streets with no other ally but himself, thus explained to me the motive for this economic reform. "In the first place," he said, "the brute ate too much—sevenpence or eightpence a day; and in the next, as the roads are stony, I was constantly having it new shod. One day, when I had bought it a set of shoes, I noticed that mine were in a very bad state, so I resolved to get rid of my donkey, and have better shoes on my own feet. I now pay the cobbler what I used to pay the farrier, and find myself better off." Though rather large, the army of street-sellers is limited by the competition of the numerous shopkeepers who also sell the article. English table-salt enjoys a European reputation, and deserves it, for the fineness, purity, and solid nature of the bricks, which resemble sugar-loaves of a flattened or elongated shape. The consumption is enormous: it is calculated that in France each individual absorbs annually nineteen and a half pounds of salt, while the inhabitants of Great Britain consume twenty-two pounds a head. A distinguished economist, MacCulloch, attributes to this fact a certain influence on the food of the two races. According to him, it is the reason why an Englishman eats more than his neighbour across the Channel.

Salt represents the conservative principle in nature: it communicates an eternal youth to the waters of certain lakes, and especially of the sea, which, were it absent, would have been for millions of years a sink of corruption. It is also in its character of a condiment that salt plays the highest part in the public nourishment: the use of this substance, at once natural and artificial, responds in civilised peoples to the feeling of saving and foresight. While the savage gorged with meat allows the rest to rot around him, on the risk of dying of privation and want a few days later, the civilised man overthrows chance by preserving his provisions. There is possibly no nation in the world so dependent on salt as Great Britain; and you can easily convince yourself of this fact, if you reflect on the extent of its military posts, maritime relations and colonies, cast on coasts and sterile rocks to the furthest ends of the habitable world. The same substance which, in the hands of nature, has served to "pickle the ocean," now aids man in furrowing the surface of the deep. Were it not for the use of salt meats, it would have been impossible to undertake lengthened voyages, and some English vessels which cruise for three or four years in deserted seas, would lack the means to revictual. The cheapness and abundance of this condiment have given the British fisheries a development that defies all rivalry; even Holland has struck her flag before the nets of England. Agriculture, for its part, derives a part of its riches from the enormous quantity of salt meat which Great Britain consumes, or exports to the extremities of the world; and the art of preserving has attained a high degree of perfection throughout the United Kingdom. It must be observed, however, that the best salt for preserving meat and fish is not derived from the Cheshire mines and springs, but from the continental salt-works, where the sun performs the office of boiler. The English import for this purpose three thousand four hundred bushels of salt annually from the coasts of Spain and Portugal. Salt, moreover, is not applied solely to the usages of domestic life: it is employed in manufactures, to compose a great number of chemical products and medicinal drugs; it pays a tribute to the arts by entering into the preparation of painter's patent yellow; it aids in the manufacture of glass, the varnishing of earthenware, and bleaching linen; and is also used to temper steel, and render iron malleable. I will dwell on this last order of its services, and choose, as the scene of the metallurgical labours in which salt figures, the town of Sheffield.

Sheffield has been christened by the English the metropolis of steel. When you arrive by the railway, the town, which is, so to speak, only one immense forge, situated at the mouth of the collieries, seems to be struggling for breath in a dense cloud of smoke; trees, houses, sky, all are black. Seated on the confluence of two rivers— the Sheaf, to which it owes its name, and the Don, which enters the Sheffield territory at Wardsend—this sombre manufacturing town also receives some other streams descending from the adjacent hills. These laborious waters render more than one service to the factories and forges, and especially supply by their fall an immense and cheap motive power to the wheels. I must say that they bear the punishment of their utility, for they are all of a perturbed and muddy hue: recently, drinking water has had to be brought in, and reservoirs formed at a vast expense, for the domestic use of the inhabitants. Trade has equally depopulated all the streams and rivers round Sheffield. A miller showed me sorrowfully a rapid brook which turned his mill-wheel, and in which he remembered having caught trout when a lad. Now-a-days, these waters work too hard to produce any living thing, and fish have . withdrawn from them in proportion as trade poured into them its strange or deleterious elements. It is, besides, curious to follow along the sides of the Sheaf—which deserves even more than the Tiber the epithet of *flavus*—a double unbroken line of forges and factories, of every description, distinguished by grand and quaint buildings. I will notice among others the Wheel Tower, a vast and gloomy building whose chimneys are towers, and which, situated near a bridge, affects the style of the old mediæval fortresses: here, the roaring of the wheels and engines never ceases night or day; and here, too, the chronicles of artisan life have had to register gloomy dramas. The rivalries between the different unions, the jealousy between the free and the associated workmen, have more than once broken out under these sinister-looking vaults, and produced sad crimes. Most of the low streets of Sheffield have a character of sorrow, wedged in as they are between the houses of the workmen and the wall or chimneys of the forges. People would choke there of smoke, and I believe die of *ennui*, had not nature cast over all this a festive air, by opening all around smiling views. The town is surrounded by a girdle of green hills rising like an amphitheatre, and whose gently sloping sides are covered with trees, fields, and country houses.

The result is, that from nearly every street the denizens or walkers can console themselves by the sight of fields or wooded heights. Formerly, there were even forests round Sheffield, but trade has destroyed them: charcoal was required to melt the iron. It has been observed that this mineral is found most abundantly in well covered places, and that nature enriched the forests to their own destruction. If the environs of Sheffield, however, have lost much of their wood, the soil is still very rich in minerals; such as iron, coal, and stone, and it is to the latter circumstance that the origin of the factories and industrial character of the inhabitants is referable.

I will only say a word about the history of the town. Sheffield was formerly commanded by a castle that served as residence to the Lords of Hallamshire. With time this castle was to a certain extent invested by the development of factories and forges. It was a struggle between the feudal system and the new power of trade; one must conquer the other, and it was trade that won the day. In 1647, at the end of the wars between the Parliament and the Royalist party, a decree of the House of Commons demolished the old castle, of which only a few arches now remain; but for all that, a large portion of Sheffield is held at this hour by a descendant of the Lords of Hallamshire, the Duke of Norfolk. I saw in the town a brick mansion to which the name of the Lord's House

is given, but his grace does not reside there. As
it is a principle of the English aristocracy never to
part with land, the present lord grants leases for
twenty-one, ninety-nine, and even nine hundred
and ninety-nine years, according to the nature of
the estate. Nine hundred years! who can help
being struck by the feeling of eternity which distinguishes noble families in Great Britain.

When I landed on English soil, I expected, on the
faith of books, to find there only castles and hovels,
lords and poor; but it does not need a lengthened
residence on the island to convince oneself that
the strength of the nation and the government
of the country rest in the hands of the middle
classes. It is particularly at Sheffield that you
can form an idea of the power created by trade:
the proprietors of the forges and great factories,
these steel lords, rival the oldest families in luxury
and influence. There are a thousand rich country
houses to one castle, and this strength of capital
and labour, to which we may give the name of
legion, everywhere limits the ancient prerogatives
of birth. It is, besides, just to allow that the
English noblemen do not recoil from considerable
sacrifices to improve the towns and extend their
popularity. Thus the Dukes of Norfolk have
given to the public of this said town of Sheffield
a vast and splendid park, where the verdure of
the trees, the peace and the silence, only interrupted by the song of birds, form a pleasant con-

trast with the noise of hammers and saws, the
smoky streets, and the black dens of the forges.
To them the town is also indebted for a market
covered with an immense arch, possessing that
character of Roman grandeur which the English
impress on their architectural works.

What I especially sought at Sheffield was the
relation existing between iron and salt; and to
trace it, we must follow the transformations of the
metal from the moment when it arrives by canal
in the town, to the instant when it leaves the
forges and factories. This canal, made in 1815,
terminates at Hull, and forms a direct line of communication with the German Ocean. It is so
covered with boats, that you cannot even see the
colour of the water. All parts of the world pay
their tribute to the various Sheffield trades. The
elephants of Africa, the buffaloes of India, and the
stags of Russia and Germany, furnish their tusks,
their horns, and their antlers for cutlery, but the
boats chiefly bring in coals, deals, and iron. It is
a curious sight to see all this raw wealth discharged
on the muddy banks of the canal, which has justly
been christened one of the fiords of the Baltic.
Bar-iron comes from Russia and Sweden, but the
most esteemed is the Norwegian. It is carried
straight from the banks of the canal to the forges.
The type of these establishments is a large factory
known by the name of Sheaf-works, which stands
on the bank of the river, and whose low and

conical chimneys flame in the night like the eye of a Cyclops.

The labour may be divided into three parts: the bars of iron are first piled up in a closed furnace between layers of charcoal, and subjected to an immense heat; this is called making the metal suffer. After fifteen days of purgatory, when the iron has absorbed a certain amount of carbon, and is hardened and purified in the fire, it is taken out of the furnace, and from this moment is no longer iron, but steel. The next operation is to weld or cast it. In the first process, it is placed under an enormous hammer moved by machinery, and called the tilt-hammer; when it strikes, you might fancy it an enormous ram's-head chewing red-hot iron. The hammer works to weld together several bars of steel into a single one, which is then called sheer steel. The metal intended for casting undergoes a very different preparation: the bars are broken in pieces, and the fragments are placed in clay crucibles. There are few sights in the world more appalling than that of these men, or demons, moving about with pincers in the interior of a low room, a real volcanic crater—those fiery urns which pour forth fire. Cast steel leaves the mould in a purer state than the welded steel does the hammer. From this point the steel is made, but it is kept for three or four years in a cellar before being employed; like wine, it is improved by age, and is even better for crossing the sea; all it loses in weight it gains in quality. From this simple fact an idea may be formed of the vast capital required in England for keeping the forges at work; indeed, they are less factories than villages, with muddy streets, strange buildings, huts of smooth earth, caverns in which water, wind and iron toil, and where the fire-serpents writhe between the naked legs of the workmen.

The steel manufactured at Sheffield passes through several hands, and is employed for various cutlery works. It has an important trial still to undergo, that of hardening, for tempered steel assumes a peculiar hardness, and will break but not bend. The processes vary with the different purposes to which the metal is put, and I will only allude to the hardening of saws and files. These two articles of commerce hold an important place in the steel trade, and the Sheffield mark causes them to be accepted all over the world. The excellence of these articles depends, in a great measure, on the manner of hardening them; when the file has left the hands of the engraver, who has cut the teeth with a chisel, it passes into those of the hardener, who plunges it red-hot into a solution of salt and rain-water. The workmen call the hardening the christening of the file: henceforth it bites everything and nothing can bite it. Salt is of extreme importance in this branch of metallurgy. The success of English files and saws recently occasioned some competition; steel manufactories have especially sprung up in Germany, but the dearness of salt on the Continent offers an obstacle to their efforts, while the cheapness is, in the hands of the Sheffield makers, a privilege they will not easily lose. The latter, however, complain that the Germans, not satisfied with counterfeiting their productions, also give them English trade marks, and files made in Germany, and of inferior quality, are sent to foreign countries with the names and arms of the first Sheffield firms. A manufacturer of that town thought he would foil the defrauders by printing on his packets a ticket containing his name, trade-mark, and the words, " Imitating my articles and signature is a felony." The counterfeiters copied the ticket and the rest without forgetting the word felony.

The life of the makers and workmen at Sheffield offers some interesting features. The steel lords arrive in the morning, in their carriage or on horseback, at their gloomy and sad-looking factories, with their fissured walls, their tottering wooden staircases, and the damp and smoky workshops, in which the laws of Hygeia have not always been respected. At night they return to splendid houses surrounded by gardens, and built in that part of the town which stands on the hill-side. Some of them live some distance out in splendid villas, where the scenery around them puts on an air of elegance and ceremony. Walks covered with asphalte, and dry even in winter, meander through the fields at the pleasure of the rambler; in the houses, the panes, made of one piece of glass, allow a glimpse of rare flowers, ladies in pretty dresses, and all the pomp of family life. The ideas of these merchants do not extend beyond the horizon of business, though I am free to confess that this circle embraces a considerable range. One of them explained his pleasures to me in these words:

"At night, when I have my feet on the fender, I fancy I am dining, in the person of my knives, with the kings and great ones of the earth; that my saws and files are at work in both worlds; that my fine steel scissors are cutting rich and delicate embroidery in the hands of beauty; that my razors are travelling over the noble chins of youth; that my knives are making pens destined to run under the fingers of celebrated authors and statesmen; and that my steel hoops lend the ladies of the most aristocratic classes certain forms which nature has refused them. I go to sleep after, that more satisfied, and forget for an hour the cares of trade."

The file-smiths form a very powerful organisation, and the more skilful among them gain two, three, and even four pounds a week. To limit the competition of hands, they can have only one apprentice, or two at the most—the result of which is, that their union is small, and does not increase. The members pay weekly into their fund a sum proportionate to their wages, and this capital, now amounting to the enormous sum of twenty thousand pounds, is intended to support the sick, defend the interests of the trade society, and keep up strikes, if necessary. These workmen are accused of having more than once exercised a pressure on the masters, which may become ruinous to both within a given period; for the high price of handicraft in England has produced, it is said, on the Continent, a competition which slight concessions on the part of the Sheffield workmen would have annihilated. Wisdom decreed that they should not sacrifice the interests of the future to those of the present, but this consideration was despised by the file and saw cutters, who haughtily rest on their old resources. It must not be supposed, however, that because the men of these unions earn so much money, they are the better educated, or richer on that account: there are at Sheffield useful institutions, schools, and libraries, but, up to the present, education has spread but slightly among the working classes. On the other hand, opportunities for dissipation and irregularity abound, and too often reduce the wages of the best paid trades. I will not allude to the sources of foolish expense found elsewhere, but there is at Sheffield a true living curse for workmen's houses in the Scotchman. This is the name given to the tallyman, who gets into the houses and unrols his bale of goods to tempt the coquetry of the wives and the self-esteem of the husbands. This light-footed Mercury may be met in all parts of the town, but chiefly in those districts where the working classes reside: his visits, his perseverance, his offers are indefatigable, his baits irresistible. He sells on credit, for an agreed-on payment by the week or month, and I may add, that he takes high interest for the credit! The result is, that with the aid of the demon of dress, the earnings of the week too frequently evaporate in ruinous trifles.

Still, I should not like all the Sheffield workmen to be judged by this general portrait; there are some who combine with handicraft skill those qualities of order which preserve the fruits of toil. The latter have their gardens, too; strips of land enclosed by walls or hedges, where they go on Saturday afternoons or Sundays, and these gardens, cultivated with taste and grouped together, form, when seen from a distance, a pleasant mass of verdure. Moreover, all the workmen do not live in the town, and I visited a file-smith who has built himself a small house in the suburbs, on a piece of land he has rented for twenty-one years. He found on the spot the requisite material for building his cottage: for grey sandstone prevails as much at Sheffield as red sandstone does in the neighbourhood of Chester, and is found generally on the surface. This excellent stone supplied him with the foundations and roof of his house; and in fact there are now in the town several houses covered after a similar plan. His house built, the smith divided the land left over into three parts, the orchard, the flower, and the kitchen garden. All this was arranged with perfect taste, and there was even a greenhouse for delicate flowers. A young wife and three children enlivened this modest interior, where labour, cleanliness, and a certain ease spread around the perfume of domestic virtues and happiness. On Monday morning the Sheffield workmen return to their shops, and the town at that moment offers a curious appearance : the extinguished fires of the factories have been kindled again on the Sunday night, and you see on all sides a cloud of smoke rising in the pure sky, which envelopes the rising sun, and ends by obscuring it. After all, this smoke should be respected, for it is a sign of labour. The thousand chimneys which breathe and send up one after another into the blue atmosphere their black breath, are a prelude to the grand concert of noises, the bubbling of the boilers, the clashing of the wheels, and the shrill or hoarse shrieks of the engines, which form the glory and prosperity of Sheffield.

Salt plays an important part in trade; but it also renders signal services to agriculture. Spread in too great quantity over the earth, it destroys the verdure, and leaves at the spots over which it passes only a brown and wrinkled surface.

This circumstance was known to the ancients: and in various passages of the Holy Scriptures we find the words " sowing salt" employed as a metaphor to symbolise desolation and sterility. The same biblical image reappears from time to time in the history of the middle ages, and of the sixteenth century: in 1596, King James IV. threatened to raze the city of Edinburgh, and sow salt where it had stood, to punish it for the seditious conduct of its inhabitants ! This same substance, however, which, if lavished, dries up all vegetation, becomes a source of fertility when employed in a certain proportion. The idea of applying salt to agriculture was proposed, more than two centuries ago, by Napier, the inventor of logarithms; but the attempt has only latterly been made, and already this manure is in great demand throughout England. When combined with soot, it acts as a stimulating element in vegetable life; and it has been found especially adapted to sandy and ferruginous soil. A few years back, Lord R. Manners hit on the idea of watering his estate with salt dissolved in water: the attempt was successful, but a rigid limit had to be observed: an ounce of salt to a gallon of water fertilised the root of the grass, while two ounces destroyed it.

This mineral is also employed, on a great scale, for fattening cattle. It is calculated that one million tons of salt are annually given to the cattle and sheep in Great Britain. The Anglo-Americans have, before all others, extended the practice of this method: in Upper Canada, the cattle spread over the woods and virgin pastures, where they find a wild abundance of grass, but, once every fortnight, they return spontaneously to the farms to obtain a little salt; after eating which, they bury themselves anew in the solitudes. Salt, in these free countries, forms the connecting link between man and the domestic animals; better than the lyre of Orpheus, it collects in the heart of the desert the wildest rams, the half-tamed oxen, and the horses, which run up from all sides and quit the depths of the savannahs at the sight of the colonist who distributes this dainty to them. No other substance—and the fact has been proved—exerts to the same degree as this talisman a species of attractive and irresistible power over the least tamed animals. In 1829, three million and a half bushels of salt were exported from England to the United States and the English colonies of the New World; and the greater portion of this cargo was intended for the cattle.

We have seen what England owes to her geographical position, and one of the mineral riches of her territory. She has only to dip her finger in the sea, or dig for a moderate depth beneath the surface of certain districts, to extract salt, as necessary as bread for the life of the inhabitants. This branch of commerce gives rise to a considerable trade, creates on the coast a nursing school of sailors and fishers, and furnishes the useful arts with a germ of development, wanting, at any rate on so extensive a scale, to the great civilised nations. Salt played an important part in the ancient religious rites and ceremonies : it was offered to Divinity in the sacrifices. It was the privilege of domestic economy to transform the mystic character of this substance. There is also something religious and sacred in the labour which ransacks the depths of the mines, in the trade which purifies and whitens this conservative manna of nourishment and animal life, and in the commerce which exchanges the elements of comfort, and consolidates the bonds of peace between nations. In the middle ages, salt was a symbol of alliance and fraternity : even at the present day, in some Eastern countries, the men who have shared and exchanged this present of nature are henceforth inviolable to each other. May it become the same between the societies of Europe!

CHAPTER VIII.

MILITARY TEMPER OF ENGLAND—THE BRITISH SOLDIER—WOOLWICH
—THE ACADEMY—ROYAL ARTILLERY INSTITUTION—ADDISCOMBE
—SANDHURST — COUNCIL OF MILITARY EDUCATION — THE COLD
SHADE.

THE notion has been too lightly spread that
Great Britain was not a military nation. The
movement which has taken place during the last
year in the United Kingdom sufficiently contra-
dicts that opinion, which, at a given moment, may
become dangerous to the other European states.
On what do people rely, moreover, when they
recognise in England only a maritime power of
the first class ? Have not English soldiers, though
few in numbers, sufficed for all the great eventu-
alities of history ? Has not for ages the weight
of their arms been felt when the destinies of the
Continent were placed in the scale ? Every time
when victory was needed, have they not conquered ? I will not evoke irritating reminiscences;
I will not write down the name of a great battle
so painful to the self-esteem of the French: suffice

it for me to remind them that recently England recaptured India with a handful of men.

Instead of denying history, it would be better to discover by what bonds the British character is attached to the group of martial nations. The Englishman is not warlike through inclination: he does not like war for the sake of war, he does not keep up an army for the ruinous pleasures of seeing bayonets glistening and ensigns waving. He has an army to defend his territory, his trade, and the immense ramifications of his external affairs and relations. Experience has more than once demonstrated to him the necessity of placing the pride of wealth under the protection of courage. At a meeting where I was present, an English speaker, laying a stress on the necessity of certain sacrifices intended to increase the means of national defence, had recourse to the following comparison :

" Look at the cottages, they defend themselves by their poverty: but the mansions, the factories, the shops, are surrounded, and rightly so, by an army of watchmen. Well, then, it is the same with states, which are the more menaced the more prosperous they are. England is not in vain the great storehouse of Europe: riches and civilisation produce obligations. By the side of the army of artisans whose products excite envy, let us have, then, a powerful army of soldiers, who will cause us to be feared and respected."

The character of the English soldier is based
on this ideal: he possesses less enthusiasm than
coolness.   On the battle-field he dies as he lives
—resolutely, and through a sense of duty.   Im-
movable, he feels weighing on his weapons the
responsibility of labour which has made England
an opulent nation.   The military element offers,
therefore, in Great Britain peculiar and interesting
features.   And then again, very recently, a new
independent army has sprung from the soil to
support the regular army;   yesterday it only
existed in embryo, to-day it fills the town with
the call of its bugles; it has reviews in Hyde
Park and Holyrood, it covers the plains with the
smoke of skirmishers.   I allude to the volunteers,
or riflemen.   We must seek the origin of this
movement in the influence it has already excited
on English manners, but before examining the
army and volunteers ought we not first to study
the military schools and arsenals?   From the
schools come the officers who exert so great an
influence over the morals of the English soldier;
from the arsenals the army derives the munitions and engines of war, which now play so
important a part in battles.   This study, a necessary complement to the preceding, cannot be called
untimely: at a period when all the nations of
Europe are observing each other, and when rumours of war spring up, die out, and are born
again from moment to moment, it will do the

French no harm to know the strength of their neighbours.

In all ages, England has attached great importance to the education of the officers, and the state imposed on itself, in order to form military leaders, sacrifices which have not been fruitless, and yet, during the Crimean war, sharp complaints were raised in the country as to the manner in which operations were conducted before Sebastopol. Public opinion, annoyed by the length of the siege, instead of taking obstacles into account, attracted attention, I should say criticism, to the superior branches of the war administration. The army had not deteriorated, but it had not conquered quickly enough to satisfy the popular self-love. Influential organs, the *Times* itself, which has often rendered the English army a service by being severe to it, pointed out as the root of the evil the patronage which at that time gave commissions to young men of family. The advantage of free nations is that they know how to profit by their faults or the frowns of fortune: discussion may sometimes exaggerate in England the character of the wounds discovered, but, at any rate, it calls in the remedies. The government was aroused by the temper of the country, and, in 1856, a committee was appointed by Lord Panmure to reorganise the education of the officers. This committee proceeded to the various military academies in England, carefully inspected similar institutions in France, Prussia, Austria, and Sardinia, and collected all the documents of a nature to throw light on its researches; the report is a marvel of learning, taste, and impartiality. The authors of this inquiry, Colonel Yolland, Colonel Smythe, and Mr. Lake, of Oxford University, pointed out what needed reform in the English system to raise the military educational establishments to the height of that inevitable progression demanded by modern times. They also recommended the formation of a board of military education, which, placed beyond and above the teaching corps, should direct the studies of youths intended for the army. From these varying influences, the pressure of public opinion, the committee appointed in 1856 by the government, and, above all, the board of education, came the happy changes of which we shall find traces in the military schools of Great Britain. These schools are three in number, the Royal Academy at Woolwich, and the Military Colleges of Addiscombe and Sandhurst.

Woolwich is a thorough depôt of arms : barracks, military hospitals, and arsenals, impart to it a rather stern character, contrasting with the peaceable air of most English towns. The town itself, commanded by the brick chimneys of the dockyard and arsenal, squeezed in between the walls of their two great war forges, intersected by monotonous streets which grow gloomier as they

near the Thames, has nothing gay or attractive
about it, but in front of the barracks extends an
immense open plain, the English Champ de Mars.
The grass, though down-trodden by the horses
and soldiers, is, for all that, green and close, for it
is visited by fresh breezes. To the right of this
plain, better known as Woolwich-common, stands
the Rotunda, built by the orders of George IV.,
then Prince Regent, in Carlton-gardens, to receive
the allied sovereigns. Transported to Woolwich,
this stone tent, with a slate roof, now serves as a
repository for models of naval and military buildings; for trophies, among which is a complete suit
of armour that belonged to Bayard; and for inventions and weapons of war, which, collected from the
infancy of the art, form an interesting history of
the way in which men have killed one another at
various periods. On the left, and at the end of
the common, is the Royal Military Academy.

This brick edifice was built in 1815. In the
centre is a solid square building, with four towers,
crowned with octagonal domes, and two wings
extending on either side in a straight line. All
this forms an undecided *ensemble*, a medley of
the Early English and Elizabethan styles, which
I prefer, though, to the solemn coldness of some
stone erections. Six-pounders, drawn up in the
entrance-yard, indicate the character of the institution. Better than the architecture is the
situation the building commands ; in front is

Woolwich-common; behind, runs the wooded range of Shooters Hill, in the centre of which stands out the gloomy and old tower of Severndroog Castle. It may be remarked here, that the English have generally selected picturesque sites for their great civil and military schools, for, in their view, scenery is also a means of education. The rustic beauties of nature dispose the mind to meditation, and the free air of the woods and fields, while developing the physical powers, infuses a species of vigour on the health of the mind.

The origin of this academy, so celebrated in the military annals of Great Britain, dates back to the reign of George II. It was established in 1741, at Woolwich Warren, in a house where the Board of Ordnance assembled, and near another formerly occupied by Prince Rupert.· This school was intended to instruct officers, sergeants, corporals, cadets, and even soldiers, in the different branches of mathematics relating to the artillery and engineer services. In 1761 the institution was limited to the instruction of youth, and about 1777 the study of the classics was introduced. There is a very curious book written by Colonel Wilmot on the history of Woolwich Academy, with plates representing the uniform of the cadets at various periods. This title of cadets, which now serves to indicate pupils, is derived from the habits of Old England, for, in noble families, where the law confers on the eldest son the estate of his ancestors, the younger sons or cadets were most usually destined to the Church or the profession of arms. Originally, Woolwich Academy was subjected to military discipline, and there are in the chronicles of the institution cases of bad conduct tried by courts-martial. Up to the year 1831, the whole expenses of the academy fell on the English government; but, from that date, a scale of annual payments to be made by the family was laid down. The age of admission varied between fourteen and seventeen. Prior to 1855, the candidates were nominated by the Master-General of Ordnance, who was, at the same time, head of the academy. Those chosen, nearly all belonging to the aristocracy by birth or fortune, had to undergo, after nomination, an entrance examination, but we may easily assume that this trial had nothing very serious about it. Two perfectly irreconcilable principles were present— patronage and control. Would it not have been derisive to give with one hand a favour which was withdrawn with the other? The course of study was divided between theory and practice, the first fixed by regulation at four years, the second at one year, which was passed in Woolwich Arsenal.

I will not assert that the school, thus constituted, did not turn out very good artillery and engineer officers; but, for all that, something was wanting. Those cadets who seriously devoted themselves to study, were too often branded with the energetic epithet of bookworms, while the others displayed a marked preference for games and gymnastic exercises. Foot-races, dangerous leaps, lumps of lead cut through with a sword, and other feats of skill, recalled on certain days the golden age of merry and chivalrous England. Prizes were given, and the most honourable reward was a silver bugle, which sounded at the end the successes of the victor.

Such was the state of things when the late war with Russia called the attention of the government to the reorganisation of the military schools. In 1855, a grand reform was effected: an admission by examination was substituted for the nominating system. A circular of the minister appealed to all the candidates, without distinction of class, who wished to enter the Royal Academy: public examinations, open to all youths and directed by examiners independent of the instructing body, succeeded those conducted by the professors within the school walls. Competition had come to dethrone privilege. In any other country, such a change would have seemed to be the overthrow of society: in France, it required nothing less than a revolution to make the upper grades of the army accessible to the middle classes: in England, however, the institutions are endowed with an elastic force, allowing them to expand and yield to the movement of public opinion without any change in the nature of the government. I will not go so far as to assert that this liberal measure met with no opposition, for it found it, and very sharp, among old officers and pupils of the academy. It was accused of assailing the distinction of birth, to which the English traditionally, as it were, attach the privilege of courage. It was, they said, new blood infused in the army, which must obscure the privilege inherent for centuries in the corps of English officers. Some of the cadets, who had entered the academy during the reign of patronage, affected for some time to draw a line of demarcation between themselves, the children of favouritism, and the new comers, the children of their works—between the "gentlemen," and "persons."* This resistance had been foreseen: the government had the good sense to persevere in the path of progress, and if at the present day all the old and lively prejudices are not suppressed, they are at least disarmed. Public opinion and a vote of the House of Commons have consecrated the principle of competition so effectually, that what has been done can never be undone again: the happy effect of this measure on the military studies is incontestable, for it has cut away at the

---

* To understand better the nature of this distinction, I must mention that the old nominations were addressed to *gentlemen*, while Lord Panmure's announcement stated that every *person* who fulfilled the conditions required would be admitted to examination.

root the tree of privilege, and substituted personal merit for the pressure of influences.

Still, we must not exaggerate the influence of the change which has excited so much apprehension. The barriers that closed the officers' career to the majority of citizens have been lowered, but other limits exist, the more insurmountable because they are defined by the very nature of things, and graven on the manners of the people. These limits are the preparatory education, which in Great Britain demands heavy pecuniary sacrifices : the high price of the academy, and, above all, the military code of English officers, who will not admit among them any but young men of good family. During the age of nominations by the Master-General, the son of a quartermaster was admitted into Woolwich Academy on the recommendation of the Duke of Wellington. The cadets were doubtless ignorant of the latter circumstance, for, on his entrance, the new comer was badly received, sent to Coventry and bullied. Advised of what was taking place, the Duke went, himself, to Woolwich and defended his *protégé.* "It was I," he said to the other cadets, "who recommended him, through respect for the memory of his father, an humble but brave officer, who did his duty in the campaigns we fought together, and whoever of you in future ill treat this young man will have to answer to me." It required nothing less than this high intervention to efface the distance between the quartermaster's son and the other pupils. In another case, an intruder was put in Coventry by the cadets, and everybody was forbidden speaking to him in play-hours. One alone generously refused, and he was blamed and menaced by the other cadets, when the Marquis of Anglesey, then governor of the academy, brandishing his cane and leaning on the only leg Waterloo had left him, empha.-tically praised the young man's conduct. We see from this what the force of resistance formerly was in the corps of English officers: and though competition may have modified this resistance, it has not conquered it, and even on this point the fears of the conservatives were exaggerated. In principle, access to the military schools has been opened to all since 1855: practically it remains restricted to a certain class we should call in France *la haute bourgeoisie.*

The entrance examinations take place twice a year at Chelsea Hospital: they are held under the superintendence and direction of the Council of Military Education, in a long hall decorated with old flags of all nations, venerably bullet-torn, and taken by the English in different battles. The sole conditions demanded of the candidates who present themselves are guarantees of morality, and exemption from certain personal defects which would render them unsuited for service. The programme of subjects is rather extensive: it embraces mathematics, pure and applied, history, geography, and English literature, the Greek and Latin classics, French language and literature, German, the experimental sciences (chemistry and physics), the natural sciences (mineralogy and geology), geometrical draughting, and landscape drawing. Each candidate, however, can only select five subjects: in this way it was hoped to repress in youths that unlucky avidity for getting a smattering of all branches of education and knowing none thoroughly. The result of the examination is made public, and those aspirants who have failed in the first trial may make another attempt six months later, till they have attained the age of twenty. Destined not only to control, but to raise throughout the country the level of classical acquirements, these examinations exercise an indirect influence on the civilian schools from which the candidates come. Competition has put a bridle on ignorance and mediocrity, which were too often excused (if it be an excuse) by titles of nobility or a brilliant fortune.

Another no less important reform was the order of the Minister of War, which raised the age of the admission for candidates, and it was fixed between sixteen and twenty. The inconvenience of submitting young men at too early an age to military discipline was most wisely recognised by General Portlock, who was of opinion that the character of lads demands a more delicate training than

may be expected from the officers commanding
in a military school; for in their eyes the pupil,
however young he may be, is a soldier, and they
treat him almost as such. They certainly teach
him his manual exercise excellently, but it is a
moot point whether they have the experience and
the qualities needed to perfect his moral education. Another consequence of premature admis-
sions was the introduction of a species of confusion
and uncertainty in the system of instruction: at
the present day a marked distinction is made between the studies preceding and those following the
entrance to the academy. It has been considered
that a military college stood at the cross-roads of
life—between a good general education completed
and the professional service which is commencing.
The character, mind, and manners of the student
are supposed to be formed according to the customs of society: he has reached the age when the
man chooses his future career. Up to this point
his classical education has but slightly differed
from that equally fitting for the church, the bar,
or medicine: on this general education the instruction of the military academy now grafts practical acquirements.

We know when and how pupils enter Woolwich Academy: let us now see what they do
there. The house is directed by a governor (at
present Colonel Wilford), an inspector of studies,
an assistant inspector of studies, and a chaplain.

On their entrance, the cadets all put on uniform; their time is divided between theoretic studies and the management of the musket, gun, and horse. The highest mathematical professorship has always been held by eminent men, such as Derham, Simpson, Hutton, Olinthus Gregory, Barlow, and the present professor, Mr. Silvester. Among the other branches of study more directly referring to the profession of arms, I will mention military history, the art of fortification, and the science of drawing plans. There are altogether thirty-five professors, among whom eight teach the living languages. It is unnecessary to dwell on a syllabus of studies which is nearly the same as that of all the great military schools in Europe: I should like solely to describe precisely the moral character of English education, which proposes before all (I quote from Dr. Olinthus Gregory) to discover and fecundate in man the heavenly springs of self-government. With the Englishman knowledge is power; and he neglects nothing to develop strength of will simultaneously with the resources of the mind. In order to learn better how to command some day, the cadets begin first by learning to obey, and discipline is maintained inside the school walls, partly at least, by the students themselves. The monitors, selected for their good conduct among these youths, are called corporals, and they exercise a species of authority over the other cadets. Dismissal from the school,

arrest, stoppage of leave, a written or verbal re-
primand, such is the descending scale of punishments proportioned to the nature of the offence.
These punishments, moreover, are only inflicted
with considerable reserve, and the feeling of human
dignity is always regarded. Through a laudable
respect for the uniform, General Portlock, when
inspector of studies, went so far as to propose that
the faults of the students should be tried by the
cadets themselves, forming a jury of honour. A
trait of the English character is the gravity attaching to a charge of falsehood, even when brought
by a master against a pupil; the British blood revolts at the idea of being suspected of an untruth.
Doubting the word of a cadet would be an insult
to the national honour, and the Queen's colours,
in which the cadet is clothed.

The entrance of the building displays a certain
grand architectural character, and you specially
notice a splendid dining-room, darkened by richly
painted glass. Additional buildings are now being
added to the wings. During the hours of recreation the cadets spread over the common and town,
where everything renders them remarkable—their
elegant and light uniform, their youth, and that
interest which is felt by all classes of society for
the growing flower of the English army. The
habit of not confining the pupils within the school-
walls during play-hours is general, and extended to
all schools, and an Englishman gave me this reason

for it. "We must," he said, "form at an early hour
in man the feeling of liberty, if we wish him to learn
how to employ that privilege of our nature without
abusing it." Sports have lost much of the old
splendour that distinguished them at Woolwich
Academy; though the cadets still indulge in
gymnastics, and challenge the officers of the garrison to a game of cricket, more serious studies
have been substituted for the old displays of
strength. The cadets pass two to two and a half
years in the academy; and every six months an
examination takes place, proving the progress each
has made. Formerly these examinations were en-
trusted to the professors of the academy, but since
1859 the Council of Military Education have sent
their own examiners to control the final examination of the most advanced class. Those of the
students who come victors out of this trial receive
their commission in the army; up to this time, the
two branches of the scientific corps have been
blended in the same round of studies, but from the
final examination the separation begins: those
who have most distinguished themselves are at
liberty to join the engineers, while the others are
attached to the artillery. The advantages attached
to the former arm are chiefly pecuniary, the pay
being ten shillings and sixpence *per diem*.

The baptism of these young officers gives rise
to an interesting ceremony. The Duke of Cambridge, accompanied by a numerous staff, goes

twice a year to the Military Academy of Woolwich; the students are inspected in front of the building, and very admirable is the way in which these young men go through their evolutions and manœuvres. The duke then enters a hall, where a *vivâ voce* examination takes place on the art of fortification; this completed, the cadets form square, and the prince, followed by his staff, goes to a table on which the prizes are arranged, consisting of a sword of honour, telescopes, mathematical instruments, and books. The Vice-President of the Military Council of Education then reads the names of the cadets of the first class who are to receive their commissions in the engineers and artillery; and, finally, the duke makes a paternal address to these young men who are about to pass from the ranks of the school into those of the army. Such is a short summary of this academic *féte*, to which the brilliancy of the company, the rank of the persons present, and the joy depicted on the faces, impart a delightful and yet solemn character.

The young artillery officers who have obtained their commissions, generally pass a few months at Woolwich, where they learn the practical branch of the science thoroughly, and are at liberty to attend the lectures given at the Royal Artillery Institution. This establishment is due to the individual efforts of some meritorious officers: since its foundation, the institution has received support

from the State; but it still provides for its main-
tenance by voluntary contributions.   As the artillery opens a field of considerable study, a very
fine library, a chemical laboratory, a natural history collection chiefly geological, and professor-
ships of the living languages have been formed to
respond to the wants of an age which progress
has rendered more exacting.

The young officers specially appointed to the
engineers proceed to Chatham, where they are
to some extent still under a species of tutelage.
Chatham is another military town, formerly a
Norman camp and cemetery: the large military
and naval establishments are situated at a place
called Brompton, some distance from the town,
from which it is separated by a line of fortifications.   Here are an arsenal, barracks on a large
scale for artillery, enginéers, infantry, and marines,
as well as magazines and storehouses for arms.
All this is in perfect harmony with the ruins of
Upnor Castle, an ancient and picturesque tower,
which proudly wraps a mantle of ivy round its
wounds.   This castle, built by Elizabeth on the
opposite bank of the Medway, had the honour of
repulsing a portion of the Dutch fleet, when the
vessels of Admiral de Ruter appeared before the
walls of Chatham; but at the present day, this
historical veteran has some difficulty in supporting
itself on its ruined base.   The Engineers' School
at Chatham was founded in 1812: the Committee

of 1856 expressed a wish that the period of residence here should be lengthened from fifteen to eighteen months; that courses of lectures in geology, mineralogy, chemistry, and photography, should be annexed to the art of fortification and mining; that all these studies should be crowned by a final examination, and that all engineer officers now on service might from time to time stay at Chatham, in order to rub up their knowledge, grown rusty through want of use. Only one part of these reforms has been introduced. After completing their period of novitiate, the young engineer officers are generally sent to some English colony. While some, as we have seen, came from the Military Academy of Woolwich, others issued up to this year from the Military College at Addiscombe.

This institution was a branch of the Indian tree. Addiscombe, situated near Croydon, stands in the midst of a landscape, of another character from that at Woolwich, but even better adapted to please the eye. (I will remark *en passant*, that the sober and chaste style of British landscape has exercised an influence over the descriptive art of the best English poets, who have generally displayed discretion and reserve in their enthusiasm for nature: while the poets of the South, treating the indulgent nature of their country like a courtesan, have too freely raised every veil.) Addiscombe was formerly the residence of the

Earl of Liverpool; in 1809, his house was purchased by the East India Company to be converted into a military school, and the rebuilding
and new edifices added to the original house cost
more than forty thousand pounds. This college
for artillery and engineers was, to the Indian
army, what the Woolwich Academy is to the
English army, with this exception, that since
1825, young gentlemen were trained there for the
infantry service. Up to very recently, the establishment was under the charge of the East India
Company, and was governed by a political and
military commission, whose authority extended
over the whole staff of the house. This haughty
Company, which made peace and war, having
been shipwrecked in the great revolt that threatened to detach India from the mother country,
Addiscombe passed into the hands of the English
Government. One of the first acts of the Minister
of War and the Council of Military Education, was
to inaugurate the competitive examination for
admission to Addiscombe, which had borne such
good fruit at Woolwich. Up to that time, the
candidates were nominated by the East India
Company, and their nomination was rendered dependent on an examination, or, to speak more correctly, the examination was dependent on the nomination. As the course of studies at Addiscombe
is now entirely similar to that of Woolwich, it is
needless to dwell on it, but we may mention one
branch of knowledge referring of yore to the pecu-

liar object of the institution—Indian history, geography, and languages. The cadets learned to speak Hindostani, and to write in the two ordinary characters, Persian and Nagari. Statesmen and moralists have frequently insisted on the advantage there would be in a thorough knowledge of India, to maintain the conquest of that vast colony: young officers, strangers to the language, manners, and customs, often take with them prejudices, which the study of a civilisation so different from ours, but after all ancient and venerable, would have toned down. The programme of the English government to avoid the faults which have been committed, is clearly laid down: hold with the sword, and enlighten by example. The cadets, generally one hundred and fifty in number, had to spend formerly a year at Addiscombe; they entered, after this period of time, according either to merit or inclination, one of the three arms. Such were the principal features of this military institution as long as an Indian army existed; but Addiscombe College is merely a temporary dependence of Woolwich Academy, which involves a course of studies relative to British possessions in the East. The Indian service, no longer distinct from any other, will be, nevertheless, sought after; for that life of adventures, the bivouacking in jungles, the tiger-hunting, the imposing prospect for the imagination which the struggles with men and animals offer, and the dazzling image of a sunny world, seen through the fogs of Great Britain, will ever appeal to one phase of the English character, the spirit of enterprise.

Another military school, the Royal College of Sandhurst, prepares officers for the cavalry and infantry of the English army. This establishment was founded in 1799, at High Wycombe; three years later it was transferred to Great Marlow, and finally settled at Sandhurst in 1812. As the English like to withdraw their centres of study from the contagion of cities, the college stands thirty miles from London, in the sterile and ferruginous sands of Bagshot Heath. Gloomy gorse, pools of greenish water stretching over a muddy soil, a few scrubby patches of firs—the only trees which like this poor land—naked and desolate plains, barren hills, from which the abodes of man have kept aloof, offer the sadness, but also the grandeur, of solitude. It is in the midst of this desert that the Military College of Sandhurst, and the rich plantations surrounding it, stand, like an oasis formed by human hands. A thick curtain of firs hides the edifice from the visitor; the professors' houses are drawn up along the old western road, from which they are separated by a hedge; these double houses, detached from each other by equal spaces covered with verdure, have an air of calmness, freshness, and elegance. You presently enter a park, intersected by graceful avenues, and adorned by three lakes;

one of them, on which swans swim about, running in front of the college façade. The building with its two wings, one of which serves as the residence of the lieutenant-governor, the other, as hospital for the cadets, has a grand entrance. A portico supported by Doric pillars, and a vestibule adorned with piles of arms, introduce you into vast passages leading to the schoolrooms, modelling-rooms, and upper floors. At the time when I visited Sandhurst, a young lady in a riding-dress, with a greyhound lying at her feet, and a horse, of which she held the bridle, was standing on the steps of the gallery connecting the various parts of the building, and seemed, in the midst of this solitude, like a mediæval graceful spectre attracted by the call of the bugle, which sounded the school inspection.

In spite of the gloomy Bagshot sands, the vicinity of Sandhurst has many pleasant walks. I went a few miles, in order to see Pope's tree, at Binfield: tradition has it that the poet, who lived close by, composed some of his poems under a clump of beeches commanding a hill-side. An admirer of Pope, Lady Gower, wishing to perpetuate this recollection, had engraved on the bark of one of these trees, under which stood a bench at the time : "Here Pope sang." I could find neither tree nor inscription, and was retiring somewhat disappointed, when an Englishman, to whom I told my ill-success, said, with considerable good sense, "Our Lady Gower did not know what she was doing. The names of poets must not be engraved on trees, but on the hearts and memory of men."

At Sandhurst you find, under the same roof, two very distinct institutions—the Staff College, and the Royal Military College, which is a preparatory school for officers of the infantry and cavalry. Sooner or later, the Staff College* will be detached from the common building; and in the pine wood, surrounding the building like a girdle, I saw the mighty foundations of a new mansion, which will belong to the former of these two departments. The Staff College, also called the Scientific Department, may be justly regarded as the coronation of military studies : the pupils of this establishment, who have all, before entrance, undergone a competitive examination, are already officers: they have even served several years in the active army, some of them having gone through the Crimean and Indian wars. In 1859 one of these officers had received eighteen or nineteen wounds from the Pandies, and bore on his face the honourable but fearful scar of a sabre-cut which had laid open his eye. I was surprised to find in this college aspirants to the staff who speak and write French in a way that would do

* M. Esquiros gives a quaint definition of this word, "Staff= support ; as one would say, the staff of my old age." Can he mean any malicious allusion to our Crimean generals ?—L. W.

honour to many a French officer. The English
find an advantage in thus receiving into the ranks
of the service young officers of talent and energy,
who wish to rise to the higher ranks of the army,
for, with the knowledge of their profession, these
picked soldiers already combine extensive attain-
ments, which a second education still further con-
firms and develops. Besides, it will be allowed
that it needs a certain moral strength to return,
after several years of command, to school benches,
in order to follow a varied course of study, and
undergo rigorous examinations, which preclude all
idea of promotion by favour, fortune, or birth.

Sandhurst Military College is, like Woolwich
and Addiscombe, a cadet school, where the abuses
of patronage have also been recently combated by
competitive examinations, which will alone, for
the future, grant admission to the school. The
cadets, one hundred and eighty in number, are
distinguished by their uniform—a red tunic, em-
broidered with gold on the collar; grey trousers;
a shako, and, in undress, a small blue cap. Everything is done, both in and out of school, to promote sports and gymnastic exercises: in summer,
the students bathe in one of the three lakes so
poetically bordered by the trees that surround
the building, or pull on the other pieces of water;
while in winter they skate on the sheet of ice
formed on the lakes. The studies, as in the other
schools we have reviewed, refer to the various

branches of the military art, but with slight alterations determined by the difference of the arms
the Sandhurst cadets join.   After a residence of
about two years, a number of Sandhurst students
who have gained a certain amount of marks in
the final examination, receive their commission;
others, less successful, buy it. Economically speaking, Woolwich and Sandhurst are self-supporting, and cost the government scarcely anything.
This fact, in no way foreseen at the outset, results
from two relatively recent measures : the gradual
withdrawal of the subsidies formerly granted by
Parliament, and the entrance of the sons of rich persons not connected with the army. The latter pay
a high schooling fee, and contribute in this way towards the education of the other cadets, who, being
the issue of soldiers, enjoy certain immunities. In
England, it is considered just that the services of
fathers should benefit the sons: according to this
principle, the debt contracted by the state towards the men who have served their country is
paid to the sons by civilian families.

Young men, however, who have not passed
through Sandhurst school, can be received as officers into the infantry and cavalry, but on condition
of undergoing an examination and purchasing their
commission. As this system severely injures the
development of the Sandhurst Military College, it
has several times been proposed to abolish this last
relic of the ancient regime ; this is the opinion of

the Duke of Cambridge, who, agreeing in this with the Minister of War, desires that in future no one should enter the English army save through the gate of a military college.

Up to this time we have only seen the members of a grand system: the unity dwells in the Council of Military Education, which forms to some extent the head of the education. The influence of this council, composed of eminent men, radiates through the several schools, introduces changes and useful reforms, directs the public examinations, and, in a word, communicates the impulse to the military studies throughout the United Kingdom. The civil and religious element is represented in it by one of the most learned of English clergymen, Canon Henry Moseley; the other members are generals and colonels, belonging to the different corps of the army.

England enjoys, we thus see, a system of military education which can stand a comparison with that of any other European nation. The principal features of this system are a good civilian instruction up to the age of sixteen or seventeen, then a short military instruction, and, after several years' service, the completion of the studies in the senior department. We must not, however, consider the present state of things, though happily modified by the new competitive principle, as the extreme limit of progress. I desire too greatly, in the name of liberty, that Great Britain should

maintain her rank in the world, to flatter impro-
perly her self-love, or lull to sleep her aspiration
for reforms. She has done much in late times, but
much remains to do, and she knows it, in order to
elevate her officers to the heights of modern times,
when education is so spread throughout all classes.
Here, as in other countries, progress meets with
resistance: here, more than elsewhere, the government is bound to be in the right, and trample
down, by the wise measures which public opinion
accepts, that cold shade which cannot be conquered in a day. After all, I do not distrust
nations that advance slowly, I only doubt those
which recoil, or advance rashly beyond the limits
of the road.

War is carried on with technical acquirements,
but also with arms. In a study on *le Passé et
l'Avenir de l'Artillerie*, signed by Louis Bonaparte, I read that the old British archers, the best
regiment of light infantry that existed for a long
period, owed a portion of their success to the skilful arrangement of their bows. The English have
wished to transport the same superiority to the
manufacture of the weapons now employed in war.
It is within the walls of Woolwich arsenal that
we can form an idea of the labours and murderous
inventions, which—I love to believe the English
statement—serve to maintain peace.

CHAPTER IX.

WOOLWICH ARSENAL — THE WARREN — ARMSTRONG'S GUNS — WHIT-
WORTH — THE CARRIAGE DEPARTMENT — THE SAW-MILLS — THE
LABORATORY—THE SHELL FOUNDRY—COLONEL BOXER—WALTHAM
MILLS—ENFIELD GUN FACTORY.

IN England, where all is done on the principle
of liberty, the characteristics of the soil, and what
may be called the geographical relations, have
exercised a greater influence than elsewhere on
the localisation of the civil and military establishments. The proximity of London, and the assistance of the Thames, which flows past the town
in a powerful stream, bearing large vessels on its
bosom, doubtless determined the formation of the
arsenal and dockyard at Woolwich. The arsenal,
however, did not occupy at the outset the site
which appears to have been destined for it by
nature. There was at Moorfields, in the reign of
Queen Anne, a royal foundry, at which bronze
guns were cast, and it was employed in 1716 to
re-cast some guns in a bad condition captured by
Marlborough from the French. A great number

of officers, curious persons, and people of rank,
assembled at the spot to witness the experiment.
At first all promised to go on well, but among
the spectators was a young German (some say a
Swiss) of the name of Schalch, who did not at all
share in the general confidence. Andrew Schalch
was just out of his apprenticeship, and according
to the fashion of artisans of his country, was travelling to fortify himself in his art before he could
set up as master. Alone in the crowd he had
noticed a circumstance which escaped the eyes
and thoughts of all: he discovered that the moulds
into which the bronze was about to be run were
damp, and he said to himself that the steam
engendered by this humidity brought in contact
with the boiling metal, would be strong enough
to produce an explosion. Schalch, therefore, con-
ceived the greatest fears for the success of the
experiment and the lives of the company; he com-
municated his doubts and alarm to the persons
present, but, seeing that he was not listened to,
he sent a message to Colonel Armstrong, Master-
General of the Artillery, and to the Duke of Richmond, who was head of that department. His
warning being despised, the young German there-
upon withdrew quietly with his friends. A few
minutes after his departure, all London was
alarmed by the noise of a terrible explosion; a
portion of the roof of the foundry was blown off,
the galleries intended to receive the spectators

were destroyed, and a great number of workmen received severe and even mortal wounds. What Schalch had predicted, happened; the moulds had burst under the compressed force of the steam, and the boiling metal had rushed in every direction. To this accident is owing the origin of the arsenal now existing, though no longer at London.

The English authorities sought for the young German who had so cleverly foreseen the consequences of the error. An advertisement in the papers invited him to present himself to the Artillery Board, sitting in the Tower of London. Schalch went there, and after going through an examination, he was offered the superintendence of a new gun factory. In the name of the government, Colonel Armstrong requested him to choose in the vicinity of London a site more favourable than that of Moorfields, and a short time after this interview Schalch was at Woolwich, studying with a searching eye the advantages of what was then called the Warren, about eight miles from London; a river to ship and unship guns, a vast extent of open ground to make dangerous experiments, and all around an uninhabited country, so that the establishment could remain without hurting anybody's property. After examining all this, he said to the government, "This is the place." His plans were adopted, a gun-factory was built at the desolate spot he pointed out, and Andrew Schalch, having given further proofs of his talents, was appointed Master-Founder. He filled this office for nearly sixty years, and died in 1776. I saw his tomb in Woolwich churchyard.

At the present time, Woolwich arsenal is a town within a town, with a floating population of ten thousand workmen, a river, a railway, buildings following buildings, immense squares, paved streets, along which tumbrils rattle, an enclosing wall extending far into Plumstead, a school, a library, neat houses, inhabited by the civil and military officers, magazines, museums of arms, a chemical laboratory; in a word, all the elements of an industrial city. Here are manufactured, as it were, the means of national defence, the fortune of Great Britain on the field of battle. Externally, you perceive nothing but enormous brick chimneys towering over the town, buildings half concèaled by other buildings, and open spaces on which the eye surveys a mass of verdure. Here and there, amid the luxuriant grass, stand guns, mortars, and other bronze instruments, the wild flowers of these stern plains, on which, however, a few cattle browse. It is curious to see the workmen go in and out, ten minutes before two, after the meal that divides the day; a large bell fills with its powerful note the neighbourhood of the arsenal, summoning to work. Artisans of all ages then besiege the three entrance gates, one of which is at the other end of Woolwich, while the other two open in the Plumstead-road. This population with its look of business, its serious air, and hands hardened by work, rushes into the establishment. To observe these artisans more closely, and enter the arsenal, a written permission from the War-office is required, and twice a week, on Tuesday and Friday, visitors flock in. What strikes you most, on first entering, is a character of grandeur and immensity in the labour; at least a day is needed to visit attentively these two hundred and sixty acres of ground, covered by gigantic workshops, docks, and every variety of industry. To avoid confusion, I will divide this Babel into three distinct departments: the royal gun factory, under the orders of Colonel Wilmot; the royal carriage department, where carriages and tumbrils are made, at the head of which is Colonel Tulloch; and, lastly, the royal laboratory department, where the munitions of war are prepared, and directed by Colonel Boxer.

Formerly one of the marvels of the arsenal was the gun. foundry, built by Vanbrugh, and which, surmounted by a species of belfry, stands on the left at some distance from the principal entrance: I said formerly, for in the present era of progress, casting guns almost belongs to ancient history. Two years ago I witnessed this sight, one of the most startling industry has to offer; in one of these furnaces, capable, as I heard, of containing eighteen tons of metal, the bronze could be heard seething with a hoarse roar, resembling that of the sea in wrath. It was a solemn moment when the tap was turned of the vessel in which the melted metal was growling; the liquid and dazzlingly white mass rushed like a stream of silver into a sort of pit, where it filled the gun and howitzer moulds, leaving everywhere on its passage marks of incandescence. At the sight of these fiery furies, I was no longer surprised that Milton placed the cradle of artillery in Hades. Within the moulds, which grew red-hot, and over the surface of which an angry flame played, the captive metal assumed the form intended to be given it; and it took two days ere the new-born grew cold enough for a man's hand to be applied to it. The moulds were then broken, and the gun or howitzer sent to other divisions of the arsenal, where the "dead-head" was removed. Three-quarters of an hour sufficed to reduce the gun to the shape it was to assume, and it then passed through the hands of other workmen, and, if I may use the expression, of other engines. At about one hundred yards from the entrance gate, you were introduced into a workshop where a certain number of yellow and round bodies were slowly revolving on their axis; these were guns in various stages of development. When their external toilet was completed (which took two days) they were bored; six-and-thirty hours later the piece of artillery was ready for service, but it still had to undergo severe trials. About twenty

artisans and boys could run in the foundry twelve
to eighteen pieces a week, and with the machinery
the arsenal had at its disposal, thirty-three of these
weapons could be finished in the same period.

At the present day, gun-casting has lost much
of its importance; the furnaces are extinguished,
and a dead silence has succeeded the tempest of
bronze, for since Sir W. Armstrong's discovery,
cannon are no longer cast, but wrought; we must,
therefore, proceed to another department, the new
gun factory, in order to follow the progress of
this branch of manufacture. Certain parts of the
system are still shrouded in mystery, and the entrance to some workshops is forbidden to strangers.
Sir William, however, recently allowed, himself,
that his invention was no longer a secret, and the
history of the gun is now so well known, that we
need only dwell on it shortly. Mr. Armstrong
began his experiments with the new rifled guns in
1854; his first cannon, finished in the spring of
the next year, though constructed on the same
principles as those he now follows, did not give
satisfactory results on trial, and more than once
the inventor had to recognise what an enormous
distance separates theory from practice. He required three years to surmount the resistance and
difficulties opposed to him by the manufacture of
a rebellious and complicated arm. In the middle
of summer he made his experiments on the sea-
shore, between three and six A.M., the only mo-

ment of the day when the beach was deserted. Doubtless, through respect for the quiet bathers, whose slumbers he disturbed, Mr. Armstrong next transported his head-quarters to the marshes and flats of Allenheads, where the only risk was that sheep or grouse might be struck by the projectiles, or aroused by the explosions. After three years of struggling, trials, and progress, the discovery at length appeared to have attained some degree of development, and Mr. Armstrong constructed, at his own expense and responsibility, some guns after the new system. In 1859, a committee was appointed to examine generally into the invention of rifled ordnance: for five months the committee witnessed experiments, the result of which is known, and it is enough for me to say that the success obtained with Armstrong's gun bordered on the marvellous. Since that period, this arm has made further progress both in range and accuracy; at a distance of six hundred yards, an object of so small dimensions as the mouth of an enemy's gun may be struck almost at each round. At three thousand yards, a target of nine square feet, which at that distance only appeared like a dot in the blue sky, was hit in calm weather four times out of ten rounds. The English government rewarded Mr. Armstrong's discovery by knighting him and giving him an annual salary of two thousand pounds as engineer. At Woolwich arsenal, where he does not live, but of which he is one of the directors, Sir William has a vast department for the formation of his guns, which are intended to supersede the old ordnance of the English army. By the end of 1860, it was estimated that the artillery would have received a reinforcement of one thousand pieces on the new system.

The Armstrong gun is made entirely of wrought iron: it is composed of separate pieces of an average size, which are welded, as it were, one by one, for, according to the inventor's expression, his is a built-up gun. This system, it is said, ensures the weapon a high degree of strength and solidity; and we can understand that, to manipulate the iron and render it docile, engines and tools of extreme power are required. One of the objects that arrest the eye in the new workshops is a monstrous hammer: the face and handle of this hammer weigh four tons, and I leave my readers to conjecture the blows it deals, which can be rendered faster or slower at will. At one moment it falls with a solemn gravity befitting such a mass, at another it deals two or three hundred crushing blows a minute: its precision and perfect command are only equalled by its size. By turns delicate or rough, it can as easily crush a mass of red-hot iron with prodigious violence, as deftly crack a nut. The other machinery by means of which the various parts of the rifled cannon are welded, twisted, rolled and fastened together, are no less remarkable, and this metal, which has the reputation of being harsh, allows itself to be cut, filed, and planed with unequalled docility by the steel which is animated by the living force of steam. The shreds of iron are detached from the block just like apple-peel pared off with a knife. When the fragments are welded, the Armstrong gun represents a roll of massive iron, which is bored, like other guns, by a perforating implement, which plunges and advances in the body of its victim like the beak of a vulture. The tube is then covered on the upper part with iron bands successively growing wider. I saw in the workshops an Armstrong gun nearly finished: the shape is not very elegant, and artistically I greatly prefer our old bronze guns to it; but beauty is not required in this case, and all demanded of an arm in our positive age is to kill the greatest number of men. It is easy to perceive at the first glance that this gun constitutes a notable progress on the old artillery.

In one of the streets of the Armstrong department, the projectiles of the new guns are piled up against the walls of the workshops. According to our classical notions, it is difficult to conceive a cannon-ball that is not round: nothing, however, can be less round than those of the new system; they are cones of the size of a sugar-loaf, with a short bottle neck, and are made of cast-iron slightly coated with lead; they may be employed either as solid shot, or shell. Their resistance is so great that these missiles have gone through a mass of oak nine feet thick without breaking. When employed as shells, the same projectiles scatter into forty-nine pieces of regular shape, and a hundred of indefinite forms; the explosion takes place at will, sometimes when they near the object, at others when they come in collision with it. Gifted with a species of intelligence, owing to the arrangement of the means of percussion, they know, if I may venture to use the expression, when they are in a friend's or an enemy's country. In the former case, they restrain their deadly fury so well that they may be hurled on the roof of a house without bursting; in the second case, they are so susceptible and malevolent, that the slightest contact makes them pour forth fire and flame. Matters can also be so arranged that the shell may burst and scatter on leaving the gun's mouth. In the latter case, the pieces of the projectile spread in a fan of fire and play the part of canister. In an experiment made before the Duke of Cambridge, two targets, nine feet in width, were placed one thousand five hundred yards from the gun: seven shells were fired at them, the two targets were struck in five hundred and eighty places, and that with such force that one of the targets, though three inches thick, was pierced through and through. Similar results have been obtained, some at much greater dis-

tances, and we can thus form an idea of the gaps
such discharges would make in the ranks of an
enemy's army.

At first, Sir W. Armstrong only made guns of
small or moderate calibre : now he is turning out
seventy and even one hundred-pounders. At the
arsenal you can see pyramids of monstrous iron
rolls piled up outside the workshops, and intended
to form the chambers of these new guns. One
of them was tried during the winter at East-
bourne, where stands, or I should say stood, a
martello tower, considered very strong, and
which, being regarded as useless, was employed
as the mark for these experiments *in animâ vili*.
The Duke of Cambridge went to the spot at the
head of a numerous and brilliant staff. The principal object of attack was the face of the tower
looking on the sea: it was a mass of brickwork
and masonry, nine feet in thickness. Forty, seventy,
and hundred-pounder guns commenced the fire
at a distance of about one thousand yards; and
shot on shot, shell on shell, hurtled against the
old tower, which offered, I am bound to say, a
valiant resistance. Soon, however, the shells piti-
lessly attacked this sturdy building: the portion
supporting the roof was carried away by the
tempest of fire, and crevices resembling the gaping
mouth of a wounded giant opened along the line
of parapet. Neither stones clamped to stones by
iron, nor blocks cemented to blocks, could defend

this portion of the wall, which fell down in lumps like a wall of planks. The parapet once destroyed, the tower itself, or at least the face fronting the sea, was so battered and injured that it could no longer serve as a shelter. A breach of about fifteen feet wide by seven high offered the gloomy and yawning appearance of a vault growing narrower as it ran into the building. This ruin, which appealed for mercy, was spared, and the result of the day was to confirm more fully than ever the confidence of the English in the power of the new rifled guns and projectiles, which tear asunder stones and bricks like pasteboard. In their eyes, this old shattered tower stands over the sea like a witness of the destructive character any European war will in future assume.

Praised by some enthusiastically, criticised by others with reference to its complicated nature and the expense of its manufacture, the Armstrong gun has already a rival in the Whitworth. The latter has not yet found its way to Woolwich Arsenal, and is still in the period of doubt and trial. Some of the experiments, however, have been so successful, that professional men do not hesitate to place it, in certain respects, above the other rifled gun. I must not prejudge the question, which will soon be decided by an artillery committee. Mr. Whitworth, whose factory I visited a year ago at Manchester, is celebrated already for other inventions: a son of the work-

shop, he has not those brilliant qualities which
distinguish Sir W. Armstrong as a man of the
world and speaker: but, after all, it is the weapon
which must have the word here, and not the
inventor.   I will only mention one experiment,
which took place in the month of June last, in the
presence of the Duke of Somerset and the Lords
of the Admiralty, at the mouth of the Thames. It
was a very unfavourable day for trying a gun:
the thunder, lightning, hail, rain, and wind raged
over the sea, whose waves broke short and
agitated. Loaded on board the *Carnation*, the
Whitworth gun was pointed at the iron-cased
sides of the *Trusty* steam-battery. The first
round was fired at a distance of two hundred yards; so soon as the powder-smoke had
dispersed, it was seen that the projectile had
pierced the iron and was buried in the oak-casing
of the vessel. The second shot was even more
successful; the flat-headed projectile this time
forced its way through the iron, wood, and all the
other means of resistance, and rolled madly on
the deck.   The gun was fired five times, and with
the exception of one round which passed over the
bulwarks, the iron pierced the iron, in addition covering the deck with splinters of metal and wood,
which, in the case of an action, would have
hurled terror and death around. This result
was greeted with a species of surprise mingled
with enthusiasm: the cannon-ball whose effect

against floating-batteries had been doubted, had regained all its value as a destructive agent. It was now proved that there is no vessel of war invulnerable, since the life of man was no longer in safety behind a shelter of four inches and a half of iron. The conclusion arrived at by the Lords of the Admiralty was, in fact, that other and more energetic means of defence must be devised. At a period when no longer men but vessels are covered with an iron coat of mail, this armour itself must be protected by a new system of construction against the effects of the Whitworth gun. If I am correctly informed, however, the artillery committee is not favourable to the gun, though it is possible that, by fresh thought, Mr. Whitworth, who is a man of fortune and energy, may free his cannon 'from the defects urged against it. On the other hand, the wish of the artillery officers whom I have consulted is, that a third inventor may appear, skilful enough to combine the advantages of the Armstrong and Whitworth guns, and simplify both. After all, the field is open, and the state spares no sacrifice to favour the ameliorations that relate to ordnance. Since 1852, private persons have been paid the large amount of 72,769l. for artillery experiments.

But it is not sufficient to cast or build up fieldpieces; they must be mounted. This second part of the task falls in the arsenal upon the royal carriage department, where, besides gun-carriages, tumbrils and ambulance carts are made. Imagine a suite of workshops as large as churches, with a multitude of machines: here iron is no longer the sufferer, but wood. One of the forces of this department resides in the saw-mills; you find them of every shape and size, from the steel ribbon that executes the most delicate work and cuts wood like lace, up to the circular-saws whose pointed, bent, and terrible teeth saw asunder the trunk of a tree with groans of rage. One of these saws specially deserves our attention: a few steps had carried me to a plank platform resembling the empty stage of a theatre, where my guide made me a sign to wait, and whispered, " She is coming." Who is she? In answer, an enormous log was thrown along the stage: a man turned an instrument, and I saw a steel disc emerge from a groove in the floor, armed with a circle of teeth, displayed one after the other as the disc emerged from the ground. This metal wheel advanced, leaped on the log, walked straight through it without halting, and then, its work being completed, it returned remorselessly to its den, like a monster which has devoured its prey. When the saw disappeared, I asked leave to visit the case in which it lay hidden: I went down a deep staircase, where I saw in the gloom this shark-toothed thing, still warm with the results of its massacre, and which even when calm seemed animated by a feeling of hatred.

This collection of machines has something startling and wonderful about it. At first sight, man feels humiliated before these creations of industry, whose superior strength insults his weakness; like the alchemist in the German poem, he trembles before the beings of steel and bronze, to which he has, as it were, given life; but as, after all, these monsters toil under his hand, he soon sees in them only the auxiliaries and conquests of his genius. A trait of the English character is, moreover, the love of the English artisans for the machines; they speak of them as the Arab does of his horse, with a species of pride and admiration. With what delicate attention, with what maternal coquetry do they perform the toilet of these saws, and those other living tools, whose teeth leave a deep mark on all they attack. One of them, from whom a steam plane had carried off two fingers, said to me, with a flattering look at the machine: "It is ill-tempered at times, but it must be pardoned, for it is so beautiful!" Motion is produced here without the aid of man; I do not mean merely the mechanical motion, but also certain actions which seem to imply a will. I saw, for instance, pieces of wood pass from one workman to another along travelling bands of leather. As this department of the arsenal chiefly has to do with carriages and limbers, a portion of the machinery is naturally employed to make wheels, which are turned out by thousands. In this series of works, we shall find matter subduing

and fashioning matter; the wood yields to every
desire of the machinery, and, at any rate, has the
excuse to offer that iron, copper, and other metals
offer no better resistance than itself. When the
various parts of the wheel are made, they have
to be joined together, and this is effected by an
instrument which is an astonishing mechanical
power. You stand as if stunned by the sight
of six iron rams or blocks which advance to
connect the detached pieces; the wood groans
under this pressure like women squeezed in a
crowd, but the tyrant insists, and does not loose
his hold till it has given the victim a character of
unity.

The third division of the arsenal, the royal
laboratory, is devoted to the preparation of all
the projectiles now employed in war. There is no
stranger, I believe, who is not struck and plunged
into a sort of dumb stupefaction on entering the
great gate of the laboratory. As far as his eye can
reach, above, below, around him, he sees nought
but iron, he hears nothing but the noise of iron, he
only dreams of iron and steel. Dazzled, stunned, he
believes himself transported to a world where in-
animate nature acts and does the work of a million
arms. There are certainly in this room six to seven
hundred workmen, but if they represent intelligence, they are not the strength, which resides in
the machinery; and there are no workshops in
the world where such a collection of automatic

instruments can be found. The laboratory is an immense building, whose iron carcase is covered at regular distances by a roof of wood and glass. The thousands of revolving wheels, the bands of leather transmitting life to the cylinders, the motion of bands and machines, the variety of the productions which seem born as if by magic, all exalt and sadden the spectator at the same moment; for has he not before him the progress of science and industry applied to the art of exterminating humanity? But as, after all, war may break out at certain moments of history in the interest of civilisation, we cannot blame those peoples which employ the leisure of peace to perfect the material on which the fate of armies frequently depends.

The projectiles and munitions of war prepared at Woolwich are also manufactured in the other states of Europe, hence I will not dwell on them; I am only desirous to give an idea of the mechanical power inherent in the English arsenal. When reflecting on fertility of production wedded to perfection of work, I cannot pass indifferently by the collection of machines that make Minié bullets. Each of these self-acting machines cuts seven thousand bullets an hour, and as there are four of them, they turn out 300,000 bullets a day; but as such artisans have no occasion for rest, the production may be doubled by letting them work through the night. The lead destined for bullets enters in a boiling condition a species of hydraulic pump, or cylinder presser, whence it emerges in the solid shape of a rope. This leaden cord runs round a pulley fastened to the machine, which, by the aid of two iron fingers, seizes at each movement a piece of the cord, which falls, cut and modelled, into a box. Four workmen, with a great outlay of combustible matter to keep the lead in a liquid state, cannot make more than six hundred bullets a day, that is to say, a thousand less than each machine turns out in an hour. An English friend of mine, a great statistician, calculated that, during the ten minutes we spent in front of one of these machines, the death of a dozen men would have been settled in war, and he only counted one bullet as mortal in five hundred! The same activity, with even more precision and delicacy, is found in another group of instruments, those which cut caps. Animated by a species of appetite for copper, these machines greedily champ the thin plates of copper handed to them, and tear them with incredible eagerness; not satisfied with cutting, they give a perfect shape to the morsel they have carried off. One of these machines (bearing the name of the inventor, John Abraham), small, but endowed with extraordinary energy, makes by itself fourteen hundred caps a minute, or more than a million a day.

The cartridges, or at least the coarse paper employed for their case, is also manufactured by an ingenious process. In the paper manufactory there is a wooden instrument armed with fingers, each of these being gloved, so to speak, with felt. The implement is plunged into the pans, when the paper pastes round the glove, thus assuming a circular shape, with an opening left at one of the ends to receive the powder. The cartridge made, all that is left is to fill it, and that is done by children. I found myself in a room resembling a school, in which five hundred lads, from ten to twelve years of age, were seated on benches along immense tables. In order to stimulate the zeal and activity of these children, the number of cartridges he filled during the past week is placed before each little workman. Although this branch of manual labour possesses none of the marvel of the machines, it interests the novelist; for all these young and busy hands are partially removed from the temptations of want. There are no scourges without some compensation: if war makes widows and orphans, it, at any rate, provides labour for lads, who, without it, would probably seek on the highway the bitter bread of charity.

There is in the arsenal a retired spot, separated from the rest of the works by a canal communicating with the Thames, surrounded by trees, and isolated from all buildings by commons covered with scanty verdure: here silence dwells;

a silence that contrasts with the sound of the hammers on the anvils, the whizzing of the machines, the clank of iron against iron, with which the visitor is stunned in the workshops—it is the east laboratory. The workmen admitted into this building doff their every-day clothes, which they hang up in a dressing-room, and put on the "safety dress of the War Department." The few strangers allowed access to these forbidden spots leave their boots at the entrance and put on leather slippers. These precautions and the style of the buildings warn us that we are at the headquarters of danger; from this place come the rockets, which have been the object of study and improvements ever since the Crimean war, where, however, they were so successful, that all the Christian governments (I therefore except Turkey) have tried to penetrate the secret of the English manufacture. Shells have equally appealed to the skill of British engineers in late times, both to fix the moment of explosion as well as to fill them with a formidable material. The history of these projectiles is curious to follow, from the moment when they leave the shell foundry up to that when they are pierced and charged, by mechanical means, with all the destructive luxury which the genius of war has invented. You see men, black as demons, carrying the liquid metal in buckets, which they pour like water into the moulds: the shell then passes from hand to hand, from machine to machine, until it has received and hidden within it the mystery of death, which will be revealed by the mouth of the howitzer. They are of all sizes and of different patterns, but the most terrible shell, and one peculiar to Woolwich Arsenal, is the diaphragm shrapnel, improved by Colonel Boxer; on the battle-field it bursts at the desired moment, and produces in the enemy's ranks, as an old English soldier told me, the effect of a charge of small shot in a covey of partridges. Some of the preparations for the shells are kept secret: with the information and means of analysis science now possesses, I have no great faith in the duration of war arcana; but I should be more inclined to believe that the secret, if secret there be, consists chiefly in the skill of the workmen, which defies the rivalry of foreign hands. Once they have emerged from the laboratory, the messengers of death—shells, rockets, and other inflammable projectiles—are placed in covered gondola-shaped barges, which convey them to the magazines. The sight of these boats on the gloomy and sleepy water of the canal has something sorrowful about it.

Such is the general aspect of Woolwich Arsenal. I pass in silence over many other branches of labour, which, for all that, occupy a considerable space. What most strikes the visitor, is the life and movement that buzz in this great hive, where

iron, bronze, and the chemical compositions the
art of war employs are distilled. The transports
either take place on paved ways, or on trams, by
means of horses and large mules brought back
from the Crimea. Nothing can equal the obstinacy of the latter animals, save their strength and
zeal: they are led by artillerymen, who assert
that the ordinary mules are docile and tractable
brutes by the side of these. It is curious to see
the arsenal workmen handling and stacking the
balls, those apples which fall from the tree of the
knowledge of good and evil, according to the
expression of a workman. On seeing them so
piled up by thousands, you would say that Great
Britain could stand a siege against the whole of
Europe. In the last war, ten thousand five hundred shells issued from the machines in twenty-
four hours.

Woolwich Arsenal, in ordinary times, employs
from ten to twelve thousand workmen, and according to the habit of all English factories, they
are paid at the end of each week. The paying is
also a scene by no means deficient in interest, for
so extensive an affair demands a mechanism distinguished by order and speed : owing to the
great number of workmen, the paying wages
begins on Friday at one o'clock, and ends on
Saturday at two in the afternoon. All the men
collect in their turn—that is to say, by a series of
letters and numbers—before a wooden office stand-

ing in the middle of a yard, called the ticket-office. As soon as the number of the series is announced, the men form in a line, and enter the office one after the other, where they show a ticket, delivered to them the previous day by the foreman. Their money is all ready, and deposited on a sort of tray with the number over it: a clerk calls the number, while another takes up the money and hands it to each man as he passes. It is impossible to follow without interest the application of so simple and expeditious a system, especially when we reflect on the great diversity of the wages. Youths receive from four shillings to eleven shillings and eightpence per week; the men, from fourteen shillings to two guineas, with the exception of the foremen, who earn a larger sum—three and four pounds. The government spares no sacrifices, and offers certain advantages to secure the best hands. After three years' service, the arsenal workmen are paid during one month of illness; and if they receive a wound while working in the shops, their pay goes on till they return to work. If they lose a limb in the service of the establishment, they are never discharged, save in the extreme case of ill-conduct. After twenty years, the workmen who have not left the arsenal have a claim to a pension. These pecuniary advantages are not the only ones the state offers: the directors of the arsenal, intelligent and large-

hearted men, have paid attention to the moral
well-being of the workmen. There is a school at
which the younger fry can study eight hours a
week, without losing any of their wages, and
some of those who follow these classes have
made remarkable progress in mathematics; evening lectures are also given now and then on different subjects. The library is open to all the
workmen, and the labourers pay fourpence, the
artisans sixpence, a month, for leave to take books
home. The arsenal also provides work for girls,
who receive about twelve shillings a week: it
may be little, but the establishment gives them a
daily dinner of soup, meat, potatoes, and bread,
for the sum of three - halfpence. There is a
butcher attached to the arsenal expressly for the
purpose. A tragical event, two or three years
ago, furnished a proof of the kindly sentiments
prevailing between the master and workmen: one
of the civil officers was thrown from his horse and
killed. I never saw a more royal funeral; I do
not allude to the pomp of the procession, the
guns, or the panoply of military mourning, but
the true and profound emotion which was displayed by the crowd that followed the hearse.
A monument has been erected in the humble
Plumstead churchyard, with this inscription:
"Erected by the voluntary subscriptions of the
workmen of the arsenal."

These workmen inhabit cottages round the

walls of the establishment, at a weekly rental of six or eight shillings. The horror of the English for barracks is so great, that they despise the pecuniary advantages attaching to the assemblage of several lodgers in the same building. The sentiment of self, which constitutes one of the pronounced features of the national character, has exercised a powerful influence over the entire architectural system. The poor man likes a home as well as the rich : hence there are for each class of workmen cottages built of brick, two stories high, with a very small front garden, and a large back one, where a few vegetables are grown, or chickens and a pig reared. Plumstead and Woolwich, being in some measure grafted on the arsenal and dockyard, the village and town have followed the development of these two great arenas of labour. Streets spring up daily, as if by enchantment, and houses—nearly all on the same model—spring up from the ground to hide the old meadows. On Saturday, after two o'clock, a holiday air spreads over the town : the workman, who has received his week's wages and enjoys a half-holiday, goes with his wife and children to lay in the Sunday dinner. It is no longer a market, but a fair : traders of every description, quacks who sell infallible powders to cure every illness, and comical cheap jacks, arrest the mob, which flows all along the streets. At midnight begins the great day of rest. Too

little is known in France of the blessed influence
which the observance of the Sunday (I am not
looking at it from a religious point of view) exerts
on the family life of the English workman. The
man who has been absent from home all the week,
finds himself on that day in his own kingdom,
amid his wife and children, whom he likes to see
clean and tidily dressed. After a week of fatigue,
he enjoys rest through his heart. One of the great
principles of the Protestant religion is *crescite et
multiplicamini*, and it is enough to look at the
swarm of heads buzzing round the houses of
Plumstead, to see how fully the Divine precept is
observed in England by the working classes. The
population of the arsenal is only distinguished
from other factory hands by a character of ease
and serenity. A superintendent, however, drew
my attention, with a certain degree of physiologi-
cal tact, to the taciturn influence large workshops
exercise on certain bodies of the state. Amid
the deafening noise of the machines, which drown
and defy the human voice, the mechanics end by
resigning themselves to silence, and gradually contract the habit.

A question has been recently mooted: Is the
arsenal really well placed at Woolwich ? When
old Schalch pointed out to the English government the Warren as the most favourable site, he
only had in view the presence of the Thames, the
proximity of the Thames, and other topographical

advantages. In his time it was right to dwell on
such considerations, for Great Britain then considered herself sufficiently protected against invasion by her fleet, the sea, and the belt of rough
coast bordered by shoals and storms. Now-a-days
the conditions are changed: steam, introduced
into the art of navigation, and other causes, have
shaken the old confidence England placed in her
maritime forces and her geographical position.
In the event of war, a rich depôt of arms and
ammunition like Woolwich Arsenal, would not fail
to tempt the ardour and covetousness of an invading army. Regarded from this point of view, the
situation of Woolwich ceases to be irreproachable.
Seated in Kent, and at a very inconsiderable distance from the mouth of the Thames, that town
may be easily attacked by the enemy. In that
case, the loss of the immense resources, or even a
simple suspension of the works, would entail consequences for the United Kingdom which the
English do not regard without terror. To prevent such disastrous chances, it was proposed
some months ago to transport the arsenal to the
north of England. This expensive scheme has
been abandoned; but still the emotion of the
country since that time has only increased at the
idea of a hostile army being able some day to
tread the soil of the inviolate island, and lay hand
on the Palladium of the English armies. In the
month of June, 1860, a committee was appointed

by the Minister of War to examine into the condition of the national defences: the committee replied, that the territory was not sufficiently protected against a descent, or the progress of a hostile army which had once disembarked on shore. The attention of generals and engineers was especially directed to the seaports, and the mouth of the Thames, and the Woolwich Arsenal and dockyard. The committee, therefore, proposed to government to construct detached forts to cover the most menaced points, on account of the importance given them in the strategic system. The outlay for purchasing land, building the defensive works, arming the fortifications, and making bomb-proof barracks, amounted to the enormous sum of twelve millions. This sum, since reduced to nine millions, frightened neither the country nor the parliament, which had already voted money on account. The state, not satisfied with protecting the arsenal from a *coup de main*, by crowning the heights of Shooters Hill with fortifications, has decided on establishing one or two other depôts, to divide the munitions and material of war now concentrated at Woolwich. This demand for funds is at present popular in England: the least timid consider that no sacrifice should be spared to cure a great nation of the evil of fear, especially when that has as its object the phantom of a foreign invasion. A member of the peace party, who voted on this question with the majority of the House, thus explained his motives in a London drawing-room: "I regret that so much labour and money are expended here to defend the country from probably imaginary evils; but as, after all, the spirit of conquest may not be extinguished in the hearts of all civilised peoples, I appreciate the alarm of my nation, and seek a means to combat it. What English commerce most needs is security. I therefore regard the military preparations, however expensive they may be, as the best remedy for panics even more injurious to material interests than war itself."

The prosperity of Woolwich Arsenal, as a great factory of arms, is of a much more recent date than might be imagined on seeing the extent and multiplicity of the works. A few years back, the English government procured a great part of its material of war by contracts entered into with private firms, and in this again the Crimean campaign and Indian mutiny have exercised a fortunate influence. The contract system is abandoned in principle, and the state is striving henceforth to collect in its own hand the various branches of manufacture which were abandoned to private trade. In this reform it has found two advantages: economy and superiority in the productions. At the present time only the gunpowder and muskets do not come from the arsenal workshops, and the only powder factory the government possesses is situated at Waltham Abbey, in Essex.

Here the visitor finds himself in a landscape of the most peaceful style: meadows in which cattle quietly browse, streams on whose banks old Izaak Walton would have liked to pitch his tent, winding paths that lose themselves in woods of willow and alder trees; but from time to time barges laden with charcoal and saltpetre pass along, which recal the idea of war. Men, black as miners, seem to endure the penalty of the gloomy and dangerous works carried on in the vicinity; and although the sound of a large wheel beating the water tells us that we are approaching a gunpowder-mill, I will not stop here to describe the processes of a manufacture with which everybody is acquainted; suffice it to say, that the reputation English gunpowder enjoys on the Continent is well deserved. Two explosions, of which history has retained the date (1780, 1811), have carried terror over, and caused great ravages in, the environs of Waltham Abbey. These accidents are partly owing to that indifference which men gradually contract who find themselves in daily contact with explosive substances. The workmen at Waltham mills tell a curious story on this head. A labourer belonging to the establishment was returning from dinner, and, in defiance of the regulations, was smoking his pipe. As he approached one of the buildings called the gloom store, where the gunpowder was drying, he put his pipe in his waistcoat-pocket, but did not

extinguish the tobacco. Fortunately, a comrade
of his, of the name of old Ben Wall, perceived that
the other's pocket had caught fire: to warn him
of the circumstance would have been dangerous,
for the imprudent fellow was already on the
threshold of the magazine, and might have lost
his head. Old Ben, a man remarkable for his
coolness and courage, called the workman to the
platform by the river-side, and then with a vigorous
push sent him flying into the water: in this way
he saved the lives of a great number of persons.

The Ordnance musket factory is situated at Enfield, about twelve miles from London: on leaving
the railway station, the visitor finds himself among
damp and flat meadows, separated from each other
by ditches more or less full of water. You at
length reach the factory, a collection of gloomy
and sunken buildings, from which issue one thousand five hundred rifles per week. The manufacture of the fifty-one different pieces going to make
up a rifle must be inspected on the spot, in order
to form an idea of the difficulties this trade en-
counters, and the valiant way in which the machines remove all obstacles. I had for a length
of time fancied that iron and copper were hard;
but that is an illusion quite dispelled when you
have visited Woolwich Arsenal and Enfield factory. The establishment employs twelve to fourteen hundred hands, men and boys, and it is an
interesting sight to see this population emerge

from the factory at the sound of the bell, and spread at mid-day among the ten or dozen public-houses of the neighbourhood. These thirsty Cyclops, it may be easily imagined, do not possess the sobriety of the machines, which labour without eating or drinking. "Would to God," one of the workmen said to me, "I was like them." An hour later, the same bell which rung the hour of liberty rung that of toil: the publics are immediately deserted, and a silence peculiar to English workmen spreads over the crowd, which returns to the factory gates. Already, in fact, the steam is whistling impatiently, as if it were anxious to respond to the constant demand for arms.

The English, it will be seen from my statements, have, during the last years past, paid a primitive attention to the manufacture of arms and the material of war. Everybody recognises, now-a-days, the importance of this branch of the military art at a time when the progress of science tends more and more to efface individual strength, and substitute for it the skill of soldiers, the efficiency of manœuvres, the precision of explosive machines, and the energy of projectiles. This activity in the English arsenals succeeds, I am bound to add, a certain degree of negligence. At the moment of the Crimean war, the sword of Great Britain, as the English themselves allow, had somewhat rusted in the scabbard. The causes of this period of repose are easy to discover: during the reign of Louis Philippe, England believed in the assurance of peace given to it by the French government, and which seemed to consolidate the state of Europe. No cloud troubled the foreign political horizon, and the English profited by this truce to increase their commerce, trade, and external relations. During these eighteen years of military slumber, our neighbours took giant steps in the path of material ameliorations: read the journals and political essays of that period, and you will fancy that the gates of the temple of Janus were eternally closed. Events, to which I have no need to refer, happened to dispel these illusions. England found herself engaged, while slightly unprepared, in a war against a powerful empire, in which she was glad to find France by her side. A short time later her Indian possessions, which she believed secure, were shaken by a formidable insurrection, and that was sufficient to recal her attention to her army. The agitated state of Europe, the tone of the foreign press, certain menaces, and other causes sufficiently known, aroused from their lengthened torpor the English, who had hitherto been entrenched behind their ocean barrier. At the present day, they regard confidence as one of those leafy roofs under which the traveller may shelter himself during a short autumn shower, but which, when once saturated, do the person beneath more harm than good. Taught by the sudden changes of external politics, henceforth they trust in their armaments, forts, and arsenals. Determined to rely on themselves alone, they find in their immense financial resources the means to answer their own fears by military preparations, which have nothing alarming for Europe. All that Great Britain desires in arming herself from head to foot is to ensure peace; she enjoys too great a prosperity, the fruit of labour and a long tranquillity, to rush lightly and without provocation into war.

We know now the state of the English military schools and arsenals: this study prepares us to enter into the organisation of the army and the volunteer movement. Here a new field of observation opens: to acquire a perfect idea of the forces of England, we must now visit the barracks, camps, parks, and even the public streets. It seems to us imprudent for Europe to judge of these forces by the vague reports which attenuate or exaggerate in turn the character of the armaments. When I read the French journals, I believe that the Thames is on fire; when I read the English papers, I fancy that it is the Seine. Without dwelling on these rumours, I think that the armaments and military reforms of the United Kingdom are of a nature to inspire Europe with serious reflections. Any continental nation, no matter which, that wished to come into collision with Great Britain, ought to think twice of it. Before all, she will find before her the old wooden wall of England, which has hitherto covered the coast with an impenetrable bulwark; behind the ships, the soldiers—improving daily in numbers and organisation; and behind the soldiers, a country in arms.

CHAPTER X.

To write the history of the English army we
should have to go back to the origin of the
nation, and follow the development of an empire,
which has spread by land and sea over two
worlds; but at present, I only purpose to sketch
the principal transformations which the military
forces of the United Kingdom have undergone
during centuries. In England, as in the majority
of European states in the middle ages, all the
men were at first soldiers; all had to collect at a
given moment beneath the banners, to repulse an
attack or prepare an invasion. This primitive
state of things became modified with the progress
of civilisation, and the natural growth of society;
the principle of the division of labour having
taken root in the Anglo-Saxon character, the
military strength was detached from the civil
element. It was then that troops, more or less

regular, came into being; the first paid bands, however, had only a temporary existence limited by circumstances. Raised in the event of war, or for a peculiar object, they were always disbanded when hostilities ceased. The system of a permanent army only dates back, in England, to Charles II.

This king had resided at the court of Louis XIV.; he had witnessed the changes introduced in France into the constitution of troops kept up in peace equally as in war. On his return to Great Britain, he took his measures to support his newly restored throne on the fidelity of the soldiers; and he also sought to fix the hitherto shifting basis of a military government. As no régime is improvised, we can find precedents for this innovation in English history: two regiments, created in the reigns of Richard III. and Henry VIII., and still existing—the Gentlemen Pensioners and the Yeomen of the Guard—formed at that period a sort of transition between the system of accidental and standing armies. This last order of things was so opposed to the constitutional customs of Great Britain, that Charles II. inaugurated it very gradually, enlarging and filling up at intervals the *cadres* of his battalions. We smile at the emphasis with which the public writers of the age speak of this "formidable army," which was composed of five thousand men at the outside. The king enrolled in his newly created regiments the Cavaliers who had attached themselves to his fortune—good or bad—followed him abroad, and crossed swords in the Low Countries with the Roundheads. Nor did he despise the remains of Cromwell's brave army. The whole completed two cavalry corps and five or six infantry regiments, and as they still exist and are proud of their genealogy, their names may be quoted here. They were—the first regiment of Foot Guards, or Grenadier Guards; the Cold-streams, commanded by General Monk; the Life Guards; the Blues, whom Lord Oxford obtained from one of Cromwell's best regiments, and there-fore called the Oxford Blues; the Scotch, who had returned from France, and were enrolled under the name of Royal Scots; and, lastly, the Second Queen's Royals. Still, it is on this narrow, but solid, basis that the edifice of the English army has been successively erected.

We have seen that the same military system prevailed nearly at the same time in Great Britain and France. The two peoples, however, greeted in a very different way a novelty which changed the character of the armed force, especially in peace times. In France, under the absolute rule of Louis Quatorze, it does not appear that the es-tablishment of standing armies encountered even a shadow of opposition, but it was not the same in free England: if we may judge by the number and thoroughly British bitterness of the pamphlets this measure provoked, we are justified in the belief that the fears and doubts of public opinion were carried to an extreme. The worst reminiscences were evoked against such an institution: Richard II. overthrowing at the head of four thousand archers the liberties of his parliament, and Cromwell seizing the dictatorship in defiance of the laws, and trampling the dignity of another parliament under the heels of his soldiery. To believe one of these pamphlets (and it is by no means the most violent), a standing army implies the idea " of slavery, Papacy, Mahomedanism, Paganism, Atheism, and everything that is bad on earth." The English have recently laughed heartily at certain foreign newspapers which have taught them that liberty of the press and speech was a recent conquest of theirs, and I confess that, on perusing these political writings of the seventeeth century, in which the boldness of the language goes beyond all bounds, I could not refrain from sharing in their mirth. These stormy agitations were prolonged till the reign of George III., though no one, it is true, thought of revoking a measure of which time had demonstrated the remedy. It was evident to all, that in the face of the European armaments, Great Britain needed a standing army to defend her territory and maintain her prestige before the world: but the public mind, ever restless, was resolved not to allow any peace till it had limited the prerogatives

of the crown on this delicate point. The parliament at length succeeded in obtaining a control
over the army, and drew up in a series of laws,
known as the Mutiny Act, those restrictions
which, while respecting the rights of the sovereign, safeguarded the natural liberties. As it is
now constituted, the English army cannot possibly
become the instrument of anarchy or despotism.

This review of facts, rapid as it is, introduces
us naturally to the terrain of the military institutions at present existing in Great Britain. To
continue our study of the army, we must now inquire what is the present system of recruiting, the
life of soldiers and officers in barracks or camps,
before observing them in the presence of an
enemy.

I was one day going down Parliament-street,
towards Westminster Palace, where an important
debate was going to take place in the House of
Commons. It was a moment when the air was
laden with rumours of war, which vanished as
they came, with the clouds dispersed by the
wind, from the other side of the Channel. I
noticed in an obscure and dirty street, Charles-
street, an unusual movement: sergeants, with
ribbons of different hues knotted to their shakos,
were pompously stationed near the public-houses,
which were themselves decorated with flags and
military inscriptions. Flags attached to a rope
that crossed the street at regular distances sadly

displayed the faded colours of Great Britain;
groups of young fellows poorly clad and mean-
looking, were talking with the sergeants, or going
into the public-houses with them. Curious people
stopped; I followed their example, and, addressing
a policeman, I asked him what the matter was?
The civil officer replied, with his British phlegm,
"Nothing: Old England must be protected, that's
all." Charles-street is, in fact, the street of enlistments: the public-houses—which, by the way,
seemed to me to flourish—are veritable barracks,
in which the recruiting-sergeants hold their levees,
and where they lodge their men for a weekly
sum agreed on with the publican. These men
are recruits; that is, in common parlance, poor
devils who have accepted her Majesty's shilling.

Every individual who has accepted a shilling
from a hand attached to the recruiting service, is
by law considered a soldier, and from that moment has a right to a billet. This first step, however, is not irrevocable; and in order that the engagement may be complete, the recruit must pass
the doctor, and be taken before a magistrate to
be attested. The magistrate then asks him if
he perseveres in his resolution of becoming a
soldier. The recruit may say no, and in that case
must be set at liberty on repayment within twenty-
four hours of the enlisting money, and an additional sum of twenty shillings as smart-money, with
the expenses of subsistence during the two or three

days he has lived at government charges. If, on the contrary, the recruit answers in the affirmative, the magistrate reads over to him the oath of allegiance, the young man kisses the Bible, and the bargain is concluded. He is from that moment a soldier for ten years in the infantry, twelve in the cavalry and artillery. Any person who after receiving the enlistment-money, hides himself, or refuses to go before a magistrate within a space of four days, is considered to have taken the oath, and may be punished as a deserter.

The recruiting-sergeant is a thoroughly English type, but he must not be studied in the large towns, where everything is to a certain extent lost in the crowd. In villages remote from cities, and specially on fair days, the arrival of the recruiting-sergeant produces the same effect on the simple inhabitants as the marching in of a whole regiment does in towns. The women and children, standing in the doorways, watch him pass with widely-opened eyes, evidencing a very natural feeling of curiosity mingled with respect. All, it is true, in this new personage contrasts with the humble costume and clownish manners of the rustics that surround him. They admire the pomp of his brilliant uniform, the knot of ribbons floating from his shako, and which is to the recruiting-sergeant what a sign is to a shop; his imposing height, the methodical solemnity of his gestures—his walk greatly resembles the strut of a cock—the flourish of his military salute, and even that stiffness of carriage which with simple people easily passes for majesty. The profession of re-cruiting-sergeant demands special qualities: a sure and piercing glance, a certain acquaintance with mankind, and an imperturbable coolness. In the same way as the hunting animals, the lion and the fox, lie in ambush on the banks of streams, the recruiting-sergeant establishes his head-quarters at the ale-house, where he seeks to attract his game. There he sits in state, harangues and dazzles, and we can easily imagine that he al-ways presents the romance of military life on its brightest side. His paintings, laden with all the colours of the rainbow, have perhaps, if artisti-cally regarded, the defect of being improbable, but that is a fault to which the ignorant and the credulous pay little attention.

As one of the fears of the English labourers is of being sent to the colonies if he enlists, the orator with his well-hung tongue is most anxious to combat this wretched prejudice. To hear him, the British soldier is a tourist travelling for his pleasure at the expense of government. Then comes a description, more or less fantastic, of those distant countries flowing with milk and honey, perhaps with ale and gin. Abusing that privilege of lying granted to men who come from afar, he favours his audience with a natural history of the countries he is supposed to have seen: to

believe him, in all the spots where English garri-
sions are stationed, the plants and animals have
only one anxiety, that of pleasing, supporting,
and clothing the soldier; as for the marches over
the sterile plains of India, there is no cause to
be alarmed about them, for the sick soldier is
borne in a palanquin, like a sultana. We may
judge by this specimen of the promises this proud
and jolly fellow makes, with a certain effrontery
of imagination. Some English moralists have
branded their baits with a severity that does them
honour, and we must applaud the frankness of
General Codrington, when he said in the House
of Commons, "We seduce men into the service
by means that degrade the profession." I must,
however, observe, that now-a-days the exaggera-
tions of the recruiting-sergeants deceive but very
few persons: what I fear, on the contrary, is the
suspicious temper which such manœuvres have
aroused in the towns and country. It is certain
that, beneath the most lowly roofs, the news that
the eldest son of the family has been led away
by the wiles of the recruiting-sergeant, is always
received with tears and sobs. As, at any rate—
materially regarded—the condition of the English
soldier is better than that of the labourer, we
have cause to feel surprise at the dislike felt
among the rustic classes for the military service:
if these poor families regard the enlistment of
their sons as a calamity, may it not be because

they fear a snare beneath the illusions and influences that lead youths into the profession of arms?

The recruiting system forms one of the distinctive features of the English army, and our neighbours boast of being the only nation who have discovered the secret of levying troops without having recourse to injustice and oppression. We Frenchmen, who regard this system through the recollections of our ancient history, perhaps, too, through the bad theatrical impressions in which the recruiting-sergeant generally plays the part of seducer and traitor, find it rather difficult to share on this point the very honest opinion of English optimists. On the other hand, the English regard our system of conscription with horror; they reproach it before all with assailing individual liberty, and exercising a disastrous influence on trade and agriculture, by carrying off perforce young men who were beginning to create a useful means of livelihood. The state not recognising the right of making soldiers—in other terms, of tearing British subjects from their avocations and tastes to force them under arms—it has been found necessary to have recourse to other methods to induce voluntary enlistment. One of these means, and the most energetic of all, is a money payment known by the name of bounty. The origin of this gratification dates back, we are told, to the fifteenth century, when rich men, having influence over their tenants, engaged, for certain advantages, to supply the king with an agreed-on number of soldiers. At the present day, the bounty is a direct transaction between the state and the recruit, and it may be easily guessed that the sum which serves as a bait for enlistment, varies with times and circumstances. In case of wars, when the demand, to use the language of military economists, is large, the government has recourse to a double measure: it raises the bounty and lowers the minimum of height demanded for the service; on the other hand, in peace times, and when it is wanted to reduce the army, the sum offered is lowered and the standard raised. Thus, in 1856, before peace was concluded, the bounty was seven pounds; the ensuing year it fell to two pounds, and is at present fixed at three. I must, besides, call attention to the fact that this sum only represents a slight portion of the expenses defrayed by the state: it is calculated that, what with the cost of the recruiting-staff, the expenses of keep before joining the regiment, uniform, equipments, &c., each recruit costs about twenty pounds. A few years back the kit was deducted from the bounty money, and this reduction, more or less kept secret, gave too often rise to severe disenchantment. As the recruit did not receive in hard cash the sum he expected, he began his military career under the saddening impression that he had been duped. A just and liberal government has put an end to this abuse. This simple mechanism has hitherto

covered the requirements of Great Britain under
the most critical circumstances, and hence there
are no reasons to change it : constraint is so opposed to English manners and ideas, that it has
been impossible to introduce the law of military
conscription, and I do not hesitate boldly to pre-
dict, that it will never be planted on British soil.
Heaven forbid that I should, on that account,
blame a state measure which, in the hands of the
National Assemblies, saved France from the evils
of a foreign invasion; but I cannot, on the other
hand, blame a system which disarms all criticism
by its respect for individual liberty. An Englishman to whom I remarked that these paid enlistments might become, at a given moment, a heavy
burthen on the nation, answered me, " It is better
to give our money than attack, according to our
ideas, the dignity of our fellow-men."

In what strata of the population is the English
army recruited? To answer this question, we
must first seek the motives which, in the absence
of a coercive law, the state can appeal to, to stimulate enlistments. These motives are three in
number : patriotism, inclination, and necessity.
Patriotism is, at any rate in peace times, a feeble
resource: I will not say that this feeling does not
vibrate in the heart of Englishmen, on the contrary, it is the supreme one; still, British self-
esteem prefers to struggle against other nations
with the weapons of trade and commerce than

with the musket on the battle-field. As for natural inclination, there are certainly men in the
United Kingdom who seem born for an adven-
turous life; but they find so many opportunities
to employ their courage, their erratic humour and
chivalrous tastes, afloat and ashore, without enlisting, that the state could not trust for forming
an army to the help of these exceptional Englishmen. And then, again, every calling is ambi-
tious, and what is the perspective offered the man
who enlists as private in the ranks of the English
army? a field of promotion assuredly most limited,
since the majority of the officers come from the
military colleges. The only thing left is necessity,
and that, according to the remark of an English
officer, is the real recruiting-sergeant. Very few
enter the army by choice, but many under the
pressure of painful circumstances: if there were
no poor, Great Britain would have no soldiers.
In fact, it is only an imperious necessity which
determines the Englishman, in the majority of
cases, to alienate a privilege of which he is so
jealous—his independence and personal liberty.
These facts greatly limit, it will be allowed, the
meaning that should be attached to the words
"voluntary enlistment;" the recruits are, to a certain extent, the conscripts of hunger, and it is not
only the bounty that attracts and subjugates them,
but the prospect of finding a roof, clothing, and
food.

We can now guess in what waters the state fishes in order to maintain and renew its army. The middle classes furnish but very few soldiers; during the Crimean war, the newspapers reproached the young shopmen with not enlisting under the banner of Great Britain, and their reply was significant. "Patriotism," they wrote, "is a very fine thing, but so long as you do not ensure us a prospect of promotion for good conduct, we shall have no desire to seek the company of that class of men whom we have seen following the recruiting-sergeants in the streets of London." Nearly all the young recruits belong to the lower classes of society, and statistics teach us that out of one hundred and thirty-three soldiers, eighty-two came from the labouring classes, forty-one from the artisans, and ten from the shopmen, clerks, and liberal professions. We would say nothing of their humble origin, but experience has proved that most of them bore in their habits the moral brand of vices too often engendered by wretchedness and *malesuada fames.* The inconvenience would not be so great if, as the Duke of Wellington thought, " the greatest scamps make the best soldiers;" but that opinion is not shared in the present day by political economists, states-men, and enlightened generals. It would be unjust to say that the British government desires an ignorant army; and to contradict that calumny, we need only consider the numerous efforts lately made to spread instruction among those poor and unhappy classes whence soldiers are derived. These efforts have been crowned with real success, and we may say that the moral standard of the army has gradually risen with that of the nation. Still, there are in the force of things certain obstacles which are not easily overcome, and in the very darkness of the population a fatal instinct of resistance which opposes the diffusion of education. This fact is only too clearly proved by statisticians, for it was found a year ago that out of thirty-five thousand men belonging to the line, only two thousand could read and write, and possessed a fair knowledge of arithmetic; twenty thousand were quite unable to read and write; and while thirteen thousand could read, they could not form letters.

The three ancient states now merged into the United Kingdom furnish their contingent to the army. The sister isle, as the English call Green Erin, being the classic land of wretchedness, is at the same time, as might be expected, the nursery of soldiers. Scotland also is found, though for different causes, a depôt of ever-ready recruits, especially in times of war. This military temper is dependent to a certain extent on the blood, the geographical influences, and the history of the country. In Scotland the feudal system was maintained, under forms more or less modified, far beyond the events which produced the ruin of that

system in other districts of Great Britain: the
physical character of the country, crossed by
chains of mountains difficult of access, and protected by winding and rough defiles, through
which the national justice could not find its
road, has maintained longer than elsewhere a
régime which seemed rooted to the rocks. The
Scotch also belonged to the Celtic or Gallic
" tap," which is principally distinguished from
the branches of the Saxon family by its excitable
and warlike spirit. In old Caledonia, up to the
beginning of the last century, every man was a
soldier; he took a part in the wars produced by the
political rivalries of the nation, and when he had no
enemies left at home he went abroad to seek them.
The empire of the civil law has certainly modified this state of things, but the germs of the
old martial character still exist on the rough
mountains of Scotland. In his day, glorious Dr.
Johnson gave, with his usual good sense, the advice to respect these germs, and not allow that
valiant and chivalrous spirit to die out, whose
excesses modern civilisation suffices to restrain.
He asked himself if, courage being necessary to
preserve states, and cover as with a buckler the
prosperity of trade and cômmerce, it would not be
better to maintain in some remote provinces that
heroic ardour of old times, which grew weaker in
society with the progress of labour and political
economy. What country, in this respect, is better

suited than Scotland to become a nursery for
soldiers? At such a distance personal courage
may be displayed without troubling the interests
or the peace of the kingdom, and it may be sum-
moned from the crest of the mountains whenever
circumstances demand it. Doubtless, this instinct
for fighting is not yet a military spirit, but it
becomes so by subjecting it to discipline, and by
imparting the idea of duty. And this happens
daily with the Scotch recruits, who are distinguished after enlistment by a persistent air of
independence and national pride.

The English army also admits a certain number of foreigners. Walking one day through the
streets of Woolwich, I met a Frenchman in the
British uniform, who told me his history. He
had been a brother of the Christian doctrine in
a department of Brittany, but feeling little inclination for his calling, he had escaped at the age
of nineteen from a religious establishment directed
by the Abbé de Lamennais, brother of the author
of the *Paroles d'un Croyant*, and embarked for
England. Having no better prospect before him,
he enlisted. He had been serving for two years,
and I must grant that he did not appear extremely
proud of his escapade. • What vexed him most
was his shortness, which, according to the custom
of the British army, as he said, barred all hope
of promotion. "If I were only a foot taller, I
might rise to be a corporal or even a sergeant," he

exclaimed, as he gazed with eyes of envy at a gigantic non - commissioned officer who passed along the street at the moment, and obscured us both by his majestic stature.

At their starting on a soldier's life, the recruits who have come from various provinces, and have no other connecting link than that of ill-luck, offer, I am bound to say, an *ensemble* in no way flattering to Great Britain. I have frequently stopped at the railway stations to watch the sergeant-majors emerge from the carriages with the small band of recruits they had picked up, and these non-commissioned officers, in spite of their brass, seemed to me generally somewhat confused at the ragged state and wretched appearance of their men. If I dwell on the character of the recruit, it is because most of the exceptional laws governing the English army are derived from it; the means of making a better choice, and recruiting the soldier from all classes of society, would have the effect of democratising the army by overthrowing the barriers raised between the inferior and superior grades. This limit, however, is not insuperable, and it would be a mistake to say that the law in England offers any opposition to the soldier becoming an officer. There are two varieties of commissions: those which are purchased, and those which may be granted gratuitously by the Queen. Not finding this barrier in the law, we must seek it where it really exists—in the habits, manners, and feelings of the soldiers. During the Crimean war, at the moment when the position of the troops excited the liveliest interest, the authorities gave commissions to sergeants and corporals whose conduct had been applauded by the officers on the field of battle; but most of these commissions were declined, and the small number of those who accepted had reason presently to repent. The sergeant, on rising from the ranks, finds himself transferred to another sphere — among gentlemen whose birth, education, tastes, fortune, and conversation, condemn him to a state of isolation. Even though the other regimental officers are too generous to keep him aloof, he feels by the very nature of things a vacuum formed round him, and a sort of inferiority weighs like a remorse on his daily relations. We can understand, then, that under such conditions the good sense of the non-commissioned officer prefers an humble grade to a promotion which throws him out of gear. Thus regarded, the gulf that separates the army into two classes, of which one is almost interdicted to the recruit, is deeper than if it had been dug by the law, for this gulf it is not even in the power of the government to fill up. The liberal intentions of the Minister of War have failed several times, and they will still fail, before obstacles which it is more easy to reprove than surmount. Still it must not be said that there is no remedy; but it will require a long series of reforms, and the action of time, to modify on this point the constitution of the English army. A great step towards the change in the military temper would be a limit to the purchase of commissions, even if that custom were not entirely abolished. The government, agreeing with the Duke of Cambridge, seems inclined to enter on this path, but it is unhappily checked by several opposing forces. Still, it is recognised as a universal necessity that, in some way or another, the attraction of emulation, which is now almost nil, should re-act on the recruiting. I will not assert, with some economists, that by opening a wider perspective to the rank and file the bounty might be suppressed; but, at any rate, money would no longer be the sole motive of attraction. The ideal, in a free state, would be indubitably a system that appealed to the tastes and feelings of the recruit by considerations more noble than those of the pocket; but we must not leave out of sight, for all that, the distance which, in the matter of military administration, separates the utopia from the fact.

CHAPTER XI.

BARRACKS—STOPPAGES—GOOD-CONDUCT PAY—SOLDIERS' MESSES—
CLOTHING COLONELS—MILITARY LIBRARIES—THE LASH—DUKE OF
CAMBRIDGE'S CIRCULAR—SOLDIERS' WIVES—SCENES IN THE PENIN-
SULA.

WE now know how and why the English
soldier enlists. After having taken the oath, the
recruits are forwarded to the regimental depôts,
or garrisons; on their arrival, their hair is cut
short in accordance with the regulations, they put
on their uniform, and they are trained for service.
Three or four months after, you would not recognise the raw elements of recruiting, changed as
they are by parade, discipline, and the management of arms. At the same time as the new
soldiers learn their drill, they are expected to
attend the regimental school, which occupies
them for two hours a day in the infantry, and
one in the cavalry. The barracks are, even more
than in other countries, the home of the English
soldier; in fact, troops on the march throughout
Great Britain, are not billeted on the inhabitants
of the towns and villages, as elsewhere; only the

publicans being subjected to this tax, of which they bitterly complain. This custom formerly existed, and even lasted up to the middle of the last century, but it produced disturbances, and the authorities thought it advisable to abolish it. Such respect shown to the liberties of the nation, naturally imposed the obligation of providing by other means for lodging the army : barracks were built, not, as in other countries, at the expense of the municipalities, but at that of the state. Certainly, the purse of the tax-payer thus provided in money what he had formerly paid in kind; but, at any rate, the principle of the inviolability of the domicile was saved, and for the Englishman that is no slight conquest. These barracks, scattered throughout Great Britain, were constructed at different periods : the plans were drawn by the Royal Engineers, and the works executed under contract by civil architects. If they all resembled Woolwich barracks, which stand majestically in a free and open space, or even those at Chatham, there would be nothing to say; but, unfortunately, most of the old barracks were built at a time when the science of public hygiene was still in its infancy. The whole English press was aroused two years ago by a courageous report, published after an inquiry that took place in several barracks, and which suddenly revealed the most crushing facts.* A

* See in the Blue Books of 1858 the labours of this commission,

sort of terror spread over the conscience of the nation, and it was asked what should be done to save from an inglorious death men who had, at any rate, the right to demand of their country a more worthy and useful end. Various remedies were proposed: the most radical, though most expensive of all, would be building new barracks, or thoroughly remodelling the old ones, according to the modern data of military architecture. That is a sacrifice which economists do not regard without terror, but to which the nation will eventually submit in consideration of the noble interests connected with it.

In the bosom of a nation, whose citizens depend very little on the state, and take on themselves the management of their own affairs, the English soldier forms a more striking contrast with the mass of other men than among other peoples, and in this he is at any rate more separated from society. In fact, he offers the unique phenomenon of a being, fed, paid, clothed, lodged, and altogether a burthen on government. In this essay on English military life, it will, therefore, be natural to investigate

in which you read the startling phrase, "the barracks are only an ante-chamber to the hospital." We will, however, observe *en passant* that it is too often the fashion of those who are bent on writing down England, to seek their weapons in these official reports. They are certainly sources of information which must not be neglected, but, as a general rule, you only find in them rare and exceptional cases. And then, after all, is there not an essential strength in a free government which has the courage to recognise the evil, and the greater courage to publish it?

the duties the state undertakes as regards the soldier, and those the latter contracts toward the state. One of the obligations of the kingdom is to put those who secure it beyond the chance of want; and it is a truly English principle, admitted by most employers of labour, that a man well paid, clothed, and fed, is worth two. This principle is also that which the government seems to have adopted as the basis of the constitution of its army. England is, of all the European states, the one which has the fewest soldiers in ratio to the population, and which, at the same time, pays them best. Mr. Barrington de Fonblanque, in his work on the administration and organisation of the English army, determines this proportion by figures. There is, in England, 1 soldier to every 128 inhabitants; in France, the proportion is 1 in 95; in Russia, 1 in 72; in Austria, 1 in 68; in Prussia, 1 in 80; in Spain, 1 in 119; in Belgium, 1 in 115; in Sardinia, 1 in 119; in Turkey, 1 in 74. The average annual pay of all arms in England, is 20*l.* 5s. for privates; 37*l.* 12s. for non-commissioned officers: in France, it is 9*l.* 10s. for privates; 24*l.* for non-commissioned officers. This pay has, however, given rise to some objections in England, for though it is nominally one shilling a day, the soldier does not receive all this money, a portion being retained for his food. This system of reductions, known by the name of "stoppages," is generally

blamed : its principal defect is leading into error
the recruits, who simply imagined that they
would receive their whole pay, and who, on their
entering the regiment, are unpleasantly undeceived. The state, of course, does not join in the
fraud, but is it so with the subaltern recruiting
agents? The truth is, that they are very careful
not to enlighten the recruit on this delicate point,
but make the shilling glisten in all its plumpness,
just as the bird-catcher dazzles larks with a bit
of glass. In spite of the stoppages, the English
soldier in line regiments has threepence a day
left for his pleasure; while the French soldier
only receives three-halfpence: where, then, is the
motive to have recourse to a fiction which injures,
to a certain extent, the dignity of the relations
between the state and the recruit ?

The daily pay is not the sole attraction the military administration employs to attach the soldier
to his duties. There is, under the name of good-
conduct money, a remuneration of one penny a
day and upwards for men who have distinguished
themselves by their good behaviour; there is also
the beer-money, and additional fatigue pay for
soldiers engaged as labourers on public works;
but all these sources of income are very small.
A more serious prospect is that of a pension: up
to the reign of Charles II. the state had not
troubled itself with providing for the fate of those
soldiers who had grown grey under arms, but in

1682 that monarch laid for them the first stone
of Chelsea Hospital, the *Hôtel des Invalides* of
Great Britain; which stands in a pleasant position
on the banks of the Thames, that wide and majestic river whose limpid waters have not yet been sul-
lied by passing through the old districts of London. This retreat, however, can only shelter six
hundred veterans, and there are more than sixty
thousand who implore the assistance of the state.

A system of out-pensions was introduced in the
reign of Queen Anne, and in 1806 an act of parliament conferred a legal right to support on
soldiers who had spent twenty-one years in the
service, or had lost a limb for the glory of their
country. At the present day there are about
sixty-four thousand veterans receiving an annual
pension. The scale naturally varies according to
the length of service, the severity of the wounds,
and other considerations, but the average amount
of each pension is one shilling per diem. I will
not assert that the old soldier can certainly rely
on this subsidy as a means of existence, but he at
any rate finds in it a considerable relief. This
system imposes on the nation an annual burthen
of one million two hundred thousand pounds, but
it is a sacrifice no Englishman regrets, so much
does he consider it a duty of justice and humanity.

The state, in the second place, had to make
arrangements for the soldier's nourishment, and
he has three meals a day, breakfast, dinner, and

supper, each meal being announced five minutes previously by the bugle. The men assemble in their rooms, and it is curious to see them in their fatigue jackets forming what is called the soldiers' mess. Five minutes later the bugle sounds again, when the party sit down. The English soldier receives a larger ration of animal food than any other in Europe. When on the march he endures any privations, but he must have his meat. In most of the barracks, camps, and garrisons, the meat and bread are supplied by contracts entered into between the government and private persons, and the cooks, accompanied by a non-commissioned officer, buy the other articles of food in the neighbourhood. If the quantity of provisions given the soldier in Great Britain is more considerable than elsewhere, we must also allow that the culinary arrangements might be greatly improved: and with whom does the fault lie? The English soldier is a very poor cook; this fact, which was very speedily discovered in the Crimean war, results from the national character, or rather from that division of labour which has so ramified through the habits of the country. The British soldier can fight, for that is his trade, but do not ask him to turn his hand to everything, as the French soldier does, with a species of juvenile ardour and innate knowledge. Still, we are bound to say, that this Crimean war, which gave so many other useful lessons to England, also exercised a fortunate influence over the cookery of the army. M. Soyer, ex-chef of the Reform Club, having been sent to the scene of action, gave the English troops some excellent advice as to the benefit of deriving advantage from the most ordinary fare, and Colonel Tulloch, now one of the three directors of Woolwich Arsenal, also laid before the committee, appointed in 1857 to inquire into the sanitary condition of the army, some excellent plans to improve the dietetic régime of the soldiers. The military authorities have already entered on this path, and at Alder-shott camp experiments which cannot be too greatly encouraged, are successfully pursued. Captain Grant has also invented a cooking apparatus for the use of the troops, which allows food to be prepared at a very cheap rate. The end is clearly laid down; generally providing the army with a greater variety without imposing fresh burthens on the state. Science having begun, it is for practice to do the rest, and direct the troops to a domestic conquest, regarded by professional men in England as of the highest importance.

As regards clothing, the English soldier is equally privileged, and is generally cleaner and better dressed than in all the other military states of Europe. Still, a great deal had to be done ere the administration disarmed all criticism on this head. Up to recently, the duty of clothing the army was in the hands of the officers, from whom it passed to the colonels: it is useless to notice here the abuses that resulted from it, as they have now ceased with the system.   In 1854, the period of the great military reforms, the government undertook the duty of clothing the troops, and from that period a certain degree of progress has been made in the form and quality of the uniforms. Most of the garments are annually supplied by contract; but the government has also established a tailor's shop, and, though the enterprise is recent, it promises to bear good fruit in an economical point of view, for, in 1857, the state produced for 7700*l.* a quantity of infantry coats which under the contract system would have cost it 10,800*l.* The future will finally decide a question which is still being discussed : Ought the state to take the place of private trades in all that relates to the equipment of the troops?   What public opinion now demands, is a wise and liberal system which will maintain the army on a respectable footing, while paring the daily shilling as little as possible by stoppages.   When certain articles of clothing have been worn their time, they are the soldier's perquisites, and he is at liberty to sell them.   This circumstance accounts for the great number of red tunics which you see at fairs, not without regret, on the backs of the mountebanks and cheap jacks.   I will not carry further the inventory of the articles of personal use which the military administration supplies to the troops, but it will be sufficient for me to say that, all considered, the English army is the dearest of all in Europe, considering the number of soldiers.* This fact is the consequence of voluntary enlistment, and of the thoroughly English principle recognised so far back as Cromwell's time. "A small number of men well clothed and satisfied with their lot, is better than a large number of suffering and discontented soldiers."

The soldier being an intelligent being, the state also owes him a certain degree of moral cultivation, and Great Britain has made notable progress in this direction, specially during the last few years. General Foy, in his Memoirs, represents the English soldier as a brute beast, animated by a species of blind and limited courage; but I find difficulty in recognising in this portrait the features of the model I have before my eyes. Either the judgment of the French general was obscured by national prejudices, admissible up to a certain point after 1815, or, as I would be rather disposed to believe, the character of the English soldier has greatly changed since that time. There is at present an inspector-general of military schools, whose duty it is to visit the barracks and garrisons throughout the kingdom :

* It may be interesting to see the proportion of military expenses expressed in figures. In England each soldier costs annually 52l.; in France, 36l.; in Russia, 13l. 5s.; in Austria, 18l. 10s.; in Prussia, 31l.; in Belgium, 38l.; in Sardinia, 32l.; and in Turkey, 10l. 15s.

he thus watches the state of education in the army
and makes known the intentions of government
for the moral development of the soldiers. There
are now about two hundred military schoolmasters, arranged in four classes, according to the
order of position and merit. In the schools, care
is taken to keep aloof from the instruction those
delicate questions which might arouse sectarian
jealousies, and the religious teaching is limited to
those universal principles which are obscurely
graven on the heart of man. It is not even obli-
gatory to attend school, and the men are at liberty
to do as they please ; but the ignorance of the
British army has, at any rate, lost that deplorable
character of obstinacy and pride which closed the
sources of progress to it in another century. It
is interesting to see, at the schools, not only privates, but also corporals and sergeants, who have
bravely fought for years to sustain before the
world the honour of the British flag, now trying
their rude organs on the elements of reading and
writing. A small weekly payment is demanded
of the adults and children who attend the military
schools, amounting to from fourpence to eightpence a month for privates, corporals, and sergeants, and a penny or twopence for the children.
The pay of the schoolmasters varies from 48*l.* to
150*l.*, to which they add, in some garrisons, a
further income by giving lessons to the officers'
children. Another recent improvement, which

merits notice, is the establishment in barracks of
libraries and reading-rooms, the inspector-general
selecting for them those books, reviews, and peri-
odicals which are best adapted to the tastes and
wants of the profession. Here, for a penny a
month, the soldier can spend useful hours, and
profitably employ the leisure which he might
otherwise devote to the pothouse. It has been
objected, I allow, that, owing to the bad local
arrangements of the old barracks, some of these
reading-rooms are cold and gloomy. Much remains, doubtless, to be done, but the principle is
good, and, although limited by material arrangements which it is difficult to modify in a day, it
has already exerted an excellent influence over
the mind and inclinations of the army. What is
next wanting in the English barracks—and it
could be hardly believed in a country where physical strength is the object of assiduous cultivation
—is gymnastic instruments and exercises. Some
officers, struck by such a want in the means of
recreation, and the sanitary régime of the soldier,
have tried to make up for this forgetfulness at
their own expense; but the state can no longer
rely on chance or the generosity of individuals,
and must soon take in hand a system which has
elsewhere produced such excellent results. The
only game of skill in which the troops indulge at
intervals is the world-famous cricket.

I have described the obligations which the

state, under the free régime of enlistment, had
contracted towards the stranger, and the mode in
which it fulfilled them. It would be superfluous
to dwell on the duties of the English army, for
they are usually the same as those of all civilised
armies, but there is a unique feature which must
be taken into account, and which distinguishes
the British troops—and that is ubiquity. Whenever I cast my eyes over the map of Europe, I am
surprised to see the two small islands which have
extended so far the network of a power disse-
minated to the confines of the world. Like the
rich man of whom Jean-Jacques Rousseau speaks,
England is thus menaced over a greater surface,
and needs all the energy of her army, small as it
is, to protect her immense possessions. This geographical condition imposes hard trials on the English soldier; for, with the colonies and establishments she holds in hand, Great Britain is nearly
always at war, even in time of peace. Then, to
the labours of war, the English soldier must add
long sea-voyages, marches and countermarches
through unknown countries, and a contest with
the most varying climates, from the rock of Gib-
raltar to the flowery groves of Malta; from the
happy group of the Ionian Islands to the savannahs
of South America; from the mysterious and parch-
ing solitudes of India to the black forests of Canada. Under what a soft image do his dear native
isle, his village, his cottage, where he left an aged

mother and sisters, appear to him at that distance!
He sees them again at last, but for how long? He
must set out afresh for China or Australia. These
voyages, privations, fatigues, and contrasts of tem-
perature, form a portion of the debt the soldier
has contracted towards the state, and, strategically regarded, they have the advantage of hardening him. If the French army during the reign
of Louis-Philippe tempered its strength in the
African campaigns—as most people readily believe—ought we to despise another army bronzed
under the same conditions, and which, moreover,
on its cosmopolitan march, has been tried in turns
by the fires of Asia and the ice of the new world?

As discipline is the soul of armies, any violation
of military duties must unhappily be severely
punished. I will not speak here of punishments
existing elsewhere, but there is one belonging
more or less to Great Britain, and against which
for some years past the unanimous voice of moralists has been lifted—I mean the lash; which
under such grave circumstances as, for instance,
desertion, is inflicted on the British soldier. I
will not describe a cruel correction at which I
never had the courage to be present; but it would
be unjust to say, as I have read somewhere, that
this flogging belongs to the English manners and
character. Great Britain has for a long time reproached herself, and still reproaches herself elo-
quently, for a trace of the barbarous ages, which

the progress of civilisation and Christian feeling
ought to have effaced in the nineteenth century.
The Duke of Wellington has already reduced to
fifty lashes the maximum, which had been at three
hundred; and, a year back, the execution of the
sentence of a court-martial on a soldier flogged
at Windsor, under exceptional and painful circumstances, provoked a cry of horror which ran
from one extremity of the army to the other. The
Duke of Cambridge, willing to meet public opinion
half way, wrote a circular which was enthusiastically received: the army, according to the orders
of the commander-in-chief, was to be divided into
two classes, the first entirely free from corporal
punishment, except for a small number of extraordinary cases, while the second, comprising men
degraded for serious offences, still remains subjected to the old system of punishment; but it is
the wish of the royal prince that recourse to the
rigour of military law should be avoided as far
as possible, even with the latter. Fallen soldiers
may, besides, redeem themselves, for it is a purgatory and not a hell: and a year of uninter-
rupted good conduct restores them to the first
class. This reform, which introduces a moral
division in the army, and which limits the condition of flogging, was universally hailed as an excellent idea on the part of the administration, and
as an act of humanity. I must add, that public
opinion went further, and saw in this measure a

step towards the total abolition of a brutal and degrading punishment. Petitions covered with a great number of signatures, and meetings, demanded, and still daily demand, the complete triumph of a gentler legislature more in harmony with the dignity of modern times. I do not believe that public opinion is deceived in its expectations: but in England, there is no sudden leap from one established system to another, especially in a matter so grave as the discipline of the army.

Those who defend, at any rate as a transitional measure, the use of the lash as limited by the Duke of Cambridge's circular, base their arguments, moreover, on considerations which it would be unjust to neglect. The English army, they say, is placed by the very nature of the recruiting system in peculiar conditions: it receives annually a large proportion of idle, turbulent, and savage characters, who must be acted on by regrettable, though necessary, means. It has also been observed that, among the faults for which the English army merely inflicted flogging, there are some which the French military code punishes with death. These arguments, I am bound to add, have not convinced me: for it is not so much the severity of the punishment I blame, as the moral brand it leaves. Another more consolatory consideration, and in my opinion more correct, is that in Great Britain the liberty of press and speech exercises an active surveillance over the system of military punishments, whatever it may be.

Among the characteristic features of the English soldier's condition, there is another I am bound not to forget. Great Britain, as compared with France, offers us two great anomalies—a married clergy and a married army. When an English soldier has made up his mind to take a wife, he informs his officers : this formality is not indispensable, but, in the event of his marrying without their consent, he is not allowed to have his wife in barracks, and loses some advantages attached by the military regulations to the union of the sexes. Experience has proved that married men behaved better, were less frequently punished, and enjoyed better health than bachelors. A privilege of which they are jealous is messing with their wives, and the withdrawal of this favour often acts on the mind of the married soldier more than a severe punishment.

The loves of the soldiers sometimes give rise to romantic adventures. In 1811, an Irish soldier, Terence Burns, who had enlisted for seven years, received orders with his regiment to embark for an English colony. The vessel started, and had been out to sea for two days, when a pretty girl was discovered on board, who had contrived to hide herself behind some piles of ropes. She gave her name as Margaret, and said she had followed her sweetheart, Terence, the private. The fact was soon made known to the captain of the ship and the regimental officers, and they desired that this devotion should not pass unrequited. The marriage was solemnised on board, in the presence of the colonel and other officers, the ship's captain performing the duty of chaplain. Terence and Margaret lived together as man and wife during the four months the voyage lasted, but, unfortunately, the finale of this history does not harmonise with its poetic commencement. A young officer present at the marriage, and who performed the duty of clerk, managed to insinuate himself into the good graces of the young wife, and when the regiment reached Sidney, the frail and inconstant Margaret left Terence, and transferred her affections to the gallant officer, with whom she lived till his death.

The soldiers' wives constitute in barracks one of the types of military life. When girls, they were mostly attracted by the sound of the drum, the brilliancy of the uniform, and all those coquetries of glory which exert so powerful an influence on some female hearts. Only a small number of women, however, find lodgings in the barracks, and owing to the bad architectural arrangements to which I have alluded, the laws of decency have not always been regarded, as the report of the committee tells us. These women are gossiping, quarrelsome, and eager to interfere

in one another's business, so that the intervention
of the husband is at times required to re-establish
order.   They are, however, active and industrious,
and one of their great occupations and small
source of profit, is doing the washing of the un-
married soldiers.   This sort of work is so attached
to their condition, that a young girl, courted by a
soldier, and who had not yet accepted his hand,
simply confided to me the cause of her hesitation:
"I love Robinson, and a military life pleases me,
but I can't bear washing."   The most artistic
among these wives of the regiment have a decided
taste for the piano; though, on hearing them strike
the keys with a hand more bold than delicate, you
would be inclined to believe that it is not music
but noise they seek.   The English government,
while engaged in organising military education,
has not forgotten the soldiers' helpmates, and each
regiment or garrison has a schoolmistress specially
to instruct the girls and children, for it was
thought that the best mode of regenerating the
soldier was to raise, at an early age, the moral
tone and the education of woman.   Those wives
who do not live in barracks receive twopence a
day pay, and generally live in the neighbourhood.
I more than once visited on Woolwich Common,
in a corner sheltered by a few trees, and divided
from the road by a hedge, a species of village, in
which all the houses are alike, and which might
be called a colony of soldiers' wives.   Here the

cage-birds sing, but their song is too often
drowned by the voices of the children, which in
their turn yield before the chattering of the mothers. On Sunday, these women, decently clad,
walk about with a triumphant air on their husbands' arm, especially when he wears a medal on
his chest.

In order to be thoroughly acquainted with this
peculiar creature, we must not study her either
in barracks or on her native soil, but follow her
to the grand scenes of military events. The frequent departure of troops for the colonies or distant battle-fields, gives rise to touching scenes,
which have supplied English artists with their
best subjects. All the wives are not allowed to accompany their husbands on these distant expedi-
tions, and the vessel starts amid tears and parting
embraces. About four women to a company are
received on board, and follow the drum, as it is
called. Here a perfectly new career begins for
them; marriage, with all its most austere duties,
weighs down these strange creatures; but conjugal
love seems to grow in them in the midst of the
struggle against the obstacles and difficulties of
life. We may laugh at the English soldier's wife
at home, but we can only admire her on the scene
of military enterprises. She lays no claim to the
attributes of the weaker sex; and she should be
seen on the high roads, marching with a group of
children by her side, or perched on the regimental

baggage cart, with her new-born babe in her arms, and taking care not to let out of sight the little trunk that holds the soldier's estate. At each halt she forgets her own fatigue to unload her husband, take care of his haversack, change his clothes, prepare the modest meal for him and the children, and cheer him by her conversation. Sister of charity at the same time as a wife, she suffers everything with a patience and resignation illumined by a beam of strength. After every campaign, the English generals and colonels have alluded in their reports to the happy influence these heroic women have exercised over the *morale* of the troops—privations, labours, fatigues, dangers—they shared all except the glory.

During the Peninsular war, which has left so many tragic memories in the English army, the wife of Sergeant Anton was crossing a hastily repaired bridge over the Adour, and she was driving before her a small donkey loaded with baggage belonging to another woman of the regiment. At first all went well, but, on reaching the other end of the bridge, the obstinate animal stopped short. In the mean while a regiment was advancing, the passage would be obstructed, and the poor creature did not know what to do. The idea occurred to her of removing the baggage from the donkey's back, and forcing her way through, when a grenadier of the regiment that was going to defile by the bridge, casting his eyes on an empty horn, covered with masonic signs, that hung by a cord over the woman's shoulders, exclaimed, "Poor creature, for the sake of what you carry on your side, I will not leave you in the lurch." At the same time, handing his musket to a comrade, he seized the donkey and dragged it across the bridge. Another sergeant's wife was not so fortunate, who had to ford the same river with a regiment. Mounted on a donkey, she held an infant in her arms, and struggled heavily against the ever-deepening waves. A start on the part of the animal hurled the poor child into the water; the mother, wild with grief, uttered a cry, and plunged into the river to save her offspring. Both were soon carried off by the current in sight of the husband, who plunged in in the hope of rescuing them, but mother and child had departed for ever, and the soldier himself was only saved with great difficulty by his comrades. The English regiments keep up the recollection of many episodes of this nature, which give us an idea of the world of dangers and miseries into which soldiers' wives venture by espousing the wandering destiny of armies.

We have seen the military education of the English soldier commencing in the barracks, and if we wish to know how it is completed, we must go to the camp at Aldershott, where we can form a tolerably faithful idea of the English army in the field.

CHAPTER XII.

ALDERSHOTT—THE VILLAGE—NORTH AND SOUTH CAMP—THE TENTS—
OFFICERS' MESS—AMUSEMENTS IN CAMP—BRITISH PLUCK—THE
BRAVEST MAN IN THE ARMY—MISS NIGHTINGALE—HARRIET MAR-
TINEAU—THE HIGHLANDER—THE HORSE GUARDS—REVIEWS.

THE first time I visited Aldershott camp, it was
on a gloomy and tempestuous December day: the
steam-horse having deposited me at Farnborough
station, I walked the distance separating the
station from the village. A west wind blew over
a black heath extending out of range, and raising
now and then dense clouds of dust by which I
was blinded, for the road runs through the desert
which desolates this portion of Hants. I was reduced to such a state, that I blessed the rain-drops
which speedily laid the dust, and blended the low
and gloomy sky to some extent with the general
colour of these bleak, sad, and shifting plains.
The village or town of Aldershott, which has
sprung up like a mushroom in the vicinity of the
camp, is not without a character of its own. Only
a few patches of sterile land now bear evidence here

and there of what this wretched hamlet was ten years ago. To-day the ear is deafened by the noise of the saw and the trowel, the eye only perceives scaffoldings, building works, and houses springing up as it were by steam. Some speculators, finding that brick buildings did not advance rapidly enough, have put up wooden huts or zinc houses, in which they have installed their trade. All this, I allow, has rather the air of a fair, where the booths are erected in a night and theatres improvised, than of a town in process of building. The source of this great activity—is it necessary to mention it?—was opened by the installation of the troops at a short distance from the village. The soldier needs amusement, the soldier is not saving, hence it is expected that the soldier will patronise the shops, taverns, dancing-rooms, and concert-halls. In consequence, here the inscriptions and signs try to flatter the self-esteem of the British hero! You read here the names of all the victories, not excepting, of course, those in the Crimea. A railway, intended to carry coal and building materials, now runs through Aldershott, which is already overshadowed by large and lofty barracks built of yellow brick. Leaving behind me the military village, I ascended a small hill, and soon saw the whole of the camp stretched out before me. Wooden huts and groups of tents planted on a few scrubby pieces of turf rose all around me amid the black and muddy sand, while on the horizon on one side of the hill a red line, like a field of pionies, undulated: it was formed of British soldiers at drill.

In reality, Aldershott camp reminds you of an encampment of ancient Britons. When the soldiers took possession, a few years ago, of this bare, dry, and desolate soil, they were compelled to build themselves a town of canvas and wood: barracks made of planks and covered with tar are aligned so as to form streets. These huts are divided into lodgings for the officers, non-commissioned officers, and privates: in summer they are stifled, but, to make up for it, they are frozen in winter. All the huts, however, are not sleeping-rooms; for there are some which respond to the different wants of military life. I found in this colony a bath-room for the soldiers, a wash-house for the women, a kitchen with an array of turnspits, commanded by a sour-looking corporal; an hospital, the huts of which contain a dozen beds, and have the doors painted white; a children's school; an adult school; a post-office, and a telegraph station, the wires of which, agitated by the whistling wind that continued to blow, vibrated over my head like the chords of an Æolian harp. As you go along, you also see a family hut for married soldiers, where, from time to time, a man with harsh and bronzed features is dandling in his rough hand a babe, which boldly clutches him by the beard. The camp is divided into south and north camps, separated by a canal, on which artillery manœuvres are practised. The farther you go, the more you seem reverting to primitive times: in the north camp, the huts appeared to me less numerous than the tents, each of which, like an overturned teacup in shape, shelters a dozen men, who sleep on straw. With their feet collected round the centre pole, which supports the frail edifice, and their heads against the canvas wall, they represent the spokes of a wheel, and their rolled-up cloaks serve as a pillow. The soldier's dinner is cooked in the open air before a camp-fire, as in the Homeric ages; and if we may judge by the heaps of potatoes and heavy puddings boiling in the caldrons, the appetite of the warriors has not degenerated in Great Britain. Each of the divisions, north and south, has its church, a sort of wooden barn, for man can only give to God what he has, and neither stone nor brick has as yet penetrated Aldershott camp, as they would alter its character. All this hard and vigorous population, burnt by the sun, bitten by the wind, and tempered like steel in rain water, appeared to me to enjoy rude health. The intention that dictated the formation of the camp is easy to detect: the government wished to carry out there the practical education of officers and men. This object has been attained, and the

twenty thousand men who cover the heights of
Aldershott compose the nucleus of the best army
England probably ever possessed.

The life of the officers offers, in this rude school,
features which cannot be found in the barracks:
they live like the troops, in huts and tents, with
this difference, that they sleep singly. The name
of a block is given to six wooden compartments,
each of which is considered sufficient to serve as
a cell for the lieutenants and ensign; the captain
has two, and the field-officers occupy an entire
block. In these rooms, which are all on the
ground-floor, there is room for an iron bedstead,
a table, a washstand, a chest of drawers, and two
chairs, and the officers take their meals together
in the mess-room hut, built of black planks, and
with windows decorated with red curtains. The
English officer being particular as to his personal
appearance, there is a hut in which the barber
presides; and there is also in each camp a club
supported by voluntary subscriptions, where the
officers read, chat, or play at billiards. We can
already see that the range of amusements is very
limited. A few young officers go out shooting
now and then, but their principal relaxation is
rowing on the canal. It must be remembered
that Aldershott, like Sandhurst, is situated thirty
miles from London, on a savage plain; and this
isolation was calculated on to attach the officers
to their duties. It is here that we may, above

all, study the relations existing between the officers and privates: in England there is a greater distance between the ranks, and a more marked separation between officers and men, than in France, and we might almost say there are two sorts of blood in the English army. Still, it would be a mistake to take literally the word " aristocracy," too often employed in alluding to the British corps of officers: with the exception of a few privileged armies, these officers generally belong to the higher layer of the middle classes. They are the sons of clergymen, merchants, tradesmen, large farmers, and men belonging to the liberal professions. The aristocracy, therefore, does not exist in the persons, but in the constitution of the army, which raises a lofty barrier between the commissioned and non-commissioned officers.

This limit is based, before all, on education and fortune. It is only necessary to have dined in barracks at the splendid mess of the English officers, to understand that the non-commissioned officers regard promotion to the upper grades not only with indifference, but even with a feeling of alarm. At this table all is in grand style, and I would defy the Duke of Norfolk and Baron Rothschild to display on their table a greater luxury—of crystal, china, and plate—than can be found in the mess-room of certain regiments. A portion of these artistic objects has been left by

officers who have retired from the service; add
to this, exquisite cheer and fine and delicate
wines, whose bottles circulate carelessly, lying in
a little silver truck, especially whenever a stranger
has to be treated with respect. Nor must I forget the outlay for horses, dogs, civilian clothing
(for the English officers only wear uniform when
on duty), theatres, and pleasures of every description. In most barracks, the officers also give
balls, to which they invite the flower of the
aristocracy. It is easy to guess, from the style
of life, that the officers go far beyond the limits of
their pay; and they are backed up by personal
fortune, or the liberality of their relatives. The
army is less a lucrative than an honourable career,
in which young men of family find means to
gratify their tastes, and acquire consideration by
doing their country a service. In the midst of
this gilded world, how sad would a rough and
humble sergeant feel, compelled to live on his pay
as ensign or cornet! I have read in an English
story that when an Indian king was angry with
a great nobleman, he would give him a white
elephant: the distinction attached to this royal
favour demands that the animal should be fed
on the finest barley and best fruits, so that, at the
expiration of a certain time, the ruined lord finds
himself reduced to the necessity of selling his
estates. The intentions of the English government are assuredly very different from those of

the barbarous monarch; but, for all that, the non-commissioned has good reasons to regard the commission offered to him as a calamitous honour, or like a white elephant that would devour its master's substance. We may be allowed to regret, for certain reasons, this powerful division in the English army, but regarded strategically, it adds more than would be believed to the value of the troops. Accustomed to regard the officers as superior beings, the soldier follows them with a species of enthusiastic veneration, and would blush not to expose himself to danger whenever they do so. Now, it is well known that the English officers are not deficient in courage. By a sort of contrast peculiar to the English character, the same men who live at home among the luxury and delights of Capua, can, when required, go without common necessaries, and accept the hardest conditions of existence. During the Crimean war officers were seen turning soldiers voluntarily, and filling in silence (for silence is one of the dignities of British devotion) the gaps which the enemy's fire had made in the ranks of the army.*

At Aldershott camp, the non-commissioned officers and privates have their amusements too, which are more abundant in their way than those

---

* A soldier whose democratic opinions are well known, Colonel Charras, said to me one day, that unless profound changes took place in English society, he should regard the promotion of rank and file to commissions as a serious danger for the military system of Great Britain.

of the dignitaries of the army. Without mention-
ing the canteen, they find in the little military
village, games, casinos, and a multitude of
establishments in accordance with their tastes.
I should not like to say that more than one young
officer does not curse in his heart the grandeur
which forbids him taking part in these varied
amusements. It is true that many soldiers regret
the next morning having dallied on the isle of
pleasures. Intoxication, as is too well known, is one
of the vices of the English army, and the majority
of offences entailing disciplinary punishments, not
excepting the lash, have been committed under
the influence of spirituous liquors. Would it not
be a way of restraining this brutalising penchant
to cultivate nobler pastimes? The custom has
been, during the last years, of playing comedies in
the camps and barracks; and I was shown at
Aldershott a hut, with several entrances, bearing
a likeness to those strolling theatres I had seen
erected at fairs. The house could contain about
one hundred spectators; there is an orchestra, a
proscenium, slips, scenery pulled up with ropes
like the sails of a vessel, and a wardrobe for playing dramas and farces. One of these amateur
theatres was built last summer at Chatham, in the
Royal Marine Barracks; the actors were non-commissioned officers and privates of the Engineers,
and the audience was composed of the heads of
the garrison, and the notables of the town. I saw

performed here, "Still Waters run Deep," and the "Unfinished Gentleman;" the actors being called out at the end of each piece and warmly applauded. This was but just, for a burst of laughter had not once ceased to run round the house, and I do not believe that these two pieces were ever better played on a London stage. Such dramatic representations may possibly offer but a secondary attraction in most garrison towns, where the English soldier can generally pay for his seat at the theatre, but the regiment is not always in England. In the midst of those gloomy and distant solitudes to which Great Britain sends military posts, the resources of the dramatic art contribute to support or raise the spirits of the troops, and hence we need not feel surprised that the officers encourage their men in acting, and at times furnish the example. On certain nights the Artillery officers give extraordinary performances at Woolwich Theatre, when the price of admission is raised, and the good society of the town, which at other times holds aloof from the theatre, eagerly witness these performances, which are redeemed in their eyes by the character of the actors.

Poets are also found in the ranks of the British army; their works usually consisting of verses of the moment, which are preserved and sung in the regiment, like the warlike hymns of the old Saxon bards. They are rather wild flowers, but are not

without a certain military perfume. Another
more serious branch of literature is that of memoirs
and voyages: having seen much, the English
soldier would also have much to describe if he
knew how to clothe his ideas in words. In all
parts of the world (for where does not the British
empire extend) he has mingled with a class of
the population with which the officers do not
foregather. To the latter we are indebted for
excellent works about different countries of the
globe, but which are different in details, simplicity,
and popular features. Hence, it is not surprising
that the London press should have encouraged
books which, like those of Sergeant Anton and
Quartermaster Connolly, opened a new path in
the already luxuriant field of English literature.

The character of the British soldier approaches
in some points, and retires in others, from that
attributed to the soldiers of other countries, and I
will briefly point out the differences. The English army is generally Protestant, only about one-
fourth being Catholics, and this observation did
not escape the penetrating mind of Oliver Goldsmith. Even in his day a foreign invasion was
talked of, and in his "Letters of a Citizen of the
World" he brings on the scene three persons: a
prisoner for debt, a porter, and a soldier, who converse and communicate to each other the apprehensions with which the more or less probable
arrival of the French in Great Britain inspires

them. The prisoner for debt trembles for the national liberty, the porter for the burthens the French will impose on the country, and the soldier for the religion of England. I should be tempted to believe that this faith in the greatness of the Anglican religion was imprinted on the army by the strong hand of Cromwell. However this may be, the French themselves, during the first Empire, discovered these spiritual weapons, and tried more than once to turn them against their enemies. It must be remarked, that most of the Peninsular battles, and in the last instance Waterloo, were fought on a Sunday. Knowing the respect of the English for the rest of the seventh day, the French generals hoped to profit by it in their attacks. I confess that they had not always reason to praise their calculations, for the English troops gloriously broke the Sabbath. They thus justified the proverb current in Great Britain, " the better the day, the better the deed."

I insist on this characteristic, because if ever—which may the gods avert—a European war were to be rekindled, and the English army interfered, the religious feeling might exert a serious influence over it. As a military fanaticism does not exist in the nation, we must seek elsewhere the motives that set the British forces in motion at a given moment. Glory is a word which finds but a slight echo in the heart of the English soldier, but speak to him of duty, and he will become heroically impassioned. An idea that pursues him, amidst the solitudes of the old and new world, is that of the absent country: what will they think of us in England? these men, who perhaps will never tread their native soil again, ask themselves on the field of battle. This patriotism has, in a certain sense, passed into the blood. A young drummer fell into the hands of the enemy, and to be assured whether he were really a prisoner of war or a disguised spy, he was asked to beat the retreat. "The retreat," he said; "I do not know what you mean. We do not understand that word in the British army."

The English soldier is brave, but there are varieties of courage. The English have a word of their own, only known in familiar language, but which exactly expresses the shade of intrepidity distinguishing the race. This word, derived from the old Saxon, is "pluck;" it indicates the idea of energetic effort, and is as applicable to the man who uproots a tree, as to him who tears down a moral obstacle. It is employed to signify courage, but courage combined with firmness, obstinacy, coolness, and an unceasing resolution which never yields. English soldiers have other enemies to combat beside foreign armies; they have tempests, shipwrecks, climates, and deserts; they must be at once brave against men and against things. All this is pluck. The rough Saxon word indicates, moreover, a style of valour

subjected to reflection and the control of duty. My
French readers will, perhaps, be surprised that,
in speaking of camp and barrack life, I have not
touched on duelling, but it is almost unknown in
the English army. The weapons Great Britain
places in the hands of her soldiers are intended to
defend the honour of the nation, and not to serve
private revenge. What the English nation admires
at least equally with courage in the soldiers, is a
species of greatness of soul and disinterestedness
which elevates a man above self-esteem. A fact
will explain better than all comments. In 1837,
Wellington, as he was leaving Apsley House one
evening, was addressed by two gentlemen whose
faces were strange to him. They told him they
were the executors to a will made by a friend of
a very eccentric turn of mind, who had left 500*l.*
to the bravest man in the English army. They
added, that they intended handing the cheque
to the Duke, convinced, as they both were, that
they would thus best carry out the wishes of the
deceased. The Duke thanked them, but refused
the legacy, alleging, as his reason, that he knew
many men in the army as brave as himself. They
pressed him, at any rate, to become arbiter, and
point out the man he considered most worthy:
he consented, but begged a few days for reflection.
After thinking—for the task, he found, was more
difficult than he had at first thought—he named
Major-General Sir James Macdonell, who com-

manded at Hougoumont in 1815, a post which was the key of the Battle of Waterloo. The executors proceeded to Sir James, and after making known to him the Duke's choice, presented the money to him. Sir James replied, that he could not discuss a decision so honourable to him, but that he knew a man whose conduct had been at least as meritorious as his own on that day: it was a sergeant-major of the Coldstreams, a man of the name of Frazer. At the moment when the French rushed on Hougoumont with such fury that the gates of the farm were burst open and the position was threatened, the sergeant had helped the general in closing the gates on the enemy by a marvel of strength and audacity. Sir James consequently declared that he accepted the 500*l.*, but should give one half to the worthy sergeant, with whom he intended to share the reward as he had done the danger. Such facts are of a nature to make the country feel a pride in its defenders.

A question which has lately greatly occupied the public writers of Great Britain, is the sanitary reform of the army. The great mortality of soldiers, compared with the other classes of society, excited, two years ago, a painful emotion. Regarded from an economic point of view, it is estimated that the English soldier, when thoroughly found, represents 100*l.*; morally, his value is inappreciable; hence the state endures a serious loss each time the grave is opened to receive a soldier. Among the diseases of the army there are some which are fictitious, such as malingering, which we must blame rather than pity: but there are many others much too real which claim serious attention. It would not be so surprising if the health of the soldier underwent serious alterations in distant countries—by turns burning and frozen —to which the interests of his country summon him; but at home, and in his native air, the fact becomes more alarming. The surprise is increased when we reflect that the army is recruited from a class of young men who, before entering the service, had, to a certain extent, received a certificate of a sound physical constitution. These young soldiers are, for the most part, the rude sons of toil, and their comfort, at any rate in certain respects, has increased in lieu of diminishing, since the day when they passed from civil into military life. The cause of this exceptional disease has been sought, and it is believed to have been found in the bad state of the old barracks, in the quality of the food, and the absence of a hygienic service. Discovering the evil was calling in the remedy. One fact I have not seen mentioned in the reports of the official commission, and which might probably throw a light on the source of maladies that have partly remained a mystery, is the English love of independence. I have frequently seen soldiers, walking alone or in

pairs, stop and look sadly after a lark that was
flying away. The bird was an image of their
rustic youth, and, less happy than the lark, they
regretted having clipped their own wings. This
melancholy brooding over lost liberty throws a
cloud over barrack life, deprives their food of
its savour, and their slumber of its sweetness.
The remedy for this mental disease would be a
system of amusements to exercise the forces of
their vigorous natures in useful works or gymnastic sports. Two English women have been
struck by the deficiency that existed, and still
exists, though in a less degree, in the sanitary
system of the English army: one of them, FLO-
RENCE NIGHTINGALE, has immortalised her name—
sweet to the ears of the English as the song of the
bird whose name she bears—by substituting, during
the Crimean war, an active and intelligent service
for a saddening chaos, and showing herself in the
military hospitals as the angel of mercy. The
other, less known out of her own country, although
there universally respected, Miss Harriet Mar-
tineau, has offered some excellent advice in her
book, "England and her Soldiers," as to the steps
to be taken to prevent Great Britain losing her
army. The death of a soldier gives occasion for
a sad and interesting ceremony: the coffin advances, preceded by a band who play the "Dead
March in Saul;" his comrades follow, two deep
and silently, then comes the widow in mourning,

the children, and other members of the family. If the deceased belonged to the cavalry, his horse figures in the procession, and, led by the bridle, walks sadly along with the empty boots of its rider pendent on either side of the saddle.

At Aldershott camp, we can not only form an idea of the English soldier's life generally, but as the manœuvres of artillery, cavalry, and infantry are combined on the same field, we are able to pass under review certain regiments, whose origin, uniform, and military manners are distinguished by peculiar features. What strikes me most in the English army is the Scotch soldier. The first companies of Highlanders were formed in 1715, after the great insurrection that almost broke the union between the two kingdoms. Their theatrical, though somewhat gloomy, garb contrasts with the scarlet coat of the line; but the characteristics of this dress I need not stop to describe. A story is told that, when the 84th Highlanders were quartered in Nova Scotia, a ball was given to the ladies in the neighbourhood: some of them, on entering the room and seeing the naked legs of the Scotchmen, protested against it in the name of modesty. "She must be a very indelicate woman to have such thoughts," said a young Indian squaw present, "for are not her own arms naked to the elbows?" The truth is, that the dress of the Highlanders does not at all diverge from the laws of masculine and severe decency.

Attempts have been more than once made, and
with good reason, to change the attire of these
mountaineers, which does not seem appropriate to
the hard winters or the burning summers of North
America; but the Scotch cling so to their national uniform that these attempts have constantly
failed. During the last war in India, the 93rd Regiment consented to exchange the kilt for trews,
which defended them better against the stings of
the mosquitoes; but at the moment they advanced
on Cawnpore, they asked as a favour to have the
kilt given them again, as they could not fight so
well in any other garb. Another singularity of
these troops is the bagpiper, who leads the regiment on the march; and though I stopped several
times as the troops marched past, I consider I
could not detect the marked character of this
music. It seems that the notes of the bagpipe
speak a different language to the heart of a Scotchman than they do to the ears of a foreigner. This
instrument, in fact, exercises a sort of magical influence over the sons of Caledonia. At the battle
of Quebec, in 1760, the Scotch troops were re-
treating, and the general complained to an officer
of the bad conduct of his men. "General," the
officer replied, warmly, "you did wrong in pre-
venting the pipes playing; nothing excites the
courage of a Highlander as they do; even at this
moment they might be of some service." "Let
them play, then, in Heaven's name!" the general

exclaimed. The pipes, on being given the signal, struck up the famous air of Cruinneachadh, and at the sound the Gaels formed again and bravely returned to the charge. A few years back George Clark was still living in London, who had been piper to the 71st Highland regiment at the battle of Vimeira: wounded by a bullet in the leg, and unable to advance, he sat down on the grass and shouted, "Lads, I am vexed that I am unable to follow you, but at any rate, on my soul, you shall not want for music." And with an ineffable joy he blew up his pipes, whose warlike accents electrified his comrades. During the last years of the Empire the French soldiers had learned the power of this talisman. At Waterloo, a piper, whose bellows had been pierced by a bullet purposely fired, rushed furiously on the enemy, and would not survive what he called " the soul of the regiment." A Scotch officer, of whom I inquired the cause of the magical charm wielded by this instrument, answered me, " I attribute the effects of the bagpipe to the family life, which is very strong on our mountains, and whose bonds are drawn closer instead of being relaxed by absence. The Highland soldier gladly sends his small savings to his parents, and this filial attachment is so deeply rooted, that the threat of writing to their father or mother has often acted better than any remonstrance or punishment on men of the regiment whose con-

duct was not irreproachable. Well, the Scotch
soldier finds all this again—his infancy, country,
family, perhaps even his early love—in the notes
of that instrument which sounded his first steps
in life. There were formerly in Scotland bagpipe
seminaries, and some of these schools, whose traditions still exist, enjoyed a great reputation for
several leagues round. No other regimental band,
however fine it might be, would equal in our eyes
this national music."

The Scotch, with their picturesque costume,
their music of the mountains, their rough and
weather-beaten features, add a grand external
character to the English army; but their manners
afford a no less interesting study. Among some
old Highland regiments may be found a species of
clannish reminiscence in the relations existing, or
which did exist a few years ago, between officers
and soldiers. More than one story of their pro-
bity has been handed down: thus, a soldier of
the 91st, who fell on the field of Vimeira, just
before expiring, gave his comrade his watch and
purse to carry to a friend, to whom he owed some
obligations. For twelve years the friend kept the
deposit about his person, and resisted all the
temptations that assailed him. At length he
found the man for whom it was intended, and
gave him the sacred trust. The Highlanders,
however, must not cause us to forget the Guards,
horse and foot, who compose several picked corps,

and among whom we find the most perfect types of that masculine beauty peculiar to the Anglo-Saxon race. The first regiment of Foot Guards, celebrated in June, 1860, the two hundredth anniversary of its existence, at a banquet presided over by Prince Albert. The history of this regiment is glorious: during its career, it has fought, afloat and ashore, against the French, Dutch, Spaniards, Moors, Turks, and Russians. In the folds of its standard, it envelopes such memories as those of Blenheim, Ramilies, Oudenarde, and Malplaquet. The Guards have performed eminent services to their country, for which they enjoyed great privileges, reduced recently, but against which the voice of the newspapers is still raised.

I must not neglect in this essay the relations between the army and the state, for this is a new point of view, which will place us in a better position to judge the part played by the troops in Great Britain. The seat of the military government is in Whitehall, that quarter of London so celebrated for its historical reminiscences. Here stands, under the name of the Horse Guards, a building in very poor taste, built from the designs of Kent, and at the entrance of which two immense sentries on horseback, perfect equestrian statues, constantly mount guard in a species of niche. The mansion was hardly built when Hogarth represented in one of his immortal caricatures the royal carriage drawn by a headless coachman passing under the centre arch, which is certainly deficient in elevation and grandeur. In the interior and around the Horse Guards are the offices of the war department: the head of the state is by the constitution chief of the army, and has a delegate who acts as governor of the forces, in the person of the commander-in-chief. The tie between the military administration and the civil government is established by means of the secretary at war, whose residence and offices are in Pall-mall. If I were satisfied with appearances, I should be led to believe that the British army belongs to the Queen; but if I dig into facts, I soon see that it is nothing of the sort; the Queen cannot have soldiers without the annual and positive consent of parliament; she cannot pay a shilling to these soldiers until the legislative power has voted the subsidies. During the whole last century it is true that the situation of the army was uncertain, and we may attribute to this very uncertainty the lengthened unpopularity of an institution which has, however, caused the glory and strength of Great Britain. Among this nation, so jealous of its privileges and liberties, the soldier was regarded with alarm, as it was not exactly known whether his colours were those of the executive power or of the nation. At present, all indecision has ceased : the Duke of Cambridge, with a disinterestedness and a respect for the principles of representative government, which cannot be too highly praised, declared, himself, a few months ago, before a committee of the House of Commons, that the consent of the minister of war was necessary for all the great measures that affected the army. Now, this minister, alone responsible for the actions of the sovereign, who can do no wrong, is placed, as everybody knows, under the authority of parliament, which can give or refuse him a vote of confidence. In this state of things I can only see the oath, which is a serious bond between the army and the crown; but if this oath ensures the chief of the state the fidelity of the troops, it does not give her the supreme administration. In fact, the Queen reigns over the army, as she does over the country, by the lustre of her title, by certain prerogatives, and, before all, through the confidence and affection of the troops; and I will not be the man to deny the extent of this influence, whose limits it is, however, easy to perceive. Owing to a grand division of power, the English army is, what an army should be in a free country, the rampart of the throne and the nation : in no event can it become an instrument of political domination. Could this impartial character which the law assigns to the force of the army be altered under certain extraordinary circumstances, as, for instance, in the hands of a general who had saved the country? I have read, in the *Mémorial de Sainte-Hélène*,

T 2

that Napoleon, from the top of his rock, predicted sombre destinies for English liberty, and trusted to Wellington to make the English pay dearly for Waterloo. Either ideas have been attributed to the Emperor which he never had, or he badly understood the genius and institutions of Great Britain. No country rewards military services better than she does, and the Duke of Wellington was an example of that liberality; but the wider the circle of honour extends before the ambition of an English soldier, the more he is convinced that he will find beyond it only emptiness, resistance, and inevitable ruin.

These reflections were necessary to explain the absence of military pomp from the great cities of the United Kingdom, even in royal ceremonies. A foreigner may have resided in London for three years, and imagine in perfect good faith that there are no soldiers in England. A few rare sentinels posted at the entrance of the Queen's palace, and from distance to distance, before a few public buildings—such is nearly all the armed force seen. The isolated soldiery accidentally met in the streets, are mingled with the rest of the population, so quiet and inoffensive do they look. Unarmed (for they have been deprived of all temptation to use their weapons), they mostly walk about with a small switch in their hands. You are at liberty to consider that, from a picturesque point of view, this simple dress does not display the external character of the soldier; but does it not also

testify an idea of respect for the dignity, or, if
you will, the jealousy of the other citizens? The
court festivities, such as marriages, births, and
christenings, equally take place without any military display or bustle; but the absence of troops
does not result from any feeling of indifference,
but from the clear division between the war department and the civil order. There are, it is
true, from time to time, reviews in Hyde Park,
where cavalry and infantry march past with a
great pomp of uniforms, and the sound of bugles
and drums: but everybody feels that this exhibition of forces does not take place to amuse the
public or excite the martial ardour of youth: it
is a social duty performed, but not a spectacle.
Where shall we find in the capital any traces of
a military intervention intended to protect the
state? English institutions guard themselves by
their majesty. To my knowledge, there is only
one public building which has demanded any
strategic arrangements, and my readers can easily
guess that it is not the Queen's palace. The sole
fortified point is the Mint: at a corner of the
Tower of London, an old soldier showed me some
guns on the ramparts, which in the event of a
sudden attack, would sweep the open square in
front of the adjoining building where gold and
silver are coined. The only insurrection against
which it has been thought useful to take any precautions in London is an outbreak of thieves.

The character of an army entirely devoted to

the defence and interests of the country will aid us
in understanding the kind of sympathy given the
British troops. In peace time, the Englishman
regards the soldier with considerable indifference:
at such a period the great wings of the nation are
trade and commerce: but if the arms of the United
Kingdom are engaged at any part of the globe in
a question of honour or influence, all changes at
once. A hundred-voiced press anxiously follows
the movements of the forces on the field of action:
women of all ranks, sharing in the public emotion,
hasten to send the soldiers Christmas plum-puddings, flannel shirts, tobacco pouches, and jars of
whisky. Subscriptions are opened from one extremity to the other of the kingdom to aid the
widows and orphans whom the battle-fields put
in mourning. On the other hand, if the national
independence considers itself menaced, whether
justly or unjustly, even in peace times, all eyes
turn with even greater anxiety to the means of
defence, the arsenals, and the army. The country
revolts from no sacrifice, and the state, in dipping
into the purses of the taxpayers, only obeys the
impulse of the national feeling. We know how
greatly the war budget was increased in 1860.
Now, when we speak of the army, the finances of
Great Britain must be taken into account. Let
us not leave out of sight that England, during her
struggles with the Empire, only remained erect
on her island by immense sacrifices, of which the

national debt still bears the burthen.   At length, not content with sacrificing its money when circumstances demand it, the nation offers its blood. Despairing of raising its army in a moment to the height of the perils, true or fictitious, which their startled imagination fancied they saw a year ago, the citizens have become soldiers themselves, and have ranged themselves by the side of the troops to strengthen the barrier which defends Great Britain from a surprise.

The army of volunteers demands a separate essay.   Before relating what there was sudden or strange in that national movement, I am bound to point out an error of the French press. Wishing, doubtless, to save the two countries onerous burthens, some writers thought to calm the apprehensions across the water by talking a great deal about the generosity of France, who would not abuse her strength against a defenceless nation. I do not judge intentions, and am willing to believe in such generosity on the part of my country: but the form was at least clumsy, and displays a profound ignorance of the British character, or, if you like it better, pride.   A great nation like England will never consent to repose on the magnanimity of a neighbour, or even of an ally: the more such language is held, the more the insulted nation will seek for weapons, if only to combat a phantom.

CHAPTER XIII.

THE forces of Great Britain are now composed
of two distinct elements : the regular army, which
represents discipline, and the army of volunteers,
which represents devotion. The latter constitutes
a thoroughly English type: on passing through
Boulogne, I heard some riflemen who happened
to be there called *Gardes Nationaux*, but ought
I to feel astonished at this confusion of ideas,
which, however, displays a great ignorance of
both institutions, when I bear in mind the mistake so often committed of considering the social
creations of other nations derived from our example ? Need I recal the fact that in France the
Garde Nationale issued from the middle classes, to
enforce certain guarantees in the early days of the revolution, between the people and the crown ? The
English volunteers have been formed under very
different conditions: they arose, about a year ago,

at the idea that their country was menaced. They do not mount guard, they do not patrol or exercise any control over the order or police of the towns. It is an army of guerillas, waiting with firm foot for the enemy to come, and may Heaven grant that they never come! The organisation of such a force presupposes two things, which were never combined elsewhere : a government powerful enough to rest on the support of the nation, and a nation which has sufficient confidence not to abuse the right of bearing arms.

There is a connecting link between the army and volunteers in the militia. This is a force principally raised in the country for the internal defence of England, and is recruited voluntarily, like the army. An act of parliament in 1852 determined that every man who enlisted in the militia should receive a bounty of six pounds : if, however, the number of volunteers be not sufficient in a county, the state can have recourse to a species of conscription by ballot, which embraces all individuals from the age of eighteen to thirty-five. Need I add, that for a long time the English government has abstained from employing the power accorded to it by the law on this point? The militiamen were not even called out last year, and the minister of war is engaged in preparing great reforms, which will modify the character of this arm. As these reforms, however, are not yet known, I will abstain from speaking of them, though, if I have properly understood the minister's idea, he is desirous to include in the militia, when reorganised on a new basis, a class of society which has not joined the volunteer movement, and whose members approach more nearly than the rest, by their mode of life, to the manners and condition of the soldier.

Our attention must be here concentrated on the volunteers, properly so called: though this name has certainly given rise to some criticism, for it is asserted that in Great Britain both the army and navy were filled with volunteers. There is, however, a very great difference between the recruits of the regular and the civilian armies: the first receive money, the second pay it; those are drawn into the service by the bait of a reward, these by the attraction of disinterestedness and sacrifice. Another characteristic which, both before and after enrolment, distinguishes the true volunteers is the absence of all compulsion. This army, which is self-supporting, only obeys its own free will. To understand the movement which has been developed in 1860, and in which all has been done by individual initiative, we must take a retrospective glance at the volunteers of the past. We shall thus be better prepared to catch the spirit of the institution, and what it adds to the character of the English: the object is to make every man a soldier for the defence of the country, and it is hoped that the time is approach-

ing when it will be a disgrace for any son of Great
Britain not to know how to handle his arms. To
the organisation of these free bodies are also attached other bodily exercises which must increase
the strength and power of the race. We shall
have to follow the volunteer movement in London
and all over England: but it is at Hythe school
we shall study one of the most interesting applications of the new defensive system.

On June 23rd, 1860, I witnessed the grand review of the volunteers in Hyde Park. Having
gone at an early hour to the spot where this imposing spectacle was to take place, I had time to
observe not only the arrival of the different
coloured regiments in turn, but also the no less
curious sight of the mob that grew momentarily
larger. The cleverest people, having foreseen
that the crowd would form an impenetrable wall
round the field of manœuvres, had already selected
in the vicinity lofty situations whence they could
survey the plain. One of the gates of St. James's
Park, opposite the principal entrance of Hyde
Park, and surmounted by the equestrian statue of
Wellington, was all black with heads, and some
spectators, reduced by the distance to the size of
pigmies, were standing under the very stomach
of the bronze horse. In Hyde Park, the colossal
statue of Achilles, standing on a species of mound,
could not, for all its menacing looks, intimidate
the flood of invaders. The mob had taken all

the eminences by assault: the old trees of the
Park were invaded by young workmen, who, with
the strength and agility of Quadrumana, had succeeded in clambering from branch to branch to
the top. Thus perched, they carelessly awaited
the arrival of the Queen, while the lower branches,
more and more escaladed, sank and groaned under
the fresh clusters of curious spectators. The immense lawn which stretched out round the spot
reserved for the troops and favoured ticket hold-
ers, though protected at distances by rather tall
iron hurdles, began to grow covered with people,
for men and women boldly leaped over the barriers. As nothing yet fixed the attention of the
masses, the Cockneys, strangers, idlers (and all the
world was idle on that day), went, came, returned,
stopped, sat down on the grass, or bought the
programme of the festival, which the sellers declared to be a wonder. Swarms of young ladies,
some of whom had come to see, and others to be
seen, with their long hair confined on their necks
in silken nets, shook their wings—I mean their
lace—as they walked through the groups of talkers,
now beginning to assemble. In one of these groups,
containing several uniforms, I noticed an old man
of about seventy, whose features expressed the
most lively emotion each time new regiments of
volunteers passed through the Park gates with a
great sound of brass instruments. There was
nothing of the soldier about him, however: he

was a City merchant who had retired from business, and now lived in a country-house near London. If his heart was agitated, it was because the present review reminded him so strongly of the one which he had witnessed at the same spot in 1803.

"Though I was only fourteen years of age then," he said, "I can remember it as if it were yesterday. I stood nearly on this spot, and I fancy I still see our old regiments marching past. The volunteers of that period did not at all resemble those of to-day: they had powdered hair, and wore a *queue*—a very long *queue*, I confess. Their uniform was red, with white braid and facings; an enormous stiff and heavy shirt-frill bristled on their chest, whilst huge epaulettes pressed down their shoulders. Their lower limbs were imprisoned in short narrow breeches, to which long buttoned gaiters were fitted. A three-cornered hat, with a feather, whose shape would now seem to you ridiculous, in other cases an antique helmet, surmounted the powdered and pomaded edifice of their hair. They had not light and elegant rifles like those I now see passing on the arm of our modern volunteers, but fine old flint muskets, the real Brown Bess, with all its primitive simplicity." As this description of the volunteers of 1803 produced a smile among his audience, the old gentleman continued gravely: "Do not laugh at them, for they saved the country. To those who talk to us now about the dangers of an invasion, and the evil designs of our neighbours, we septuagenarians can answer that we saw plenty in our time. You should have lived in that day to know what England is when attacked: everybody only talked about the camp of Boulogne and the flat boats. What a burst of patriotism then took place, and how well we saw what the nation of shopkeepers was capable of when any one dared to threaten it! I was present, as I told you, when George III. held a review of volunteers in this very Park, which lasted two days. I cannot exactly remember the date of the month, but it was in autumn, and I wore a dead-leaf coloured coat. At half-past nine in the morning the volunteers deployed in a line, which extended from Buckden Hill to Kensington Gardens. The King, at the head of a magnificent staff, was saluted by a discharge of artillery, and by the air of 'God save the King.' At a given signal all the battalions discharged their arms, and the plain was soon one cloud of smoke. I will not assert that the manœuvres were excellent, or that the firing responded to all the rules of art; but the earth shook, hearts bounded, and an immense shout burst from the lips of the three hundred thousand men who witnessed the review. It was a sight that could never be forgotten. I can still see the king bare-headed on his horse, the queen and princesses standing in their carriages, apparently electrified by this touching scene. There were Frenchmen present, too," the old gentleman added, turning to me. " I remember that General Damouriez, on horseback, and some other exiles were pointed out to me. I do not know what passed in their minds, but assuredly they could not blame us for defending our soil, our hearths, and our institutions: they would have done the same in our place. As they went home, everybody exclaimed, ' Oh! if Bonaparte could have seen this sight!' I cannot say whether he was intimidated by the report of this national manifestation, but the fact remains the same—he did not come. Thank Heaven, no comparison can be drawn between those unhappy times and the present period, for this time the enemy is not at our gates. Still, it would be unjust to forget that our fathers gave the example to the present generation, and if I may judge by what I see to-day of the British volunteers, the British spirit has not degenerated; I am happy to find that the blood of the volunteers of 1803 still courses through the veins of John Bull." The old gentleman was in the right: the rifleman movement, which has astonished Europe so greatly during the last two years, and to which some people wished to give the character of a mania, is, however, no novelty in the annals of Great Britain. It is a principle, anterior even to the English constitution, that, in the case of a foreign invasion or danger, every man is bound to take up arms and become a soldier for the defence of the country. We may go back a long way in history and find that this law of public safety was more than once put in practice. When the famous Spanish Armada menaced the coasts of Great Britain, the citizens rose and ran to arms in order to repulse the invader. Towards the end of the last century and the beginning of the present, events aroused, together with the latent forces of the nation, the example of what their ancestry had done. To us Frenchmen, the period from 1798 to 1815 is the history of yesterday; for the English, who have a tenacious memory, it is the history of to-day. It cannot be gainsaid, in fact, that the recent panic, whose agitation still endures, and which so disturbed, two years ago, the peaceful atmosphere of Great Britain, was only the counterstroke of the alarms the English experienced half a century ago from the state of France, the gloomy military preparations, and that appetite for conquest which grew with what it fed on. The same fears must necessarily evoke the same means of defence, and hence in the movement of the volunteers reviewed by George III. we must seek the root of the new militia which England has recently acquired.

Nor is the invasion of the British Isles a novel idea in the military history of France, for there exists, I am well informed, in the presses of our war ministry, plans and sketches dating back to the reign of Louis XIV. The theories of professional soldiers were even twice practically tried: towards the close of the last century, circumstances were extremely favourable for the success of such an enterprise, and I may recal the facts in a few words. The American war was just terminated—not exactly to the honour of the English; George III. was displaying a touch of his madness; Ireland was agitating and threatening a separation. A recent publication* has thrown an unexpected light on this age of corruption, which the genius of William Pitt could not entirely subdue; on the weakness of the court; on the just unpopularity of the Prince of Wales; on the false strategic system of David Dundas and his creatures; on the sad condition of the army, the monopoly of which the king persisted in holding; on the incapacity of the generals and officers, who nearly all owed their

* *The Cornwallis Correspondence.* Marquis Cornwallis had served with distinction in Germany and America: he was afterwards governor-general and commander-in-chief of the forces in India, and on his return home filled for some years the office of Master-General of Ordnance. In 1805 he was employed to negotiate the peace of Amiens. The work just published contains the notes and letters of this eminent man, who was closely connected with all the great statesmen and politicians at the end of the last century, and he refused to enter the cabinet when invited by William Pitt. His historic revelations could not have appeared during his lifetime owing to the independent character that distinguishes them: but they will be gladly welcomed by all persons who are curious to penetrate into the mysteries of an epoch of history.

promotion to favour; and on the disorders of the soldiers, who had become an object of alarm and terror to everybody, excepting the enemy. It was in the midst of these causes of weakness—the year 1796—that a French fleet, commanded by Admiral de Galle, set sail from Brest to the Irish coast, bearing aboard General Hoche and fifteen thousand men. A furious tempest (it was in December) dispersed the vessels, and only a portion of the expedition reached Bantry Bay. Owing to the storm, the vessel that bore Hoche was missing at the place of rendezvous: after struggling for several days against wind and fog, it had put back to France, where Hoche found the rest of the fleet, which had returned before him, though not without attempting a descent on Ireland. Of the vessels, some had all but been wrecked on the sand banks, while others had run a risk of falling into the hands of the enemy; and the Irish, on whose aid in disembarking the French had built, had not shown themselves. Still, the attempt, though unsuccessful, had been chiefly a failure owing to the intractable caprice of the elements, and hopes were maintained for the future. One fact was at least gained, that, owing probably to the neglect of the government of that day, a force of fifteen thousand French had been able to traverse the seas and reach the coasts of a British island, without having sighted or been checked by the English cruisers.

In 1798 (two years later) the insurrection broke out in Ireland. If we may believe Lord Cornwallis, " the violence of the men in power and the religious character they had the madness to give the war against the rebels, added still more to the ferocity of the English troops, and rendered any attempted reconciliation more difficult." Such a state of things was certainly of a nature to renew the projects of invasion, which, on the part of France, had not been given up, in spite of the last check. On August the 22nd of the same year, three frigates, mounting English colours, slipped into Killala Bay: they cast anchor, and like the wooden horse of Troy, were soon delivered of an armed force. Eleven hundred French soldiers landed, under the command of General Humbert, who seized the town of Killala almost without resistance, and established their head-quarters in the palace of the Protestant bishop, Dr. Stock. The latter has left an interesting journal of all that happened in the town during the French occupation, and from this source I will draw some information as to the character of an expedition so strange and so little known. It is curious to notice in this narrative the simple amazement of the inhabitants of Killala and the good bishop himself, at the appearance of the republican soldiers, pale, thin, almost livid, and badly clothed. The majority of them had served in the Italian campaign; others were the relics of the army of the

Rhine, and all bore in their injured constitutions
traces of the glorious sufferings and campaigns
followed by victory. At the first sight it might
be thought that these short-statured men, with
their air of weakness, were incapable of supporting the fatigues and privations of war, but their
conduct soon gave the most powerful contradic-
tion to appearances: they ate bread and potatoes,
drank water, made their bed on the stones of the
street, and slept with no other covering than their
clothes, or other roof than the sky. The bishop
does full justice to their intelligence, activity, invincible patience and courage, which was allied
to a strong feeling of duty, and prefers them greatly
to their Irish allies. Humbert had declared that
his soldiers would abstain from all violence, and
only take what was necessary for their support,
and this promise was religiously kept. The extraordinary sight might be seen of an English bishop
and his little flock guarded by the invaders, and
protected by them against the rapacity of the Irish
rebels, who continued to agitate the country.

It was, however, on the Irish insurrection that
Humbert calculated to support his *coup de main*,
but he arrived too late for that: the rebellion had
just been crushed by a terrible defeat. The place
of landing was also badly chosen; the invading
force should have gone further north to find a
basis of operations in the state of public temper,
and the bands of insurgents who still resisted.

The French general had brought in his vessel arms, ammunition, and uniforms, which he distributed to the peasants of Mayo, but they were a simple and almost wild race, ignorant of the use of fire-arms, and whom the report of a cannon must put to flight at the first engagement. Reduced to his own weak resources, Humbert did not hesitate, but advanced on the day after his arrival on Ballina. The English garrison at that place fled on the approach of the French, and Humbert, encouraged by this success, pushed on to Castlebar. His small army was now reduced to eight hundred men, for he had been obliged to leave two hundred soldiers at Killala, and one hundred at Ballina, to guard those two towns. In the mean while, General Lake, who had received information of the landing, and the march of the French, awaited them near Castlebar with at least eighteen hundred infantry and cavalry, ten guns, and a howitzer. The action commenced at dawn: the position of the French was extremely critical, for they were about to attack an enemy far superior in numbers; and in the event of defeat their retreat on Killala and Ballina was cut off by two corps, respectively commanded by Sir Thomas Chapman and General Taylor. Humbert, however, was not afraid of risking the attack— one of the boldest and most desperate history has ever recorded. The French remained masters of the field, all Lake's artillery fell into their hands, and the English troops fell back in the greatest confusion. Lord Cornwallis, informed of the progress of the invaders and the defeat at Castlebar, resolved to march in person against the enemy, at the head of all the troops he could collect, and thus Humbert, who still advanced, fighting several skirmishes, in which he gained the better, found himself, on September 8, 1798, surrounded by twenty-five thousand men, on the plain of Bally-na-muck. With extraordinary coolness, he formed his small army in line of battle. His rear guard, attacked by Crawford, surrendered; but the remainder of the French troops defended themselves for half an hour, and even tried to take prisoners; but, at length, crushed by numbers—overwhelmed, but not conquered—the republican troops laid down their arms, having lost about two hundred men since their arrival in Ireland. This hazardous enterprise, whose success had only been interrupted by unfavourable circumstances and the imposing military force slowly collected, threw a sort of consternation over the country; and all asked what England might not have to apprehend from such a government and such an army, if a handful of invaders could rout picked troops, take several towns, advance more than a hundred and twenty miles in the interior of the country, and maintain themselves for seventeen days, with arms in their hands, in a kingdom which contained at that time more than a hundred and fifty thousand soldiers.*

The English nation had not, however, awaited this event to prepare its defensive means. In 1777, after Burgoyne's capitulation at Saratoga, a great agitation spread over the country, which, proposed to come to the help of the crown by furnishing troops. Manchester and Liverpool had, at that time, each formed a regiment of a thousand men, and in some other towns, and even in the country, meetings had been held suggesting a levy *en masse*. In London, however, and most of the counties, the cry to arms had met with but a slight echo ; and people contented themselves with opening subscription-lists to enlist recruits for the service. This movement was not thoroughly developed till the end of the last century (1798—1799), and this time all eyes were open to the dangers that menaced the country. The treaty of Campo Formio had left England standing alone, sword in hand, opposed to France, who had conquered or reduced to impotence the other humiliated nations; and a French army of a hundred and seventy thousand men, drawn up along the Channel coast, was a day's march at most from

---

* I have allowed M. Esquiros to give his account of these events, but my English readers will be good enough to make the necessary amendments. The best account I have read of the Humbert foray will be found in Lever's "Maurice Tiernay."—L. W.

the ports of embarkation. These preparations roused the British Lion,* and the national feeling broke out in acts of devotion: the army, fleet, and militia were augmented, and, moreover, a parliament bill urged the citizens to raise volunteer corps all over the kingdom. An immense enthusiasm responded to this appeal of the country in danger, and soon extended throughout all classes: the Bishop of Winchester authorised the clergy of Hampshire, and especially of the Isle of Wight, to take up arms. Although all ranks of society offered their services, it was, however, thought advisable, at that day, to make a selection, and known and respectable citizens were alone admitted into the new phalanx. The officers must have an income of at least 50*l.*, derived from landed property, and reside in the county where the corps was raised. In spite of these restrictions, which evidence the suspicious spirit of the government of the day, in less than three weeks one hundred and fifty thousand volunteers were embodied and armed. They drilled six

---

* I may observe, on this head, that the poets and writers of the first Empire incessantly spoke of the "tooth of the leopard." When I arrived in England, I in my simplicity sought for this famous leopard on the arms of the nation, and was astonished to find a lion there. I have since read on this subject a long heraldic dissertation, written by an Englishman, whence it results that old England always had the "king of animals" as its symbol; but that, in the infancy of art, the inexperienced hand of blazoners probably produced dubious figures, in which the ignorance or jealousy of other nations fancied it recognised the features of the leopard, an animal which, in the classification of naturalists, belongs, by-the-by, to the same family.

hours a-week, and those who thought proper to do so, could claim a shilling for the time they devoted to learning the trade of a soldier. The expenses occasioned by the new-armed force figure in the budget of 1799 as 350,000*l*. Seven months had scarce elapsed since this appeal to arms, when the King declared in his speech on opening parliament, that the demonstration of zeal and vigour from all ranks of the English nation had prevented the enemy from carrying into effect his vain threats. Must we place perfect faith in this official language? I confess that, on consulting the opinion of the English generals of the day, I find a difficulty in forming a grand idea of these irregular troops. Perhaps, though, the severity of their judgment may be explained by the species of disdain with which soldiers regard combatants who do not belong to their profession. More impartial officers, however, allow that these new levies, badly disciplined and but little used to arms, would have offered but a weak resistance to French battalions, but they, at the same time, assert that, in the event of a retreat, they would have severely handled the flanks of the defeated army.

The old volunteer movement relaxed between 1799 and 1803, as the danger of foreign invasion retired, but Bonaparte's declaration of war against England suddenly revived the languishing ardour. Placards affixed on the walls of the most remote

villages announced that the enemy might per-
chance come: and ninety thousand pikes were
served out among the labourers. The farmers
voluntarily engaged to supply men, horses, and
waggons to carry the troops down to the coast;
a chain of signals, composed of combustible matter,
not only ran along the English shores, but crossed
the country from hill to hill. At the least alarm, ·
they were fired, and those English still living to
remember the time, speak with emotion of the
armed tumult which in such cases spread over
the island, which was illumined with a gloomy
flame.   At Pevensey, bands of workmen were
held in readiness to cut the sea wall, and inun-
date all the surrounding country, doubtless in
memory of glorious Holland: in the maritime
counties, the deputy lieutenants had the horses
killed which, in the event of a surprise, might have
fallen into the hands of the enemy; sawed through
the cart wheels, and destroyed the wheat and
cattle which could not be removed. They promised the owners that the State would presently
indemnify them, but no one would listen to this,
for each forgot his own interests, and had only the
salvation of the country at heart.   The customs
officers received orders to remove into the interior,
or set running at the first alarm all the wine,
brandy, and other spirits stored along the coast:
the churches and theatres were converted into
barracks, and patrols of citizens, especially in sea-

port towns, went day and night about the streets, fens, and sands. Whenever the tide was high, the wind light, and the fog thick, all eyes were fixed on the sea with feverish restlessness; at each moment they expected to see the enemy's fleet appear, and all the English vessels of war held themselves ready to cut their cables. In the county of Norfolk, the nobility placed poles on the roofs of their houses, and were to hoist a red flag in case of danger, so as to give their tenants the signal to fall in. The martial vigilance and order were no less in the interior of the island: in the provincial towns, the mayors, excited by the holy fury of patriotism, ran about the streets, themselves beating the drums, in order to call the volunteers under the banners. They flocked in from all parts, and a report of the war ministry, dated November 11, 1803, gives their number at 335,307; thus divided: infantry, 297,500; cavalry, 31,600; artillery, 6207. The English army, including volunteers, regulars and militia, was at that time composed of 500,000 men; an enormous amount at a period when the population was not quite half what it is now. I must remark that the number of volunteers was singularly augmented by a circumstance which has not been sufficiently taken into account. Parliament had ordered a levy *en masse*, which would comprise all men between the ages of seventeen and fifty-five; but the volunteers were exempt from this species of

conscription. The result was that the people enrolled themselves by thousands in the free army:
some from no other calculation than patriotism,
others to escape the levy *en masse*. The government, in fact, declared at a later date that the volunteer movement rendered the conscription useless. Old men, quite incapable of serving, took
to the constable's staff to proteet the towns, while
their fellow citizens would go to meet the enemy
in the open field. Those who saw the state of
the country at that period, say that is impossible
to form an idea of the glow of patriotism, the
terror, the gloomy defiance, the alarms, in a word,
of all the confused feelings which agitated the
population, no less growling or less perturbed in
their island than the ebb and flow of the sea
that surrounded it.

The cry to arms was raised perhaps with even
more clamour in Scotland, and echo was borne
from one mountain to the other. The Duke of
York appealed to the loyalty of the old families,
and raised a great number of battalions, each
having at its head the patriarchal chief of a clan.
Thus the Macdonalds, Macleods, Mackenzies, Gor-
dons, Campbells, Frasers, and other tribes, enrolled themselves under their respective banners,
forming a living rampart to defend the north of
Great Britain. In Edinburgh, the volunteers assembled under the order of Lieutenant-Colonel
Hope, and in this regiment the officers enjoyed

no immunity or privilege over the soldiers: they marched sturdily with all their baggage on their back, and the colonel himself gave the example by never mounting his horse, save when compelled by the duties of his command. There was no distinction of rooms in barracks, or of tents in the camps. The inhabitants of Liddesdale—the most western point the cry of danger reached— were so afraid of arriving too late at the place of meeting that they seized all the horses they could lay hands on, and after making a forced march beyond their borders, they let loose the horses, which found their way back across the mountains and reached their stables safe and sound. Sir Walter Scott served as adjutant in a regiment of cavalry called the Royal Midlothian: his lameness supplied no excuse, the less so because on horseback he looked grand and handsome. His zeal, punctuality, and merry humour rendered him very popular in the regiment, and Adjutant Scott even wrote a martial song, afterwards published in the " Border Minstrelsy;" but, as the poet had not yet been recognised, his song was only ridiculed by the majority of officers and soldiers. The beginning of this lyric, " To horse! to horse!" was repeated at night in the bivouacs with laughter and grotesque faces. No man is a prophet in his regiment, and even those who rendered justice to the young officer's military qualities treated his verses with the most supreme contempt. Walter

Scott, however, was not the less able to observe
the Scottish volunteer movement closely, and he
wrote many an interesting page about it at a later
date. He especially praises the march of the inhabitants of Selkirkshire, whose abodes were frequently a long distance from the gathering ground,
but who for all that assembled at the first signal,
and advanced over bad roads, frequently doing
thirty or forty miles without drawing bridle. Two
members of this cavalry were absent on business
in Edinburgh, and the newly-married wife of one
of these gentlemen, and the mother of the other,
a widow, sent the arms, uniforms, and horses of the
two volunteers, so that they might join their comrades at Dalkeith. Walter Scott was greatly
struck by the reply of one of the two ladies, the
mother, whom he thanked for the zeal she had
displayed in exposing her son to danger, when
she might have left him a valid excuse to prolong
his absence. She replied with all the ardour of a
Roman matron, that no one knew better than
Walter Scott that her son was the sole support
of her family since his father's death, but she
would sooner see him lying stiff and lifeless on
the floor than have it said he had been a horse's
length behind his comrades in the defence of his
country.

When we reflect that this struggle against a
formidable enemy, who was expected everywhere,
and showed himself nowhere, lasted for more than

ten years without relaxation, we cannot but form
a grand idea of the energy and persistence of the
Anglo-Saxon race. · The distrust only increased
from day to day, from hour to hour, and a proclamation of Bonaparte's which was circulated
through the whole of the United Kingdom, added
oil to the flame. I have no means of assuring
myself if this proclamation, which, according to
the English, was on the point of being printed at
Paris, and intended to accompany the expedition, was really written by the Imperial hand.
At all risks I quote it, in the first place, because
it was at that day considered authentic throughout Great Britain, and next, because it powerfully
contributed to excite a national movement, which
I content myself with describing as a simple his-
torian of facts. "Soldiers," this order of the day
said, "we have crossed the sea! the barriers of
nature have yielded to the genius and fortune of
France! Haughty England groans beneath the
yoke of her conquerors. London is before you!—
the Peru of the old world is your prey: in twenty
days" (there were no railways then) "I shall
plant the tricolor flag on the walls of its execrable
Tower. Forward! Towns, fields, provisions, cattle,
gold, silver, women, I abandon all to you. Occupy
their noble manors, their smiling farms. An impure race, reproved by Heaven, which has dared
to declare itself the enemy of Bonaparte, is about
to expiate its crimes, and disappear from the sur-

face of the earth. Yes, I swear to you that we shall be terrible."* This proclamation, whether true or false, was greeted by England, in the same way as France had greeted the Duke of Brunswick's manifesto in 1793: a cry of execration and the clash of arms replied to it from across the Channel. The Duke of Cornwall asked the miners for a thousand men, but the solemn and hardy population of that county furnished five thousand. In offering their services, they all pledged themselves by a solemn declaration never to quit the post assigned to them in action, so long as a single armed French soldier remained within range of their muskets. In Northumberland, a lady, remarkable for her rank and beauty, presented a pair of colours to a volunteer regiment, and the young ensign said to her with thorough British conciseness: "I receive your colours with joy, I will defend them with courage, and when the bullets have torn away all the old silk, I will bring you back the staff." London did not remain behindhand in the movement: and at a period when the population was below a million, it formed thirty-five volunteer corps containing more than forty

---

* This proclamation apparently forms a pendant to the address Bonaparte is known to have made to his troops at Boulogne : "You have given peace to the Continent, and Great Britain is our only remaining enemy. I will lead you to London, where the cellars are filled with gold and silver. You shall, then, return to France, loaded with guineas, which you shall spend at home with your mistresses."
—L. W.

thousand men. An English friend of mine still preserves as a relic an old drum which beat the charge at the head of one of their regiments. In and round London nothing was to be seen but parades, manœuvres, skirmishing, and sham-fights, and the district of London alone was provided with seven tons of gunpowder a week. We must not feel surprised if terrible accidents resulted from the inexperience of the citizens who were using muskets for the first time; but nothing disconcerted the ardour of these grave citizens. A bill authorised the volunteers to drill and fire on Sunday morning, and everybody acquainted with the manners and religious habits of England, will see the gravity of the circumstances in such a derogation of the law: only an imminent danger and the sanctity of a national duty could have induced the government to tolerate such a desecration of the Sabbath. All ranks of society were blended in this movement of national defence: nearly all the king's ministers were enrolled in volunteer regiments, and the Duke of Clarence himself served as a simple private in the Teddington corps. On the other side, political opinions were effaced or reconciled on the neutral ground of patriotism: at a civic banquet Alderman Shaw proposed the health of the greatest man in England, William Pitt, colonel of the Cinque Ports volunteers. When the tumult of applause aroused by this toast had calmed down, Sheridan rose and said: "Gentlemen, allow me also to propose a toast. I ask you to drink in bumpers the health of Charles Fox, a private in the Chertsey volunteers, and the most honest man in England." This second toast was also loudly applauded, and all, both Whigs and Tories, fraternised this day in the presence of the dangers that menaced the country. On another occasion, William Pitt heard a farrier of his regiment growling at the stiff leathern collars recently served out to the Cinque Ports volunteers, and which held his neck as in a vice. "Look here," the prime minister said, "I wear one like you, and do not complain." "Ah, colonel," the farrier answered, "the case is very different; your neck ought to be the longest, for your head is the highest in the whole of Great Britain."

No one can say what resistance the volunteers of 1803, better trained than those of 1798, would have offered an invading army, as, fortunately for England, and perhaps for France, this national force was not tried. If I may believe M. de Bourrienne's Memoirs, Napoleon never had a serious intention of attempting a landing in England, for he knew too well that had he even succeeded in throwing one hundred thousand men on the British coast—and the enterprise was difficult—he would have lost at least two-thirds of his army before reaching London, while the sea, closed behind him by the English fleet, would have prevented him receiving reinforcements; and even, in the event of success, would have imprisoned him in his victory. Napoleon himself recognised that this project offered obstacles above the human will. "If I had succeeded," he said, at a later date, "it would have been by doing exactly the contrary of what was expected." The Emperor's thoughts on this point are, we see, covered, and perhaps purposely, with a cloud which I shall not seek to penetrate.

Such is the history of the old volunteers, who died out after the events of 1815, leaving a few raw regiments of cavalry as a trace of their passage in the agricultural counties; but readers are anxious to know the volunteers of 1860. Before dwelling on them, however, I must indicate the differences separating them from the other generation. In 1798 and 1803 the volunteer movement was instigated by the Tories: the fear of invasion and the spirit of national defence were allied in them to a horror of revolutionary principles, or, as they called it, Jacobinism, which, through a strange confusion of ideas, they personified in the man who had restored in France a part of the ancient regime. The organisation of the riflemen of 1860 has, on the other hand, the basis of liberal opinions. Supported by all the organs of the advanced party, they have been formed in the name of liberty, and in the presence of the gloomy shadow which despotism, as they think, casts over a portion of Europe, and their design is that this shadow shall not cross the Channel. Such opponent ideas must necessarily modify the personnel of the two movements. While, at the beginning of the century, the volunteer ranks were mainly filled with tradesmen, the solemn and weighty citizens of London, the volunteers of to-day, or at least the majority of them, belong to the class of lawyers, doctors, artists, clerks, and shopmen. Youth and new blood has spread during the past year through the ranks of the new civilian army, and the men of ripe age have generally held aloof. Strategically considered, does not this state of things constitute an evident advantage in favour of the modern riflemen? The old volunteers were, doubtlessly, good fathers of families and honest tradesmen, but there is room for doubting whether they made excellent soldiers. Hence, in the opinion of all those who saw both displays of strength in Hyde Park, the volunteers of 1860 leave far behind them the citizen troops of King George, though they do not cause them to be forgotten.

CHAPTER XIV.

THE VOLUNTEER REVIEW—FEARS OF INVASION—LORD ELCHO—DE-
FENCE, BUT NOT DEFIANCE—LADY FRANKLIN—UNIFORMS—THE
WORKING MEN'S COLLEGE—WHO SHOT THE DOG?—PRESENTATION
OF BUGLES—LADY VOLUNTEERS—THE DOCKYARD CORPS—EXPENSES
—JUVENILE CORPS—THE NATIONAL ASSOCIATION.

SATURDAY, June 23, 1860, resembled a fête
day. All faces evidenced joy, confidence, and a
certain national pride. Public opinion, oppressed
a few months back by rumours of war and dull
apprehensions, seemed to grow clear, thus following the example of the sky, which had been
stormy the whole life-long summer, though it
prepared to grow a little brighter at the moment
of the review. People asked each other, with
lively curiosity, how this army, scarce eight
months old, would perform its manœuvres, for
hitherto the regiments had only been seen pa-
rading in the London streets or squares. The
stands reserved for ticket-holders were occupied
by ten thousand persons—officers of the English
and Indian armies, members of the Houses of

Lords and Commons, pressmen, and foreign diplomatists, among whom were noticeable the Ambassadors of the Emperor of Morocco, with their snow-white burnous and turban. A parterre of ladies, enamelled with the gold of the military uniforms, steel helmets, and scarlet coats, displayed a profusion of rich toilettes, though no fresher or more delicate than the faces. Opposite these stands, at a considerable distance, ran the motionless line of volunteers, and this somewhat gloomy line of green or grey was only spotted here and there by the red uniforms of the volunteer artillery, engineers, and cavalry. The regular army, as may be supposed, took no part in the festivities: it was only represented by a regiment of Foot Guards, employed to defend the ground from the mob, and rare detachments of Horse Guards, who might readily be taken for parade troops had we not felt the weight of their arms at Waterloo. About half-past four the guns announced the Queen's arrival, and the royal carriage advanced slowly along the line of volunteers, saluting as it passed. A solemn silence, such as I never before observed elsewhere, brooded over this vast open plain, and extended, like an electric current, over the crowd, previously so tumultuous.

The Queen, after passing along the line, stationed herself beneath the great standard which floated in front of the stands. This was the decisive moment of the day ; in fact, the mass of volunteers began marching past. The column started in regular order, and proceeded at a quick step towards the centre of the Park. There were on the stands judges difficult to please—generals and old officers, who anxiously watched the movement; but the bold bearing and imposing march of the new battalions seemed to defy criticism. First passed the cavalry, in no great numbers; but the First Huntingdon were admired, remarkable as they were for the beauty of the horses and the manly appearance of the troopers, with their sabres in their hand and their carbines on their back. The horse and foot artillery excited a murmur of enthusiasm and a round of applause, to which the dull rolling of the guns responded. It was now the turn of the infantry, and all eyes were fixed on the Six-foot Volunteer Guards, a real company of giants; on the Artists' corps; on the " Devil's Own," composed of lawyers; on the London Scottish, who were preceded by a Scotch band, and of which one company wore the kilt; on the London Irish; on the Robin Hoods of Sherwood, and the various other regiments which created astonishment by their costume and martial air. The Park presented at this moment a touching scene. The Queen, surrounded by the new army the nation had offered to her, seemed overwhelmed and delighted at the grandeur of this popular demonstration. The bands played

the national hymn, which in this country terminates all public ceremonies, and the charm of
discipline was broken. The volunteers, who
had obeyed the order of the day by hitherto
remaining silent as statues, burst into one immense shout. Deafening cries were raised by all
the columns, the rifles were brandished, and the
shakos waved in the air. To this movement the
crowd responded by an energetic burst of applause, repeated for the last time by the volunteers, while along the stands an immense line of
hats and pocket-handkerchiefs undulated. This
enthusiastic exchange of fraternal feeling between
the volunteers and the populace—those arms seen
glistening for the first time since half a century in
the hands of citizens—this rampart of bayonets,
voluntarily formed round the throne and the
British institutions, to respond to vague rumours
of war—this army that burst into bud but yesterday, and whose evolutions had surpassed expecta-
tion—was not all this sufficient to intoxicate the
national self-esteem? It was a grand and glorious
sight, not only for the English, but for every
foreigner who had come to seek in England a
country in liberty.

In the eyes of all, this review was a political
event, and I heard people say around me that
peace had gained a great victory. The crowd
melted away under this solemn impression, and as
I retired, I saw on my passage the traces of de-

struction left by the violent course of the mob.
A few branches had broken beneath the weight
of the intrepid clamberers, some iron hurdles had
yielded to the pressure of the mob, and opposite
Hyde Park, a portion of the railings of the Green
Park had been uprooted, twisted, and carried
away by this ocean which rushed through the open
breach. It will be asked, perhaps, where were
the police; they were not absent, but in London
it is thought better to have some slight damage
to repair than irritate by a struggle the irresistible
force of the masses. This day singularly height-
ened the confidence of the English in their means
of national defence: during the whole review I
had not noticed in the firm attitude of the volunteers, or the free conversation of the groups
around me, the slightest trace of provocation or
defiance of the foreigner: but on the following
Monday, the tone of the English press announced
a haughty security. Turning to the Continent,
and doubtless replying to invasionary intentions,
the *Daily Telegraph*, one of the London papers
with the largest circulation, exclaimed, "Come
now, if you dare!"

Amid what circumstances and how was the
new civilian army organised which we have seen
manœuvring in Hyde Park? This is a question
which I have now to answer. Since 1855, several
trades had proposed to form volunteer corps, but
the English government had declined their ser-

vices, saying that nothing in the state of Europe
rendered such a measure necessary. Is it necessary to recal the causes which, two or three years
later, shook the confidence which these statesmen and the country had placed in the assurances
of peace? The maritime preparations of France,
which were probably exaggerated, the fortification of Cherbourg, the invention of *frégates
cuirassées*, and the warlike and aggressive tone
of certain pamphlets, which had the misfortune to
cross the Channel, suddenly aroused suspicions,
which I like to believe unjust. At another time,
these pamphlets would have passed unnoticed
among the thousand manifestations of a free press,
but, under the circumstances in which they were
produced, the threats stood out in red letters on
the dusky back ground of silence. Should we say
that the whole malady of fear came from beyond
the sea? assuredly not, for the alarm sprung up
principally in the country itself. For a lengthened
period, the inhabitants of Great Britain had professed a too absolute belief in the advantages of
their geographical position, in the might of their
race, and in the idea of an invulnerable country—
which must, sooner or later, break down. These
ideas chiefly prevailed in the country, where it is
readily believed that an Englishman is as good as
three Frenchmen, that the flag which has often
braved the battle and the breeze, must necessarily
contain victory in its folds, and that the bull-dog

spirit answers for everything. Like those Homeric divinities who, on the battle-field, escaped from the lance of the combatants by veiling themselves in a cloud, Old England fancied she could defy all perils hidden behind her fogs. How would an enemy's ships be able to approach this island, which the swallows have some difficulty in finding again in spring? Some excellent works published by professional men during the last two or three years destroyed all these illusions: the report of the commissioners appointed to examine into the defensive state of the kingdom, above all, gave the old superstitions of national honour a blow from which they will not easily recover. As always happens in such cases, the country enlightened by books, which made it see the situation under a new light, passed very rapidly from an excessive confidence to vague and confused terrors, and little was wanting for the Englishman to curse, at the first moment, the sea, the old friend and constant ally of England. It was asked, in fact, whether, judging from the experience obtained in the Crimea, an enemy who had the sea for a basis of operations did not possess a great advantage. This was a long way, we see, from the ideas of the last century about the inaccessible island; but fortunately for Great Britain, one of the blessings of free discussion is to prepare the citizens for receiving the hardest truths without discouragement. Thanks were given the men who had caused a chimera to vanish, and the nation made up its mind to consolidate by other means the almost inexpugnable system of defence with which nature had served formerly to favour the British isles.

One of these means was augmenting the army, and it was taken into consideration; but the system of a large standing army is so opposed to the spirit of the English constitution and the customs of the country, that there was but small chance of that being voted. We may almost assert that the principle of permanence has never been recognised by parliament, which lends the armed force to the executive power only for a year. In the event of a collision, which has never happened, and in all probability never will, but which it is yet permissible to foresee, between the crown and the parliament, the army would melt away in the hands of the chief of the state at the end of the year. We must not say that the nation was terrified by the new burdens which an increase of the army would impose on the budget, for I know perfectly that it would have to pay in one shape or the other the expenses of defence. In not recoiling from the enormous expenditure for the fortifications, the state showed besides, that it was much less afraid of appealing to the ratepayers, than assailing constitutional liberty. The idea of placing the English army on the same footing as the French having been dismissed, then, for the reasons I have given, the old traditions of Great Britain offered themselves spontaneously to the mind of the citizens. The Englishman holds to doing everything for himself: having created his institutions, laws and commerce, he asked himself why he should not organise war, or at least the strength for resisting the dangers of invasion. It is in accordance with these principles, engraved on the national character, and under the pressure of great apprehension, that the population resolved on bearing arms itself; though I am disposed to believe, with Lord Elcho, that the shame the English felt at feeling fear had a good deal to do with it. Is it not said that twelve cities of Greece disputed the honour of having given birth to Homer? Well, several cities of Great Britain now claim the priority in the formation of free corps, and it appears that Oxford and Cambridge have the greatest claim to the honour of having commenced the movement. Individuals boast, for their part, of having launched the idea, and lay claim in pamphlets I have read to a species of patent.* My readers will not like me to dwell on this matter of self-esteem, which, besides, excites very little interest to me: the organisation of the volunteers was a great national fact belonging to everybody. Sooner than discuss personal and doubtful titles,

---

* M. Esquiros is mistaken for once. The Victoria Rifles and the Devon Rifles were embodied long before the movement was thought of.—L. W.

then, it is better to determine the spirit of this
institution from the starting-point: the English
wished to furnish the state with a patriotic army,
equipped at its own expense, and having for its
basis the defence of the country.

The English government, which readily seconds
all the just and enlightened movements of public
opinion, could not refuse its aid in 1859 to the
creation of volunteer corps. General Peel, then
secretary of war, recognised in a circular of May
25th of what utility inhabitants accustomed to
gun-exercise would prove in maritime towns, and
citizens armed with rifles elsewhere, in repulsing
the enemy. He therefore accepted, in the name
of the Queen, the services offered by the country,
modified the act of George III., and sanctioned,
under certain conditions, the formation of volunteer corps. The government of which General
Peel was a member, and under whose auspices
the movement began, has ceased to exist; but
the same spirit is kept up. The last secretary,
Mr. Sidney Herbert, favoured to the utmost
of his power the development of an institution
which, everywhere but in England, would have
been regarded as a danger to the state, and
the under-secretary, Lord de Grey and Ripon,
also displayed remarkable zealousness in arming
in so short a time nearly one hundred and fifty
thousand men. In spite of this encouragement,
however, it is certain that the new armed force
issued from the bowels of the nation, and the

country did everything under the inspection of the government. It must be remarked that the ministerial circular was not an appeal to arms: but only the pure and simple recognition of the right the citizens of Great Britain possessed to defend themselves as they thought proper against the dangers of a foreign invasion or their own terrors. Scarce had they obtained the consent of the crown ere the English people—the most free of all hitherto from military tastes—woke up, as it were, soldiers, and began to cover the coasts, cities, and rich plains, by a rampart of bayonets. Everybody joined in the movement; the least frightened, those who least believed in any attempted descent on the part of a hostile fleet, said to themselves, that the best means of reassuring trade were to fire at the phantoms, and they followed the general impulse. The will of the nation thus came to the aid of the old national bulwarks, reefs and rocks, a species of traditional cuirass, those defects military science had first pointed out.

I have shown the origin of the movement: what I have now to point out is by virtue of what mechanism the different volunteer corps were formed and are still daily forming. The organisation commenced all over the country by meetings, presided over by influential persons in the neighbourhood, at which an appeal was made to patriotic feeling, and the advantage of forming an armed force was demonstrated. The principle being admitted, an executive committee was appointed for the purpose of raising subscriptions and defending the civil or military interests of the company. A list of voluntary enrolments was at once opened, and it was divided into three classes: 1. The effective members, who agreed to pay for their arms and uniforms. 2. The reserve corps, the members of which promised to serve in case of invasion.* 3. The non-effectives, who were to encourage the movement by an annual subscription and not undergo drill. As nothing can be effected without money, the subscriptions of all persons who took an interest in the free defence of the country, were actively collected. I see by the account of a single company, the Central London Rifle Volunteer Corps (and that not the richest), that the voluntary gifts, without counting the subscriptions of the effective members, amounted to the sum of 424*l.*, and this liberality is going on. A few months back, the treasurer of the North Middlesex Rifles received a visit from a lady in mourning, who had just met this corps marching under arms and with its band at its head to the Albany Barracks to drill. Struck by the firm demeanour and good discipline of these new soldiers, the lady announced her intention of contributing toward so noble an institution.

* M. Esquiros is generally so correct that I hesitate to alter this sentence, but I confess it is a new thing to me, though I have followed the volunteer movement very closely.—L. W.

Not satisfied by giving the treasurer a sum of money, she also requested to be inscribed as an annual subscriber or honorary member of the company, and for this purpose her name and address were required. "Write down Lady Franklin," she said. It was, in fact, the widow of the celebrated navigator, whose remains a recent expedition found in the Arctic Seas. Many other ladies of distinction also aided by their largess the formation of the numerous branches which now compose the civil army. Another mode of collecting funds is by giving dramatic representations. I was present at an amateur performance, for instance, at the Lyceum, given by the members of the Artillery Company, who thus proposed to aid the National Rifle Association. They played two or three pieces, after which Miss Kate Terry, in the costume of Britannia, recited some verses written by Mr. Tom Taylor, captain of a volunteer corps. The young goddess compared the sons of old Albion to the sons of Helvetia, and said that she hoped, on the day of danger, to find them as firm behind their chalk cliffs, as the descendants of William Tell behind their Alpine fortress.

Hitherto, the hand of the state has not been seen in anything; the corps is organized, and already enjoys an independent life, but, to pass into official existence, it must have the authority of government. The volunteers are placed by

the act of George III., and the ministerial circu-
lars of 1859, under the inspection of the lord-lieutenants of counties. These are almost irremovable
civil magistrates whose functions may be compared with those of the French *préfets*, and
through them the volunteer corps must apply
to the Secretary of War.

The only serious difficulties that have hitherto
arisen between the lord-lieutenants and certain
volunteer corps relate to the appointment of the
officers. According to the act of George III.,
all the officers must obtain their commissions
from the first civil magistrate of the country, and
this law did not generally seem to harmonise with
the progress of manners and the democratic spirit
of the movement. In the majority of companies,
if not all, the principle of election was applied in
different degrees; here, the committee proposed a
list of names for adoption by the company; there,
the volunteers duly nominated their leaders by
ballot. It was, besides, sub-understood that this
free choice would be submitted, in accordance
with the law, to the approbation of the lord-lieutenant, and it was so: but in certain counties that
official refused to confirm the election of artisans
to the rank of officers. The volunteer corps
whose votes met with an obstacle threatened dis-
solution at once, if this difficulty were not removed,
and, as far as I know, the wishes of the companies

were, after a momentary hesitation, everywhere respected. This approval of the officers by the lord-lieutenant and the Secretary of War is not the only tie attaching the armed bodies to the state, for there is another, more serious, in the oath of allegiance. I say more serious, because respect for an oath is one of the virtues on which British honour most piques itself. On this point of conscience the Scotch are, if possible, even more scrupulous, and I have heard a story that a Highlander deserted his regiment during the Peninsular war and proceeded to America; several years after, a letter was received from him containing a sum of money intended to pay the services of one or two substitutes in the same regiment. "It was," he said, "the only expiation he could offer for having violated his oath to Heaven; and the sole way of appeasing a remorse which allowed him no rest by day or night." Should we expect from the volunteers, who enrol themselves in the name of duty, less delicacy than that of the soldier who enlists for money? Hence the oath is regarded as a sufficient guarantee of the institutions of the kingdom which the armed citizens pledge themselves to defend. This oath is taken with some degree of solemnity in the presence of a colonel or general officer, who, in a short speech, dwells on the moral obligations the volunteers are about to contract. I witnessed this ceremony in the hall of an historic castle of Kent, where the walls seemed to invoke the old knights as witnesses to the oath taken by free men.

This done, the corps is constituted, and the only thing left is to equip it. Whoever has been present at a review or sham fight is struck by the great diversity of uniforms distinguishing the companies, and it is easy to see that fancy has presided from the outset over the equipment of these bodies, formed here and there almost without reference to each other.* From a picturesque point of view, this variety is certainly no injury : we only ask whether, in times of war, these groups of different colours would not have some difficulty in recognising each other at a certain distance, and some strategists have already proposed to the volunteers to adopt some common badge. This variety is very noticeable among the riflemen; some very curious experiments have, however, recently been tried with colours, more or less visible at different hours of the day, and the conditions of the atmosphere when bright or obscure, sunshiny or rainy. The result of these studies is, that grey and reddish brown are the least apparent hues, at least, in an English landscape, for

---

* The ministerial circular, it is true, invites the companies of the same county to obtain, as far as possible, a uniform type : but it left this point to the free will of the volunteers and the wisdom of the lord-lieutenants. It is easy to see in this, as in the whole organisation of this civil army, that the liberty of the individual was before all consulted.

these laws of perspective must change with the geographical situation. A great number of rifle corps have, however, decided in favour of a very dark green, which bears no resemblance to the foliage of the trees or the colour of the fields in southern France, but which, in Great Britain, where the vegetation is entirely different, blends tolerably well with the gloomy colour of the landscape. As, moreover, these corps of sharp-shooters are specially intended for hedge fighting, it is easy to understand the importance of an affinity between the colour of the uniform and that of the country. English naturalists remarked long ago with what admirable foresight nature seems to have harmonised the clothing of animals with the peculiar tone of the country in which they live, the better to protect them from the attacks of their enemies. These considerations, I am bound to say, have been left out of sight by certain companies of rifles, who have rather consulted elegance than utility. The volunteers have one enemy to be sought in their own ranks, and that enemy is dandyism, and many of them have made too great a sacrifice to fashion and military nattiness. After all, the movement is but young, and we ought not to feel surprised at these signs of childishness, which will disappear with time, especially if public opinion render them ridiculous. Experience has, besides, proved that the most simple uniform was the most characteristic: the corps I have always seen most applauded are those which wear a sort of foraging cap, a loose tunic, wide trousers and waist-belt, and cross-belt of either yellow or black leather.

According to the intentions of the Secretary of War, the arm of the volunteers should have been determined by the geographical conditions of the locality. In maritime towns, trading seaports, and the mouths of rivers, he suggested the formation of small bodies of artillerymen, assembling round one gun, whose laying and range they would be better able to study. In the country, on the other hand, he pointed out the services companies of riflemen could render, well acquainted with the nature of the country, and in which the members or comrades had been accustomed from infancy to rely on each other. I will not assert that this advice has always been followed, for here again the spontaneous instinct of the population has prevailed, and the choice of the arm has been, like that of the uniform, a matter of taste and convenience. In many cities there are both artillery and rifles, but the latter are far the more numerous; they are also best suited to the nature of the country, enclosed as it is by hedges and other obstacles which would impede the movements of a regular army. I will not mention the cavalry, formed at a later period, and which is now only beginning to be developed. Opinions differ as to the efficiency of this arm, but, as it has been remarked, England being the nation which breeds the finest horses, where those animals are best taken care of, and the men are the most perfect riders, it would be easy to raise among the farmers and country gentlemen, all more or less fox-hunters, squadrons of volunteers who, in the event of an invasion, would serve to harass the flanks of a hostile army.

After the choice of the arm and the uniform comes the drill, and this, as may easily be supposed, is the most important point in the task the volunteers have imposed on themselves. At the outset they appealed to the sergeants and corporals of the army, and the various corps generally paid for their instruction at the rate of a shilling or sixpence a head; but there are line non-commissioned officers who offered their services gratuitously. A few months back the volunteers of the Working Men's College assembled at a dinner to present a valuable sabre, as a mark of respect, to Sergeant-Major Reid, who was wounded in the Crimea, and wears on his chest the medal with the red ribbon. Captain Tom Hughes, author of "Tom Brown's School-Days," and one of the most accomplished literary men of young England, said on the occasion that, as the corps was not rich, and had no means to pay a drill instructor, the project of embodying it must have fallen through, if Sergeant Reid had not given his time and trouble for nothing. His services had not been spared, for the men of the company had drilled nearly every day, and it was owing to his attention that they had succeeded in handling their weapons in so remarkable a way. Whereupon the health of the worthy sergeant-major was drunk with three times three amid deafening applause. Need I say that the usual course of instruction has been greatly simplified in its application to the free volunteers? This course is naturally gradual, and may be divided into three sections: they begin with position drill, marching, and movements; next comes the practice of the rifle, which is succeeded by firing. The army of volunteers, we must not forget, constitutes a distinct army, which has a type of its own, a peculiar object, and a reason of existence. The English desire it to be useful in case of need on the battle-field, and acquire all proper information for that purpose, but nothing more. This programme, however, demands, as may be easily supposed, a considerable amount of effort, for professional men estimate three years as needed to make a soldier. By this calculation, the volunteers, whose oldest corps are not more than fifteen months old, would not have got very far yet; but we must remark that the recruits of the Englishmen come from an ignorant and awkward class, while the riflemen, nearly all young, well educated, and intelligent, bring with them very different minds, aptitudes, and conditions. Hence they were scarce under arms ere everybody was amazed at the rapidity of their progress. I must allow, however, that the English sergeant instructors do not admire reasoners: their principle is that in the drill-ground a man is a machine, and must obey the word of command, without thinking of anything. Consequently, more than one gentleman, accustomed at Oxford or Cambridge to ask the "how and why" of things, received a rough lesson from them. The ardour of the riflemen was not rebuffed by these trials or painful beginnings, and that will, which is the foundation of the English character, sometimes bordered on eccentricity. Thus, the story goes that a commercial traveller, compelled to change his quarters continually, always took his rifle with him, and when the volunteers of the town where he happened to be turned out for drill, he approached the captain and asked permission to enter the ranks. Such perseverance deserved to be crowned with success, and hence he was noticed at more than one place for the manner in which he performed his evolutions. The patience and zeal of the rest of the volunteers resisted with no less force of mind the almost continued rains of a deplorable summer. On one stormy day the vicar of a parish in Kent, a great admirer of the volunteer movement—and not the only one among the English clergy—was present, like myself, through curiosity at the drill. Delighted

by the firmness of these citizens under arms, who
endured the pitiless rain without winking, or even
seeming to notice it, he said to me, with a smile,
"*Aquæ multæ non potuerunt extinguere cha-
ritatem.*"

At the outset there was reason for fearing that
the novel sight of an independent army might
arouse jealousy between the soldiers and volunteers, but the contrary took place : not only do
the sergeant instructors love the volunteers as
their children, so to speak, and evince a pride in
the success so greatly owing to them, but the
other members of the regular army display a
species of admiration and respect for the disinterestedness of these citizens, equipped at their own
expense, and condemning themselves to the vexa-
tion of drill, for these worthy fellows know better
than others what it costs to learn the rude trade
of arms.　More than once I have stopped when a
new corps passed, and purposely approached the
groups of soldiers who watched the riflemen go
past with great attention, but I never once heard
from them aught but kindly remarks.　Can we
say that the volunteers have had no obstacles to
surmount?　On the contrary, they have found
them of more than one sort.　In the first place,
they had against them the old military prejudice
which denied the efficiency of citizens in a battle-
field or when opposed to regular troops.　On the
other hand, many of those who, through selfish

reasons, refused to join the movement, sought too often to combat it by ridicule. I was on Ludgate-hill when one of the first corps that appeared in London streets came marching along, preceded by its band. The excitement was extreme, and generally favourable; but, as at the Roman triumphs, a few sarcasms were mingled with it. The boys (why not call them by their right name, the *gamins ?*), who are the same everywhere, that is, impudent and mocking, pointed out maliciously that all the men were not of the same height, as is seen in a regiment of guards. An accident that happened a few months later also furnished the young scamps with darts, and presently every volunteer that appeared in the street in uniform was greeted with the query, " Who shot the dog?" The riflemen silently endured these jests, very innocent after all, being well aware that the most serious duties are not protected from criticism, and an immense burst of popularity soon declared in their favour. At the head of this manifestation of opinion the ladies placed themselves, and it has grown a point of honour with them to collect subscriptions in the towns, and even villages, in order to purchase silk colours and silver bugles, which they themselves present to the volunteers. These presentations give rise to interesting ceremonies: the corps is under arms, opposite to it stands a group of ladies in full dress—the wives, sisters, and daughters of the officers and soldiers.

From this group a wife, or young lady, steps forth, who presents the offering in the name of her companions, and who generally addresses the riflemen. The rank of the persons naturally varies with the locality: here, it is the Duchess of Wellington, whose husband is commandant of the Victoria Rifles; there, it is, as at Durham, Lady Susan Vane Tempest, who arrives on the drill-ground, with the Marchioness of Londonderry, in a carriage drawn by four greys; elsewhere, they are ladies belonging to the middle classes, whose presents and addresses, however, are not the less kindly greeted. If we wish to explain the active part Englishwomen take in the success of the volunteers, we must not let out of sight the fact that the movement is attached by very intimate ties to family life. It is to defend their hearths, it is in the name of their wives and children, and that they may repose in peace under the roof of the house or the garden tree, that the English of all classes have quitted the fireside during the winter, and run off to drill. We shall, therefore, no longer feel surprised that the women of England have sympathised with the new institution with all the strength of their souls; and this also explains the enthusiastic addresses they make to the riflemen in handing to them any testimony of esteem and encouragement. " Friends and gentlemen," one of them exclaimed, at a ceremony where I was present, "the duty of women is to attach themselves to their husbands and sons, as the ivy to the oak: it is the duty of the oak to protect us. Go, then, with weapons in your hands, so that we may remain in safety with our families. When these colours float in the breeze, when this bugle sounds, think of your mothers, your wives, your sisters, and your sweethearts, and if the day of danger arrive, be ready to defend them." This moral participation of the women in the volunteer movement, and perhaps some of friend *Punch's* jokes, have, doubtless, given rise to the belief that they thought of enrolling themselves in the new institution. A French paper announced that a society of ladies had risen *like one man* to aid the riflemen in the defence of the country, and an engraving that came from Paris even represented these riflewomen—young and pretty Amazons—in full military dress. This cut was reproduced in London by the *Lady's Newspaper*, and the English women replied to this jest with considerable dignity, through the medium of the same paper, that, although they had never had the idea attributed to them, if ever their country were menaced they would employ all their influence over the hearts of their husbands, brothers, and relations, that the latter should defend the rights and liberties of England. It is not, however, in Great

Britain, where the division of duties is as clearly
defined as that of labour, that we need fear the
part played by either sex being changed.

While in France and elsewhere the swarm of
volunteers has been represented as too numerous
not to resemble a challenge, the English complain,
on the contrary, that they have not enough yet,
and cudgel their brains daily about means to increase this element of the national defence. They
were, therefore, obliged to seek out the causes
that, in the first instance, limited the swing othe
popular movement, and the chief of all, and the
only one on which I shall dwell, is the small aid
afforded by the artisans. Might we ask whether
their services were not refused at the outset ? I
prefer believing, however, that they were kept in
the background by the material conditions of the
system. It being the principle that each volunteer must equip, arm, and instruct himself, and
procure his ammunition at his own expense, we
can easily comprehend that the classes living from
hand to mouth by their daily toil only slightly
aided in the development of the institution. However this may be, everybody now recognises the
necessity of widening the base of the movement,
by descending to those strata of the population
which have hitherto supplied but few recruits to
the civil army. The historic traditions of England
are all in favour of this view; the artisans figured
for large numbers among the volunteers, who, in

the reign of Elizabeth, repulsed the threats of a
Spanish invasion. Very few persons, it must be
allowed, have ever denied the right of the English
working classes to occupy a place in the new military organisation, for they have the same interests
to defend as the others. Have they not a home
and domestic affections? Have they not wives,
children, and aged mothers to defend? As for a
political danger it does not exist in England, for
the country has no essential liberties left to conquer,
and its institutions have nothing to fear from the
bayonet's point. The arms of progress, the pacific
arms, are in this country meetings, free discussion,
a press which dares to say everything, and they
attain the object much better without bloodshed
than the bullets of the best drilled sharpshooters
would do. It has been even observed that the
organisation of the volunteers had at once a democratic and a conservative character: for some
chartist workmen received into the ranks, proud
of the honour of bearing arms, and of the confidence of the government which descended to them,
are now distinguished before all for the ardour
with which they applaud the principles of the
English constitution. Should we feel surprised,
then, that with this state of things existing, the
liberal members of the aristocracy and the middle
classes should try to fathom the inferior waters of
society in order to reach the rich and extensive
bottom of the national resources?

On the other hand, the workmen's companies, small in number, formed at the beginning of the movement, like the artillery and rifles of Woolwich Arsenal and Dockyard, are remarkable for their handiness. After all, the gun or the rifle is a tool, and we should not feel surprised if it obey more readily hands already used to handle the instruments of labour. If we regard the other military qualities, do not the manly character, activity, strength of arm, energy, and rudeness of will that distinguish the Anglo-Saxon race, reside chiefly in the class of workmen, the primitive rock? These facts, which it would be difficult not to recognise, should give rise to serious reflections in all persons who interest themselves in the development of the new army, and they ask themselves, with Lord Elcho, whether expense is not the rock on which the volunteer movement will some day be wrecked if ever destined to be so. The amount of these expenses was needlessly swelled at the outset by a love of parade and vanity: the equipment alone cost each man, in some regiments, the enormous sum of fifty guineas! Such pecuniary burthens are equivalent to a bill of exclusion for the working classes, and hence it is surprising that, at the start, the movement was restricted to the upper and middle classes? Lowering the monetary obstacle is therefore the first method that occurred to the English mind, in order to widen the limits of the institution; but here various systems sprang up. Some wished that those volunteers incapable of defraying the expenses of equipment should be aided by the state, but such a measure would have altered the character of the new arm, whose essential feature is independence, and assimilated it to the militia. Others proposed to raise subscriptions among the rich to cover the greater part of the expense, but this was misunderstanding the pride of the English workmen, of whom many would have declined this patronage; indeed, those to whom these means of joining the volunteers were proposed, answered: " We do not desire to receive alms in the accomplishment of a duty." The last thing left was to render the price of the uniform accessible to all, and this was the plan decided on; but in this new proposition, the obstacle came from the workmen themselves. A London solicitor thought he acted wisely in offering the workmen the pattern of an uniform which, through its extreme simplicity, would not have cost more than a sovereign, and he purposed to enter the corps himself. But no one responded to his appeal, and his name remained solitary at the head of the list. We see by this that the workmen insist on being upon a footing of equality with the middle classes in the ranks of the new army, and it is now conceded that a reasonable price (2l. 10s.), best satisfied the self-esteem and pecuniary means of the working class. Again, it was not so much the amount that kept the workmen aloof, as the necessity of paying it in a lump on joining the corps, but this obstacle has been removed by taking weekly instalments, and now the accession of all classes to the movement is insured. The government has greatly aided this result by supplying gratuitously muskets and ammunition, which it had not agreed to at the commencement. Can I say positively that all the volunteers have paid for their own equipment? There are doubtless some who have received help from their comrades, but generally those who owe all to their saving—and they are one hundred to one—have a better opinion of themselves, as being in the true spirit of the institution.

There is only one question left to solve: Should the workmen amalgamate with the middle classes by filling up the battalions already formed, or constitute separate corps? These two systems have now eager partisans. Great efforts have recently been made to draw the two classes more closely together, and I will not assert that these efforts have failed. Those regiments which have celebrated men at their head, have already succeeded in drawing into their ranks large bodies of workmen, and yet, generally, the latter prefer an organisation of their own. After all, they follow in this the example of the middle classes, where the lawyers, the artists, and the clerks have grouped themselves more or less in classes. Bri-

gades of workmen are now springing up in all
parts of England, but, in both cases, the armament
of the family of labourers, without any jealousy or
rivalry, will be in the history of the volunteers
the distinctive feature of the close of 1860. In
this way a movement is completed which up to
this time has had more surface extent than depth.
Admitting the English proposition, that the civil
population as a defensive means is an excellent
mine which has not yet been explored, everybody will concede that it should be dug down to
the lowest strata in order to know its riches
thoroughly. At the bottom are found, at any
rate, strength and devotion. Indubitably, the
solicitor who leaves his chambers, the merchant
who runs from his office, the artist who deserts
his workroom, in order to acquire by a fatiguing
drill the means of being useful to his country in
the event of danger, deserve our respect and
admiration; but what shall we say, in that case,
of the workmen and artisans, who, after ten or
twelve hours of hard labour, rush to the drill-
ground and brave the icy breeze after emerging
from the dens of steam? One of them, who
works at a forge at Woolwich Arsenal, told me
with manly pride what his volunteer uniform had
cost him : he did not speak of money, but of the
privations he had imposed on himself, as father
of a family, not to abandon to others the
right of dying gloriously, if needed, for England.

Another had sold his watch to equip himself, and said with a laugh, that the report of a gun would be sufficient to announce to him the hour of danger. Hitherto, however, the movement has stopped with the workmen in towns. Should it extend to the country labourers? Here serious obstacles arise, for the British government fears lest the formation of rural corps of volunteers may injure the development of the militia.* Some statesmen think, on the contrary, that the two institutions, far from being antagonistic, will aid one another, and say that the organisation of riflemen would cultivate in the rural districts military tastes, and thus prepare the rude sons of the plough for the trade of arms. As the latter system has not yet been tried, I will refrain from pronouncing my opinion as to the validity of the opposition it meets with.

Companies of cadets are now everywhere attached to the rifle companies. At a distribution of prizes after a rifle match which took place at Montrose, Lord Elcho,† speaking about the means of perpetuating the movement, took by the hand a lad in a rifle uniform, accidentally present, and leading him to the front of the platform, said, "Here is one of the means!" Several regiments

---

* As the militia were not embodied last year, nor will they be this, this fear is very slight.—L. W.

† One of the most powerful supporters of the new army, and one of those men in high position, who has done most to enlarge its base.

of volunteers have, indeed, hit on the idea of attaching a corps of cadets, composed of lads between the ages of twelve and fifteen: these cadets pay about half-a-guinea a year, wear the uniform, are present at drill, and form, as it were, the *enfans de troupe* of the volunteer army. I met the other day, at Greenwich Hospital, one of these companies, the "First Surrey Juvenile Rifles:" having obtained the special permission of the governor, Admiral Gordon, they entered, with colours flying and their band at their head, the venerable edifice which commands the banks of the Thames. We can imagine the proud joy of these youths; but even more envious was the emotion of the old sailors—nearly all mutilated in the service of the state—at the sight of this martial ardour of lads, who reminded them of a shadow which had passed away from them for ever. In several large schools, such as Eton and Rugby, similar battalions have been formed among the pupils, and the first of these institutions recently received its colours from the hand of a lady. The battalion, consisting of three or four hundred lads, in a grey uniform with silver ornaments, marched, with the drums and fifes of the Coldstreams at its head, to the play-ground, where the young soldiers formed in square, and saluted their colours by presenting arms. In other countries it might be apprehended that these cadet corps might render the movement childish;

but in England, where serious matters are regarded seriously, this danger does not exist. What the English propose in establishing these juvenile companies,. is to inculcate at an early hour in the children a taste for military exercises, the use of fire-arms, and the feeling of discipline, so that when they have attained the age of seventeen or eighteen, they may consider the duty of serving as volunteers a natural debt they have contracted toward their country. These cadet corps are the nursing schools of the organisation, and the sight of these youths playing at soldiers with amusing gravity, arouses in the physiologist more than one reflection. May not that warlike temper which distinguishes in history young and barbarous races, be found again in the children of civilised races; or, does man only reproduce in his development the various stages of humanity ?

To judge of the intensity of the movement, we must not stop with England, for the new system of defence has thrust forth deep and numerous ramifications in Scotland. In Edinburgh, Glasgow, and a dozen other cities, all classes of society have flocked to arms, and a few months back an idea could be formed of the popularity of this institution, which has since widely extended. I allude to the review which took place in Holyrood Park, in August, 1860, and which was the counterpart of the Hyde Park review. In this old Scottish park, where the reminiscences of French history are blended with the chronicles of the country of Walter Scott, more than twenty-one thousand men marched past in presence of the Queen: there were on the ground about one hundred and fifty corps, massed in thirty-five brigades —one of cavalry, six of artillery, one of engineers, and twenty-seven of rifles. Among the latter, the lawyers' company of Edinburgh was specially noticed, one of the first formed in Scotland, if not in the United Kingdom. The Highlanders advanced to the sound of the bagpipes, and the different colours of their uniforms, their naked and vigorous limbs, their bold and rapid march which has caused them to be compared to a mountain torrent, filled all the spectators with enthusiasm. At the head of the second division of this army was General Cameron, remarkable for his military talent and noble appearance, who has since proceeded to New Zealand. It would be superfluous to institute a parallel between this review and the one that took place in Hyde Park two months previously: both, however, exercised a great influence, by inspiring the young army with energetic confidence in its strength, and by calling out fresh recruits. Ireland is, hitherto, the only island of the United Kingdom where the organisation of the volunteers has been arrested by obstacles, and they came from the English government. For those foreigners, who incessantly represent poor Ireland as crushed by the hand of her elder sister, there is a fine field for invectives and declamation. This is not the place for a discussion whether Ireland is generally oppressed or not by the English government, but we cannot blame it for refusing the right of carrying arms to a country agitated by savage religious quarrels. As Lord Palmerston cleverly said, no one suspects the courage of the Irish: on the contrary, it is feared that they may fight too well, and moreover that they may fight with one another. Need I add that everywhere save in Ireland, that is to say, wherever a civil war has not to be apprehended, the sons of Green Erin have been able and still can form volunteer divisions? To convince oneself of this fact, it is only necessary to look at the London Irish Brigade, one of the most flourishing in Great Britain.

We now know the organisation of the volunteers, and to this institution another is attached, which is, as it were, its crown: I mean the "National Rifle Shooting Association."* Do you wish to know how the education of the rifleman is completed? If you do, we must proceed to the School of Musketry at Hythe. There we shall be better able to judge of the practical science of the volunteers, and the use they expect to turn their rifles to in the event of an invasion.

---

* An institution independent of and distinct from that of the riflemen, although rooted in the same movement. Its object is to promote correctness of firing.

CHAPTER XV.

ON July 2, 1860, I, like all the curious people in London and the vicinity, bent my steps to Wimbledon, where the first great shooting-match was to come off. The two lines of railway that converge on this village, situated a few miles from the metropolis, were besieged by crowds of travellers : on the day, all distinction of classes was effaced before the attraction of pleasure, and you would see rich patricians only too glad to enter the same carriages with the *plebs*, in order to reduce the distance that separated them from the scene of the festival. Wimbledon, which I then visited for the first time, stands in a charming position in the midst of an enormous plain, ornamented with clumps of fruit-trees, rich fields, a few pools formed by the rain, and crowned on the horizon by a circle of hills, whose soft and

wooded slopes blend harmoniously with the deep
green hue and calm character of the landscape.
The village, of which I only saw a few pretty
houses separated by gardens, is one of the last in
England subjected to manorial rights: this old
feudal claim, which the inhabitants of Wimbledon
have not reclaimed, eventually passed, so I am
told, into the hands of a Jew. No great distance
off is the country-house where Voltaire lived
during his exile, and where he learned to mis-
understand Shakspere. The great attraction of
Wimbledon, and that which caused it to be selected by the council of the association for the
rifle match, is its common, or heath. It is, in fact,
difficult to find in the vicinity of London so vast
an extent of open land which has escaped the en-
closure system: as the encroaching city extends
its lines of streets in all directions, these spots
become rare, and the riflemen foresee, not without
sadness, a time, more or less remote, when London
having further increased her circumference, the
last commons will doubtless be converted into
parks. Space is the first condition for a rifle
ground, and on this head nothing can be desired
better than this great flat surface, covered with
scrubby grass and thorny gorse. To the right,
Wimbledon Common is bordered by the wall of
an immense park, that belonged formerly to the
noble house of Somerset, but which, divided into
lots, has passed into the hands of the middle

classes, which have built a large number of elegant
villas. On the left, the eye discovers no limits.
A friend, who lives in the village, had led me on
this morning in this direction to a stream surrounded by a circular brick-wall, and which bears
in the neighbourhood the name of the Roman
Well. He also showed me the Roman camp, a
circular space of ground, surrounded by a deep
ditch, in which tall trees now grow. The traces
of the old *castrum* seemed to me, I confessed,
considerably effaced: but my guide was well informed, and showed himself so convinced of the
fact, that I should have been in despair about
contradicting his antiquarian knowledge. The
proof, he told me, is, "that Cæsar in his Com-
mentaries, speaks of a camp which his soldiers
established in the vicinity of the Thames. Why
should not this camp, after all, be that at Wimbledon ?" Cæsar's idea and the invasion of England by the Romans, naturally led us back to the
programme of the day, the shooting contest,
whose well-avowed intention was to close the
soil of Great Britain for ever against the progress
of a foreign army. Already, in fact, the gloomy
heath began to be covered with an ocean of
heads.

The crowd could be divided into two perfectly
distinct currents, the walkers and the carriages. I do
not believe that anywhere but in England so large
a number of vehicles and horses could be found

assembled on one point. It appeared as if each farm, each villa, and all the houses in the neighbourhood, had turned out their teams and carriages, either elegant or rustic. The aristocracy, attracted by the novelty of the spectacle and the presence of the Queen, flocked up from all sides to do her homage. I never saw before such a luxurious display of pretty women, for the higher you rise in the social scale, the greater beauty is met with in the Anglo-Saxon race. The scene of the match was enclosed by a barrier of planks, in which four entrances were made, one for the public, one for the Queen, and two for carriages. Having paid one shilling (which caused a considerable amount of murmuring around), we were introduced on the ground—the tawny heath—on which fluttered flags of every colour, and bordered by a fringe of tents. Among the latter, that for the Queen was naturally most noticed, up to which ran a parallel path expressly formed through the gorse of the common; it was a pavilion of exquisite taste, with a dais richly covered with red cloth, and surrounded by precious flowers, supplied by an amateur of the vicinity. Opposite to us rose at a distance the butts—hillocks of yellowish earth, which, I was assured, were twelve feet high by twenty-five or thirty in width, but which, diminished by the laws of perspective, resembled piles of sand constructed by the hand of

a child. Behind the first row of butts, separated
from each other by a considerable interval, were
others even more distant. In front of the earth-
works were the targets, iron plates painted white,
half an inch thick and six feet in width, with
circles and a black dot in the centre. The last
targets were so reduced by the distance that this
dot appeared about the size of that of an *i*; but
to hit an almost invisible object was the feat
which would constitute the success of the day.
There were riflemen of all colours and uniforms,
with a few Swiss, who had arrived expressly from
their mountains to dispute the prizes with the
English. Before being admitted to compete, it
was necessary to pay at least a guinea, and this
pecuniary condition was generally blamed, as
tending to exclude from the trial a number of
artisans, villagers, and clerks, whose aim might be,
however, as certain, and their hand as exercised
as that of the richest competitors. Should the
entrance to the competition be subjected to a
money question, and, to a certain extent, tax the
bullets? At about half-past four the Queen advanced to the shooting-tent, which was situated
at some distance from her resting pavilion, and
herself began the operations of the day. A light
pull to a string attached to the trigger of the rifle
and the first shot was fired; the flags waved on
the side of the butts and announced that the magic

bullet had struck the bull's-eye; according to the rules of the association, the Queen had gained three points. The match was begun.

This shooting contest lasted for several days: the curious and amateurs seconded each other on the ground, which was saturated with the recent rain; the furze and damp grass were here and there invaded by deep pools of water, which the furrows formed during the last week by the share of a steam-plough, had not succeeded in completely draining. All the interest was now concentrated round the firing-tents, which were occupied by the competitors for the various prizes, of which the largest, the Queen's, was 250*l.* I first visited the forces at " Aunt Sally," the popular name given at fairs and race-courses to a game at stick-throwing. You pay a shilling for each shot, and the amount is divided at the end of the day among those who have struck the bull's-eye. There were riflemen who fired in turn and choosing all sorts of positions—some standing, others with one knee on the ground, one sitting, another, in fine, lying on his stomach—the way was of little consequence, provided that the mark was hit. I then proceeded to the other tents, where the excitement was the more lively, for notable and warmly-disputed victories were at stake. An idea of the distance between the pieces and the targets could be formed by the time that elapsed between the explosion of the gun and the moment when the bullet, in shape like a candle-end of lead, struck, the surface of the iron mantlets. This distance, besides, increased with the importance of the prizes and the progress of the match; it varied from 500, 800, 900, and even 1000 yards on the last day. I found it difficult, even with the aid of an opera-glass, to distinguish the black bull's-eye, really as large as a lady's parasol, but which, almost disappearing in the distance, looked like a black dot floating in space. May we not be justi-fied in the belief that habit develops in the marks-man a species of second sight, for this obscure and doubtful mark did not escape their efforts? We may easily believe that, having to deal with fire-arms of so long a range, people were not in safety behind the butts, even at more than a mile. Sig-nals of danger traced a circle of solitude all around; it was even said that a farmer in the vicinity, blockaded by the danger of stray bullets, could only leave his house during the whole week by a back door. The match was drawing to a close, and Mr. Ross and one opponent remained alone on the ground to dispute the Queen's prize. The public were panting with curiosity, and the two rivals, both Englishmen, though visibly moved, tried, with truly British strength of mind, to stiffen their muscles of steel and quell the beating of their hearts. For a moment, the chances seemed to turn against the rival who had, hitherto, stood highest in the betting; at last, a report was fol-

lowed by a restless silence, and, amid the cloud of
smoke as it settled, the black flag could be seen
waving in the extreme distance. Mr. Ross, now
proclaimed the Champion of Great Britain, had
won the medal which he proudly wears on his
chest at the dinners and meetings of the volunteers. When the fire had ended, I had the curiosity to visit the targets: they were riddled with
bullets, which were not merely flattened, but
crushed, against the wall of iron.

The intention that produced this national match
is now easy to understand: England was formerly
a nation of archers, and now wishes to become a
nation of riflemen. Who is there in this country
that does not remember the age of the Plantagenets, when every brave inhabitant of the country-
side carried his bow and arrows with him ? Each
village had then its practice-ground, where all,
even lads of seven, went to exercise their skill.
It is to this popular education that the English
are indebted for the victories of Crecy, Agincourt,
and other celebrated days; the government of
that day placed such confidence in the long bow,
as being the strength of England, that it for a
long time opposed the firelock practice that tried
to creep into the towns and the country. The
rifle, that perfected musket, was destined in its
time to meet with the same resistance: invented
about the year 1567, by a German workman, it
only spread at the outset over the Tyrolese

mountains, and the vast plains of America. During the War of Independence, the English had reasons for recognising at their own expense the superiority of this arm, for while their soldiers with the antique muskets made more noise and smoke than execution, the American volunteers, armed with their rifles, aimed at the enemy as it were, man by man, and levelled the most courageous in their ranks. From this epoch a reform in the system of musketry became the ruling question of the day; but, unfortunately, resistance to useful innovations and progress is sometimes protected by the authority of great names. The Duke of Wellington regarded the old flint-lock musket as the best weapon for war, and smiled at the idea of converting English soldiers into riflemen. Was it not with that heavy and primitive tool that they gained the battle of Waterloo? Had it not been for the Crimean war, it is probable that the English would not yet have got rid of this venerable ancestress, for "Brown Bess" was a species of personification like John Bull. Still, it is owing to the introduction of the rifle into all the regiments that England owes the prompt suppression of the last Indian rebellion, and the volunteers could not do better than adopt an arm which offers in all cases such great advantages, but especially in guerilla warfare. I will not dwell on the changes which the rifle must introduce in the mode of fighting, but there is one which deserves pointing out: hitherto, two hostile *corps d'armée* have drawn close in order to destroy each other; now-a-days, they will hardly be able to notice each other. An Englishman observed to me with a laugh, that this new system reassured his conscience to a certain point; "in the event of war," he said, "we shall no longer fire at men, but at black dots."

Rifle practice seems to be, according to the idea of the Rifle Association, the complement of the volunteer institution; but, according to the views of the government, it is the foundation-stone. A circular from the War Department declares that, before obtaining the sanction of the state, every rifle corps must have a practice-ground of at least two hundred yards in length. This condition, I grant, has been criticised, owing to the obstacles it adds to the already tedious formation of a brigade; for in England the progress of agriculture has left but very little ground uncultivated. On the other hand, a firing-ground is an unpleasant neighbour, for the farmer cannot visit his crops and cattle at any moment with that calmness of mind formerly characteristic of the British rustic. There are certainly large landholders who have liberally lent the rifle corps a portion of their domains; but parks and generous lords cannot be met with everywhere. The fact is, that in the present state of things, a few companies of a relatively old date have not yet been able to obtain a practice-ground; others have them of small range; while another section lives on the tolerance of a land-owner, and therefore hesitates at the considerable outlay required for the erection of butts. This expense is larger than might be assumed: at Wormwood-scrubs, the piece of the earth and masonry works amounted to the sum of 332*l*. The council of the Rifle Association does its best, it is true, to surmount the obstacles, and the companies behindhand, stimulated by the example of the others which have already purchased ground, spare no sacrifices. Hence, the day is not far distant when every town, perhaps every village, in Great Britain will have its rifle-ground, as it formerly had its archery butts. It is not enough to have weapons, people must learn the art of using them; and the best Whitworth rifle and the most expensive practice-ground will not make an accomplished rifleman without certain rules of art. Hence the English government has decided that it will only grant gratis ammunition to those corps of volunteers two members of which have received a fortnight's technical instruction at the school of Hythe.

The little town of Hythe is situated on the sea-shore, and, to reach it from London, you pass by rail through the rich meadows and hop-grounds of Kent. After leaving Ashford, the route offers most pleasing landscapes, the surrounding country being watered by three streams, which join before reaching Hythe. What most strikes the traveller at the outset is not so much the town itself as the recent revolutions to which all this part of the coast has been subjected. The town, situated at the foot of a cliff, only consists of one street, running parallel to the sea, with a few lanes running in the same direction, or intersecting it at right angles. There are certainly a town-house, a market, and an ancient church, of a style half Norman half English, which stands over the town, on one of the slopes of the steep cliff, with a tower having a western aspect, and a venerable crypt, in which are piled up the bones and skulls of the old Danes;* but all this cannot hide the state of decadence into which this ancient seaport has fallen. I had discovered that Hethe, Hede, or Hythe—for the town bears all three names in the old chronicles—was derived from a Saxon word signifying seaport; and it is certain that in the time of the Saxons, the Normans, and during the reign of the Plantagenets, Hythe possessed a celebrated creek, which is supposed to have been the cradle of the English navy. But, although I sought this port carefully, I could not

* Accoiding to tradition, a great battle was fought in the reign of Ethelwulf on the beach between Hythe and Folkestone. The Danes, repulsed by the Saxons, tried to regain their vessels, but lost a great number of men, and the plain was covered with their bones, which blanched under the sun and rain for years. However, some one collected them and heaped them up in the crypt of the church; several of the skulls have holes in them, and are supposed to have been pierced by iron lance-heads, or the pointed end of the battle-axes.

find it; it disappeared long ago, in the first place,
by changing its position, by taking a slip east-
ward after each retirement of the sea, and invaded inch by inch by the sands. At the present
day it is only a barren beach, with unhealthy
pools, and the town is situated a good mile from
the sea. Islets of small shingles, successively deposited by the waves, form the distinctive feature of this coast, or a few blades of grass peep
out between the stones, while a hedge of wild
broom throws here and there its thorny verdure
over the nudity of the desert. I have spoken of
the port of Hythe, which ranked, under the
Plantagenets, among the famous Cinque Ports;
but, anterior to the arrival of the Saxons in England, there was another, the *Portus Lemanis* of
the Romans, and it is to the decline of Lymne
that Hythe owes its origin. Enormous masses of
masonry and ruined walls, fastened with Roman
cement, still cover the sandy slopes of the downs
three miles from the town; and this first port was
swallowed up, as the second was afterwards, by
the silting of the sea. An Englishman, looking
from the crest of this hill, and seeing the expanse
of long grass undulating in the wind, asked himself, were they not the prodigal waves of Ocean,
returned to their old bed to make a penitent end?
But the sea does not return, and a part of Lymne,
or West Hythe port, blockaded by the waves of
sand thrown up by other waves, now forms one of

the straggling suburbs of the modern town. You see there the ruins of an ancient chapel, in which the Nun of Kent once preached and displayed her madness. Not far from the town also stand the ruins of a castle, where the assassins of Thomas a'Becket spent the night before the day on which they rode towards Canterbury to murder the archbishop. These historic reminiscences, but even more the ancient movements of the sea and earth, which constitute the most interesting feature of modern geology, were of a nature to arrest my thoughts; but on that day I had no time to be either geologist or antiquarian: the ping of the rifle bullet would have recalled me to the object of my journey, even had I forgotten it. The shingles of Hythe now serve as practice-ground, and the bullets whistle over the spots where formerly heavy vessels dragged their chains or let their anchors fall.

The school of musketry was founded by the government about six years ago, and stands at the west of the town on the Ashford road. The building was constructed at the beginning of this century, for the staff corps, and was afterwards employed as barracks. This institution was originally founded for the regular army, and to teach English soldiers the proper use of rifles, but, as the volunteer movement has since sprung into existence, it was thought right to extend the same institution to both armies, and Hythe thus found itself the head-quarters of the riflemen. Two men of each company at least go there to obtain the principles of an art which they then impart to their comrades, and this coming and going of volunteers, who spend two weeks at Hythe, and occupy furnished lodgings in different parts of the town, has singularly rejuvenated a spot that was dying of languor and solitude. You see there all sorts of uniforms, and men of all ages, from sixteen up to nearly sixty, though youth predominates. Here, all ranks of society, all classes— peers of the realm, country gentlemen, solicitors, members of the university,. tradesmen, and clerks— meet and live on a footing of perfect equality. There is no occasion even of an introduction* to become friends, for the bond of this fraternity is the common object of all—the defence of the native soil. I must even say, to the honour of the English aristocracy, that those of its members, instructed by the same sergeants and subjected to the same discipline, are only distinguished from the other volunteers by their zealousness and ardour at work. The instruction is both oral and practical: and there is a lecture-room, in which the governor of the school, Major-General Hay,

---

* By the way, foreigners make great fun of this word. In one of the German almanacks I recently read about an Englishman who might have saved another from drowning, but did not do so, because he had not been introduced to him.—L. W.

who is himself a marksman of the first rank, and rarely goes about without a rifle in his hands, clearly explains to the volunteers the main object of their institution. He tells them that for the defence of England it is better to have twenty thousand men good marksmen, than two hundred thousand only able to handle their weapons slightly, for relying on numbers instead of skill is like trusting to a rope of sand. I had hitherto believed that chasseurs and men accustomed to the use of the rifle had an advantage over others; but it is an error I was obliged to confess. The Hythe teachers prefer a man who has never fired a shot to those who have contracted bad habits in the use of a gun, which they have the greatest difficulty in the world to get rid of. The instruction imparted at Hythe is chiefly designed to heighten the soldier's intelligence, for, owing to the introduction of the rifle, he is bound henceforth to regard himself as an individuality, and no longer as a machine. The certainty of glance and firmness of hand are, according to General Hay's opinion, qualities even more necessary to free riflemen than to soldiers of the regular army. The volunteers in the open field will always be a long distance from the enemy (something like 600 to 900 yards), hence they must ensure their bullets a mortal character at that distance. Excellent lessons on the rifle itself, its component parts, and the laws governing projectiles when

launched in the air, complete the course of theoretic instruction.*

The practical part of the instruction begins with
position drill, lasting about a week; and the heads
of the school attach the utmost importance to this
manœuvre, which is the basis of the whole system.
Not satisfied with training the body to the required position, and strengthening the hand, they
educate the eye, if I may employ the expression.
What spot is better suited for this than Hythe?
The barrack walls are covered with holes, and, to
use the English phrase, seem pitted with the small-
pox. When they have learned to stand, judge
distances, aiming and firing blank cartridge, the
volunteers proceed to the shingles with cartridges
and bullets in their pouches. This is the great
day of excitement, for firing at the mark is about
to begin. At the outset, all the novices are placed
in the third class, and the first trial is not very
severe, as it is at the shortest distances. All,
however, do not emerge from it with honour, and
those who do not gain the fifteen points required
to pass into the second class, form a very downcast
group. I am bound to say that these men, desig-
nated " blinkers," " muffs," and " lame ducks," appeared to me to endure their misfortunes with a
very unequal degree of philosophy, and this differ-

* While speaking of the school of musketry, I must not forget
Colonel Wilford, who has powerfully contributed to spread a scientific
knowledge of fire-arms by his much-esteemed lectures at Hythe,
London, and elsewhere.

ence was explained to me. Men of studious and business habits readily assume their share of a failure which it was but just to foresee; but the good cricket-players, oarsmen, and all those who feel a pride in their skill at athletic exercises, make a wry face in the third, and even the second class. Those who have the good fortune to enter the first class, fire at ranges varying from 700 to 900 yards, and if the gain of a battle or a fortune were at stake, I do not believe that the competitors would have displayed more emulation than they did in making points. Their anxiety was only equalled by that of the non-commissioned instructors, who really took a paternal interest in the success of their pupils, and I saw with pleasure the general himself walk up to the unlucky and arouse their hopes with their courage by kindly remarks. This individual instruction of the sharp-shooters is completed by file-firing and skirmishing-drill. Before leaving the town, I visited a military canal dug at a vast expense sixty years ago, under the influence of the same alarms which gave birth to the volunteer movement; but soldiers of this generation did not appear to me to have any very high opinion of this barrier opposed to the invasion of the coasts. If this could keep an enemy at bay, it would be chiefly in summer, by the foul smell of its waters.

The example given by the Wimbledon rifle match and the instruction received at Hythe has

borne its fruit: at the present day challenges and
rifle contests are taking place all over England.
Considerable sums of money have been distributed
as prizes through individual liberality, and very
lately Sir De Lacy Evans, Colonel of the Royal
National Rifles, received a letter only bearing the
initials "Z. A.," and containing 50l. in bank-
notes. It was the wish of the donor that the sum
should be employed for the benefit of the brigade,
but did not specify in what way: hence Sir De
Lacy thought he acted right in employing it for
prizes encouraging rifle practice. These prizes do
not always consist of money, for one of the riflemen of the 12th Middlesex, surnamed the Gari-
baldians,* being on the point of proceeding to
Italy to see how the crater of Vesuvius was getting
on, wished, ere he started, to have a splendid
rifle competed for. His comrades, therefore, had
a match to see which of them should retain the
valuable *souvenir*. The constant use of fire-arms
will very certainly contribute to make the modern
English excellent riflemen : but will correctness
of aim be sufficient on the battle-field? Some
officers of the army still doubt it, and support
their opinion on Curran's jest; who could put out

* I may add, that the name of Garibaldi has been mixed up with
the whole volunteer movement, and the example of the Italian bands
putting to flight regular troops has excited an indirect, but considerable, influence on the spirit of the British nation. To those who told
them that the conditions were not at all the same, the English riflemen
hastened to reply, " If the Italians have a country to liberate, we have
a country to defend."

a candle with a pistol-bullet at twenty or thirty paces, but missed his man in a duel. " There is nothing surprising about it," he said; "when I fire at a candle, I know very well that the candle will not fire at me." It is also to harden themselves against an enemy's fire that the riflemen, not satisfied with shooting at a mark, hold sham fights, and the most remarkable of these took place last summer, one at Camden Park, the other at Hylands. Camden Park, situated in Kent, owes its name to a celebrated English antiquary, and was a spot well chosen for the little military drama to be performed that day to the great delight of the crowd, for it embraces one of those chalk hills dotted over southern England like a flock of sheep, and the valley which separates this hill from Bickley Wood, carelessly scattered over the sides of an opposite mount. In this wood the corps that was to begin the attack was hidden: there is a little stream in the middle of the valley, which suddenly rises towards the east, and the army of defence occupied the heights, commanding at this spot a very sharp descent, a species of hole with thick clumps of trees and a number of limekilns. Above the wooded hills undulating to the west could be seen in the distance the towers and fairy-like roof of the Crystal Palace. The hostilities commenced at an early hour, and the riflemen came out of this difficult trial much better than might have been expected. after a military apprenticeship of only a few months.

It is not my intention to flatter the volunteers: they have already perhaps been over-complimented by the English. No army can be perfect in a moment, and it was only a Cadmus who could sow dragons' teeth, and have a crop of soldiers at the right moment. I could say, for instance, without fear of being contradicted by the English themselves, that most of the officers are not yet up to their duties. It requires more time to make a leader than a soldier, and military studies are, before all, necessary, which cannot be acquired by the same means. However this may be, there is the nucleus of a grand force, and this force is daily increasing. We must not, however, form an idea of the number of volunteers England could set on foot in the event of a war, from the amount now existing—say one hundred and fifty thousand. Colonel MacMurdo, who has studied the question, estimates that at such a time, one Englishman in ten would be capable of bearing arms, which would raise the numerical power of the civilian army to five hundred and fifty thousand. With this force, he remarks, England has nothing to fear, and as for the citizens already enrolled, the colonel, who is inspector-general of volunteers, and has reviewed them in all parts of the kingdom, appears to attach great value to them, for he declares that he would not hesitate to-morrow to put himself at their head and lead them into the open field, if they were consolidated in battalions. This is, in fact, the task still left to do: the volunteers, owing to their formation here and there, at present only form groups, a considerable but scattered mass, local resources, and, if I may venture the expression, a church-steeple army. Any one who has attentively followed the movement, and is acquainted with the genius of England, will not feel astonished at this beginning. When a movement is commenced by supreme authority, nothing is more easy than to attain unity at once; but then, what sacrifices does it entail! The English do not proceed thus; they allow all their institutions to develop themselves freely, and under the influence of caprice. The natural result is, that, at the outset, their institutions seem made piecemeal, but by the very force of progress the parts are soon organised solidly round a centre. Such will be ere long, and is, indeed, already, the tendency of the volunteer army, although the movement of concentration can never efface in it the self-governing character that distinguishes it. The various bodies of riflemen and artillerymen have certain points to defend, and unless they receive superior orders, must not, even in the event of war, cross the borders of their county.

We have now to ask what England intends to

do with this national force at a given moment,
that is to say, in the case of an invasion? No
one dreams of separating the action of the volunteers from the movements of a regular army, and
the Duke of Cambridge declared some months
back at a City banquet, that the new organisation
was precious as an auxiliary, but that he should
consider it injurious to the interests of the country
if it ever tended to displace the services of the
army and navy. Fortunately for England, this
danger does not exist: the first idea was to utilise
the volunteers to protect the coasts, by drawing
round the island at the least alarm a girdle of
sharpshooters; but as great numbers of rifle corps
have since then been formed in the central counties, not only the coasts, but the whole country
would bristle, if necessary, with a wall of bayonets.
The aid of the riflemen is calculated to support
the movement of the English troops, clear the
ground, skirmish, harass the flanks of the enemy,
interrupt his communications, and, in a word, offer
obstacles of every description to the progress of an
invading army. But these services will be required for the general system of defence: we have
attended to the fortresses building on the most
vulnerable points of the island, and which the
English consider the stone keys of independence:
and as, behind a wall, every man is a soldier, a
part of the volunteers could guard the forts, and
save the militia this duty, who could thus take the

field. Moreover, if at any later date Cromwell's plan is carried out, and the heart of the nation is covered by a stone cuirass—I mean, if London is defended by a half-dozen detached forts (which is a serious question of the moment)—would they not, in the event of an attack, furnish an outlet for the zeal and good will of the armed citizens? The ambition of a great number of volunteers, I am bound to add, aspires to more direct services, and I will not be the man to discourage their efforts, for they would answer, in the words of George Herbert, " He who aims at the sky strikes higher than the man who aims at a tree." They propose nothing less than forming line with the regulars; and I need hardly add, that they spare neither time nor pains to learn the soldier's trade conscientiously. The last time I visited Aldershott camp, I met there three gentlemen who for some weeks had put up with hard beds and all sorts of privations, in order to study military drill and manœuvres at the fountain-head.

What is the true position of the volunteers towards the state, and the nature of the duties they contract? This is the final point we have to clear up. In peace, they constitute a force entirely distinct from the regular army; and, though formed under certain conditions, and attached to the state by bonds we have indicated, the institution is independent, and may be regarded as a species of insurance against foreign invasion. The members of this armed association lose none of their individuality by enrolling themselves under the banner of the national defence, and can even retire after giving a fortnight's notice. It is the English idea to hold in hand an army of soldiers at once disciplined and free, and as a devotion without organisation or system would more probably illustrate a defeat than prevent it, the leaders of the movement insist on an enlightened obedience, which differs greatly from passive obedience. Discipline in this case is based on the feeling of duty and a love of country, and it is only in the event of an invasion that the free corps would form part of the regular army, the volunteers be subjected to martial law, and treated like other soldiers. Even during war, under no pretext can they ever be sent by government out of their country, and the ocean is the boundary of their action. This clause alone is of a nature to calm the apprehensions with which the volunteer movement seems to have inspired Europe; for though a precaution may be seen in it, it contains neither a challenge nor a threat: it is an uplifting of bucklers, and not of arms. What has Europe to fear from citizens enrolled for defence, and not for conquest? This peaceful character, even in the opinion of the English, must ensure the duration of the new army, solely formed to receive an enemy should an enemy arise. The movement will not be a feverish or temporary movement, such as aggressive enterprises generally are : it was developed with the majesty of the tide, and will have no ebb. The causes which provoked a year ago the appeal to arms in England are, I hope and trust, transitory, but the institution will survive them; it is growing daily consolidated, and tends to become a permanent force. This civilian army has doubtless cost, and still costs, individuals much time and money; still, large-minded economists do not regret these sacrifices, which are amply compensated, according to them, by the protection of national interests. In the eyes of the English, confidence is a capital, and security can be purchased, and we cannot grudge our admiration of such wise policy and the acts of devotion it multiplies. Where else should we find, moreover, in an age of egotism and moral declension, an army composed of all classes of the population, an army of men equipped at their own expense, surrendering their leisure, their tastes, their private interests to the national cause? Alluding to liberty, when speaking of England, has the appearance of a common-place, still I am bound to say that the English take into account among the profits of the new organisation the defence of constitutional institutions. We must believe, after all, that these institutions possess a value, since, before the mere shadow of a menace, a force of one hundred and fifty thousand bayonets sprang from the earth to protect them.

Another interesting field of study would be to investigate the changes the volunteer movement has introduced, and must introduce more and more, in the manners of Old England. An English friend of mine went three years ago to seek his fortune in Australia, and I met him lately in London, with aged features, grey hair, and green spectacles. "You find me greatly altered," said he to me, "but somebody has altered more than I have, and that is England. I no longer recognise my country: I left it peaceful as a city merchant, and come back to find it agitated by the rattle of arms and drums, as if Hannibal were before our gates." English physiologists regard from another point of view the happy modifications the new system must impress on the temperament of the race, for soldiering is becoming throughout Great Britain a sport like horse-racing, archery, and cricket. Not satisfied with visiting the practice-ground and learning military manœuvres, the riflemen, for the purpose of hardening themselves, throw up camps on the sea-shore, or on the brow of sandy hills, and sleep on straw, or a mattress, in tents they planted themselves, and endure under a thin canvas the severity of a stern climate. Others, again, undertake long marches, whose monotony is broken by the sound of the bugle and a few warlike songs, along the old roads, which have died out since the invention of railways, and are thus suddenly aroused from

their silence. These trips suit the travelling
humour of the Englishman, and give him a useful
object. Some volunteer companies also propose
to add to the practice of arms athletic sports and
all sorts of bodily exercises, and these double
gymnastics must cultivate strength, which the
English regard as one of the essential features of
manly beauty. In the circle of commercial relations, the volunteer movement has also exerted a
great influence on the early closing of shops and
on the Saturday half-holiday. These two measures were regularly asked for some years back
by the clerks and workmen, but the interests of
the masters offered obstacles, which considerations
of the national cause have disarmed. For do not
young men require time to learn the soldiering
trade? Another consequence, which is already
felt, will be effacing the extreme distance between
the classes, drawing closer the bonds of English
society, and blending private interests in a grand
national brotherhood. What stormy meetings
were unable to effect among a people that resists
every form of constraint and violence, is naturally
developed by the new organisation: the highest
social ranks, the representatives of birth, education, and wealth, meet daily under arms with the
representatives of trade and even of manual
labour. There is no man in England, however
great he be, who, in the opinion of this nation,
does not add inches to his stature by the honour

of bearing arms in the service of his country.
The Prince of Wales is colonel of the 21st Middlesex; Lord Palmerston, in spite of his seventy-five years, has joined the Irish Rifle Corps; and
the Duke of Cambridge commands the London
Rifle Brigade. The noblemen who have placed
themselves at the head of the movement insist
daily on the necessity of avoiding personal divisions, if the institution is to be strengthened and
propagated. The principle is in force that on the
practice or parade ground every volunteer is a
gentleman: all social distinctions give way to those
which are exclusively military. Will not the new
force England has given birth to also exercise an
influence on the foreign policy of the kingdom?
Lord John Russell's recent circular on Italian
affairs may aid us in answering this question.
The movement, I am bound to say, was developed
at first without any political after-thought, and
solely to support the English government in defending the country; but, while removing the
true or imaginary danger of invasion, while showing statesmen that they had an armed nation at
their back, the volunteers also intend to supply
the government of Great Britain with the means
of proving itself firm and worthy, though always
moderate, in its relations with Europe. They
say loudly that they wished to save their country
the humiliation of courting strength.

The object of this inquiry was to dissipate cer-

tain errors as to the more or less disarmed state
of England: these errors, I allow, were propagated
by our neighbours themselves about a year ago,
and I will not blame them for it, because nations
are like men—they fall from the day when, believing themselves invincible, they defy destiny.
If the English were afraid, they are no longer so,
for, even supposing that the swarms of volunteers,
helped by the regulars, did not succeed in check-
ing an invading army, or blocking the road to
London, an organised force would still be left in
each town and village. The conquerors would
then experience what terrible truth there is in
Juvenal's words: *sed victis arma supersunt.* I
was present one day at a discussion held by some
English officers as to the state of the national
defences. They had enumerated the somewhat
improbable circumstances by means of which the
wooden wall—presently to be the iron wall—of
Great Britain could be destroyed: the rampart of
troops and volunteers was assumed to be forced,
and an enemy's flag planted on the Tower of
London. An old captain, who had followed the
imaginary march of the enemy with great coolness, quietly said, "And afterwards?" That is,
in fact, the whole question. To conquer England the English must be exterminated. Behind
England would remain Scotland, with her citadels
of granite, built by the hand of Nature, and her
rude children, who would descend from the moun-

tains like an avalanche. Great Britain would recover from her wounds, and then woe to the conqueror!

France, therefore, will do well to adhere to her commercial treaty with England. I do not write this for the French government, which, of course, knows what opinion to form of the forces grouped beyond the Channel, and which, besides, has always protested its good feelings for our allies: I answer writings which caused a painful sensation in England, perhaps, too, elsewhere. War cries were raised by the French press, and we may assume that these threats possessed force, as they alarmed the trade and population beyond the Channel. The English, for their part, seem not at all to understand these superannuated feelings of national vengeance. Why talk to them about avenging the defeat of Waterloo? People do not take vengeance for a misfortune, but for an insult. In truth, I do not believe that the invasion of the British Isles was ever a serious project with soldiers: it will be less so than ever since the organisation of the riflemen. But it is well to combat chimeras, which, at times, have more weight with the unreflecting mind of the masses than wise and prudent advice. M. Thiers said, one day, in the National Assembly, that " his lengthened experience had taught him how important it was to refute false ideas in political economy as soon as they display themselves." There are other utopias beside those of political economy, and the dreams of the national ambition are not the least obstinate or the least dangerous. These reflections, I fear, run a great risk of being unpopular; but what matter, if they be true? It is only too easy in France to flatter the love of glory, and if that is called patriotism it surprises me. The true patriots are those who, in 1812, and beneath a perfectly calm sky, pointed out to France the black point in the foreign coalition.

CONCLUSION.*

IT is, perhaps, advisable, with the termination of the essays contained in these volumes, to explain the reasons which led to their writing, or, in a word, tell the story of the book.

Exiled from France in consequence of the coup d'état of December 2, 1851, I first sought a refuge in Belgium, whence I migrated to Holland. In the latter country I was struck by the benefits spread over a small state by a national religion that offered no resistance to the development of liberty. The intensely calm prosperity and energetic character of this handful of men, who formerly disputed with Great Britain the empire of the seas, attracted my attention to a very different branch of the Saxon race. I therefore resolved to study on a larger stage the political characteristics of Protestantism, the conditions of

---

* I may be allowed to mention that this chapter is unpublished, and should be regarded as the Author's Preface.—L. W.

a representative government, and the influence of certain institutions on the moral and national life of a people.

On my arrival in England, I was struck by two things: the grandeur of the British power, and that species of manly confidence which the representative government inspired. I found here incarnated in the manners, laws, and public life that liberty which was pursued in France through so many struggles and has not yet been attained. My first idea would have been to write down my impressions on the English constitution, the mode in which it was formed, and the energy it communicates to the national character. I laid the idea aside for the present, however, owing to various reasons. Among these was the fact that a French author, formerly my colleague in the Legislative Assembly, M. de Montalembert, had already opposed the institutions of England to the present state of France in a work which will not so easily be forgotten: I did not think it wise, therefore, to follow him on a road where we should have come in collision, at least on some points. And then it appeared to me that, before studying with benefit the political life of a people, and pronouncing on the value of its government, it was necessary to be thoroughly acquainted with its character, customs, resources, territory, and the precise state of the civilisation to which it had raised itself.

Giving up, then, any definite plan or preconceived idea, I began studying without much order, and as they presented themselves to me, the pages composing the great book of English life and civilisation. My way of regarding them may be compared to that of an amateur walking through a picture-gallery. He stops before each picture, or, at least, before those which accidentally attract his attention, reserving to himself the right of forming presently a general idea of the school of painting to which they belong.

No one can be more cognisant than myself of the insufficiency of these essays, and I allow that there are visible gaps. The subjects I treated in turn, during the last three years, in the *Revue des Deux Mondes*, have not the slightest cohesion. I have described the divers aspects of English life as they passed before me, without any great anxiety about linking them together methodically. Still, I must ask that these volumes should not be regarded as forming a whole: they are a beginning, but this beginning is intended to be presently completed. My essays are going on: I still have to make known to France many other phases of the English character, and many other conquests of British civilisation, which are not all indicated in these volumes. The unity of the book must be looked for at a future day: when it is completed—and it is difficult for me now to lay down its limits—I trust that it will then respond to its title and the intentions I proposed to myself. As a French philosopher has said, "Time is a link," and it is with this link I hope to attach together those portions of my work which now appear incoherent or disproportionate.

Such as they are, however, these volumes strive to attain an object, and that—I am happy to say it—has been partly achieved. I proposed to refute, on the authority of facts, certain prejudices which prevail in France with respect to the English nation. In doing this, I not only desired to pay a debt of gratitude to a country which, after the shipwreck of my hopes, covered me with the mantle of its free hospitality; but, regarding these prejudices as one of the most serious obstacles to the return of political life in France, as well as the greatness and good intelligence of two nations, I thought I was performing a holy duty in describing, without blackening, but without flattery, my impressions as to what I saw. It is an easy task for statesmen to form on paper treaties of alliance, but so long as peace is not constituted in the minds; so long as two great neighbouring and rival nations have not learnt to know and esteem each other; so long even as they have not come to an agreement on the spirit of certain institutions which rule civil life, and the character and genius of the peoples—these treaties are effaced and torn on the first opportunity, by the slightest breath of discord that springs up.

This consideration, more than any other, determined me in publishing this series of essays in a fragmentary shape. While not imposing on the French people at present a conclusion which I reserve for the future, and which can only stand out forcibly from the complete work, I have allowed facts to speak for themselves, and these facts have proved, if I am not mistaken, that France, instead of dwelling on a few ridiculous superficialities, would have an interest in studying the sources whence Great Britain has drawn her magnificent institutions, her undeniable prosperity, her vigorous confidence in herself, and that spirit of enterprise inseparable from the feeling of liberty. A nation which had left in other hands than its own the government of its affairs, might have been able to wage great wars, and be at certain periods of its history what an ancient philosopher called a herd of glory, but would it have acquired at home the comfort, the unbending force, and, before all, the moral dignity which I set above all other blessings?

While rendering justice to England, far from repudiating my character as a Frenchman, I believe that I have done my country the only service a friendly voice and filial heart can offer it in the present condition of affairs. Nor did I consider myself bound by her display of hospitality to any sort of servile gratitude: I have written what I humbly believe the truth: I have blamed in English society all I considered to deserve blame, and I intend to use this right with equal impartiality in future.

A proud and free nation would not desire a homage that was not independent. When I wrote these essays, I had not the slightest idea that they would be ever translated into English. I was addressing France, and the best way of courting her favour in the present day is not exactly by opening her eyes to the grand events that take place across the Channel.

These essays, published in France at rather lengthened intervals one from the other, have been received by the English press with an indulgence for which I can never feel sufficiently grateful. I am bound to say, however, that certain writers of this country entertain a prejudice against which I take this opportunity of protesting. Some Englishmen fancy that they alone know, and can possibly know, England, and strangers, according to their view, understand nothing at all. I confess that certain books, hastily written about England, by Frenchmen who spent three days in Leicester-square, may justify, up to a certain point, the distrust the English entertain of a foreigner's opinion. This assertion, nevertheless, appears to me ill founded, and I ask, on the contrary, whether the English can know England? No more, to my mind, than the French can know France.

The habit of living in a country in the social medium in which a man is born, and in which he daily takes deeper root, through the slow and in-calculable power of custom, through national self-esteem and the instinct of race, necessarily en-croaches on the delicacy of perception. As judging is comparing, the elements of a comparison are wanting to every man who wishes to form a judgment on his own country: he honestly de-ceives himself about a multitude of things, in which the mistake is at once self-evident to a stranger. Who knows himself? I am in a posi-tion to prove the truth of what I say. When I lived in France I formed a very different idea of my country from the one I now hold. I needed to see Paris again after ten years' absence, and after being, to a certain point, assimilated with other civilisations, in order to be struck by a number of peculiarities in the manners, habits, and external features of the capital, which in former times I should have allowed to pass en-tirely unnoticed. I should not like to assert that on this latter visit I noticed all there was to see; for that, it would have been necessary for me to be no longer myself.

I have generally found a more correct idea of England as it is among those English who have travelled on the Continent. Having been enabled to see other manners, form different opinions, and make their prejudices clash with those of other peoples, they detect at home points which certainly escape the notice of their fellow-citizens. But in order to go further, they would have required to lay their nationality aside, to which, of course, they would never have consented, and I could not blame them.

I persist, therefore, in my belief that a stranger is better able to judge of a country than the inhabitants themselves, especially if he be careful to surround himself with those national lights and documents to which I feel myself so greatly indebted. He still incurs the danger, I grant, of confounding the spirit of the institutions he is studying for the first time with that of the civilisation under which he has hitherto lived; but English civilisation is so clearly defined, so absolute and personal, that this danger is not so great here as elsewhere. Those national enmities will remain which, I confess, still live in the heart of some men, and oppose a wall of prejudice to the healthy appreciation of facts. Thank Heaven, however, this last obstacle is being removed day by day, and the peoples may still regard themselves as the different branches of the same tree, and be anxious to maintain those differences. There may be some Frenchmen left who foster the wound of Waterloo, and regard England through the bad reminiscences of history; but their number diminishes as the feeling of humanity extends. All political parties in Europe are interested in England being great, free, and flourishing, were it only from the selfish hope of finding there a refuge, a sacred island, on the day of defeat and shipwreck.

My readers may possibly be surprised that in these essays I have dwelt exclusively on the external pictures of English life, instead of going at once to the spirit of the national character and the manner in which it was formed. It appeared to me, however, that, before seeking the causes of a civilisation, it was first right to strike a balance between the different principles which compose it. Where I have reviewed the most interesting branches of English industry — the scenes of agricultural and maritime life, the theatres, hospitals, prisons, the manners of the different classes of society, the sports, &c.—and I have much to do ere that is completed—it will be time to seek in the history and political economy of the country the root of all these complicated manifestations.

England is not merely great because she has mines full of coal, the seas covered with her ships, and her colonies extending to the extremities of the universe. All this is a great deal, doubtless, but she would never have torn from nature all her wealth, had it not been for the support and aid of her liberal institutions. Liberty has been hitherto the Cape of Tempests to the continental nations that have sought it, but to England, who has found it, and been so happy as to keep it, it has been a haven.

For France, then, I intend to continue my task. It will be for my English readers to say whether they are anxious to receive a further instalment of a Frenchman's impressions about the ENGLISH AT HOME.

THE END.

C. WHITING, BEAUFORT HOUSE, STRAND.

CATALOGUE OF BOOKS

PUBLISHED BY

CHAPMAN AND HALL,

193, PICCADILLY.

August, 1861.

August, 1861.

A List of New Works & New Editions

PUBLISHED BY CHAPMAN & HALL.

NEW WORK BY MR. CHARLES DICKENS.

Third Edition, in 3 vols., post 8vo., cloth.

GREAT EXPECTATIONS.

By CHARLES DICKENS. *[Just Published.*

NEW WORK BY MR. W. H. AINSWORTH.

In 3 vols., post 8vo., cloth, with Illustrations by John Gilbert.

THE CONSTABLE OF THE TOWER.

AN HISTORICAL ROMANCE.

By W. H. AINSWORTH. *[Just Published.*

Second Edition, in fcap. 8vo., cloth, price 3s. 6d.

TANNHAÜSER;

OR, THE BATTLE OF THE BARDS. A POEM.

By NEVILLE TEMPLE and EDWARD TREVOR.

[Just Published.

Second Edition, in 2 vols., fcap 8vo., cloth, price 16s.

LA BEATA: A NOVEL.

By T. A. TROLLOPE.

In post 8vo., cloth, price 6s.

FORAYS AMONG SALMON AND DEER.

By J. CONWAY.

In post 8vo., cloth, with Illustrations, price 10s. 6d.

OUR CRUISE IN THE CLAYMORE;

WITH A VISIT TO DAMASCUS AND THE LEBANON.

By MRS. HARVEY, of Ickwell-Bury.

In fcap. 8vo., cloth, price 4s.

OURSELVES, OUR FOOD, AND OUR PHYSIC.

By DR. BENJAMIN RIDGE.

August, 1861.

A CATALOGUE OF BOOKS

PUBLISHED BY

CHAPMAN AND HALL,

193, PICCADILLY.

ALL THE YEAR ROUND.
Conducted by CHARLES DICKENS. Vols. I. to V., handsomely bound. **5s. 6d. each.**

ALISON — THE PHILOSOPHY AND HISTORY OF
CIVILISATION. By ALEXANDER ALISON. Demy 8vo. cloth. **14s.**

A PACKET OF SEEDS SAVED BY AN OLD GAR-
DENER. Second Edition, Enlarged. Crown 8vo. bds. **1s. 6d.**

A SERIES OF DIAGRAMS,
ILLUSTRATIVE OF THE PRINCIPLES OF MECHANICAL PHILOSOPHY AND
THEIR APPLICATION. Twenty-one large Plates, drawn on Stone. With descriptive
Letterpress. Published under the superintendence of the Society for the Diffusion of Useful
Knowledge. One large folio Volume, cloth. **2l. 12s. 6d.**

ATLASES AND MAPS,
FOR STUDENTS AND TRAVELLERS; with Railways and Telegraphs, accurately
laid down.

SHARPE'S ATLAS. Constructed upon a System of Scale and Proportion,
from the more recent Authorities. With a Copious Index. Fifty-four Maps. Large folio,
half morocco, plain, **36s.**; coloured, **42s.**

SHARPE'S STUDENT'S ATLAS. With a Copious Index. Twenty-six
Coloured Maps, selected from the above. Folio, half-bound. **21s.**

LOWRY'S TABLE ATLAS. With a Copious Index. One Hundred
Coloured Maps. Large 4to. half-bound. **12s.**

SIDNEY HALL'S TRAVELLING ATLAS OF THE ENGLISH
COUNTIES, containing Fifty Maps, bound in a portable 8vo. Volume, in roan tuck.
10s. 6d.

SIDNEY HALL'S ATLAS OF THE ENGLISH COUNTIES, Enlarged
Series, with General Maps of Great Britain, Scotland, Ireland, and Wales. 4to. half-bound,
24s., and folio, half-bound, **24s.**

ATLASES AND MAPS—*continued.*

SIDNEY HALL'S MAPS OF ENGLISH COUNTIES, Enlarged Series,
with all the Railways and Country Seats. Coloured, in neat wrapper, price 6*d.* each.

SHARPE'S TRAVELLING MAP OF ENGLAND AND WALES, with
Railways and Electric Telegraph laid down to the present time. Coloured and mounted,
in cloth case, 2*s.* 6*d.*

SHARPE'S TRAVELLING MAP OF SCOTLAND, with Railways and
Electric Telegraph laid down to the present time. Coloured and mounted, in cloth case,
1*s.* 6*d.*

SHARPE'S TRAVELLING MAP OF IRELAND, with Railways and
Electric Telegraph laid down to the present time. Coloured and mounted, in cloth case,
1*s.* 6*d.*

LOWRY'S ATLAS OF INDIA. In Eight Maps. Royal 4to., Coloured,
in wrapper, price 1*s.*

1. INDIA, General Map.
2. AFGHANISTAN.
3. BELOOCHISTAN.
4. NORTH-WEST PROVINCES.
5. BOMBAY.
6. NEPAUL.
7. BENGAL.
8. MADRAS.

SHARPE'S ATLAS OF INDIA. In Six Maps. Large folio, Coloured,
in wrapper, price 2*s.* 6*d.*

1. INDIA, General Map.
2. BENGAL, &c.
3. CENTRAL INDIA.
4. THE CARNATIC, &c.
5. BELOOCHISTAN AND SCINDE.
6. AFGHANISTAN AND THE PUNJAB.

AUSTIN — TWO LETTERS ON GIRLS' SCHOOLS,
And on the Training of Working Women. By MRS. AUSTIN. Post 8vo. sewed. 1*s.*

BAGEHOT — ESTIMATES OF SOME ENGLISHMEN
AND SCOTCHMEN . A Series of Essays contributed principally to the 'National Review.'
By WALTER BAGEHOT. Demy 8vo. cloth. 14*s.*

BAILEY — FESTUS; A POEM.
By PHILIP JAMES BAILEY. 12mo. cloth. 8*s.* 6*d.*

———— THE MYSTIC, AND OTHER POEMS.
By PHILIP JAMES BAILEY. Second Edition, post 8vo. cloth. 5*s.*

———— THE AGE; A COLLOQUIAL SATIRE.
By PHILIP JAMES BAILEY. Post 8vo. cloth. 6*s.* 6*d.*

BARHAM — PHILADELPHIA; OR, THE CLAIMS OF
HUMANITY · A PLEA FOR SOCIAL AND RELIGIOUS REFORM. By THOMAS
FOSTER BARHAM, M.B. Cantab. Post 8vo. cloth. 6*s.* 6*d.*

BARRY CORNWALL — DRAMATIC SCENES, WITH
OTHER POEMS. Now first printed. By BARRY CORNWALL. Beautifully Illustrated with Fifty-seven Woodcuts, and printed on fine paper. In One Volume. Crown 8vo. cloth. 18s.

———————————— ENGLISH SONGS, AND
OTHER POEMS. By BARRY CORNWALL. New Edition, 24mo. sewed. 2s. 6d.

BARWELL — THE CARE OF THE SICK:
Being the Substance of a Course of Lectures delivered at the Working Women's College. By RICHARD BARWELL, F.R.C.S. In One Volume, fcap. cloth. 1s. 6d.

BARWELL — CHILDHOOD'S HOURS.
By Mrs. BARWELL. With Four Illustrations. Fcap 8vo. cloth. 1s. 6d.

——————— NOVEL ADVENTURES OF TOM
THUMB THE GREAT. Showing how he visited the Insect World, and learned much Wisdom. By Mrs. BARWELL. New Edition. Eight Illustrations, 16mo. cloth. 1s. 6d.

——————— NURSERY GOVERNMENT;
Or, HINTS ADDRESSED TO MOTHERS AND NURSERYMAIDS ON THE MANAGEMENT OF YOUNG CHILDREN. By Mrs. BARWELL. Second Edition. Corrected and Enlarged. Fcap. 8vo. cloth. 1s.

BELLEW — LIFE IN CHRIST, AND CHRIST IN
LIFE. A NEW VOLUME OF SERMONS. By the Rev. J. M. BELLEW. 8vo. cloth. 12s.

BENNETT (W. C.) — THE WORN WEDDING-RING,
AND OTHER POEMS. By W. C. BENNETT. Post 8vo. cloth. 3s. 6d.

———————————— QUEEN ELEANOR'S VENGE-
ANCE, AND OTHER POEMS. By W. C. BENNETT. Fcap. 8vo. cloth. 3s. 6d.

———————————— SONGS BY A SONG-WRITER.
First Hundred. By W. C. BENNETT. Post 8vo. cloth. 3s. 6d.

———————————— BABY MAY, AND OTHER
POEMS ON INFANTS. Fcap. sewed. 1s.

BENNETT (C. H.) — PROVERBS WITH PICTURES.
By CHARLES H. BENNETT. With about 250 Illustrations, fcap. boards. 7s. 6d.

BLANC — HISTORICAL REVELATIONS.
Inscribed to Lord Normanby. By LOUIS BLANC. Post 8vo. cloth. 10s. 6d.

BONER — CHAMOIS HUNTING IN THE MOUN-
TAINS OF BAVARIA. By CHARLES BONER. With Illustrations by THEODORE HORSCHELT, of Munich. New Edition. With Additions. Post 8vo. cloth. 10s.

BORDER LANDS OF SPAIN AND FRANCE (THE);
WITH AN ACCOUNT OF A VISIT TO THE REPUBLIC OF ANDORRE. Post 8vo.
cloth. 10s. 6d.

BROWNING (E. B.) — POEMS BEFORE CONGRESS.
By ELIZABETH BARRETT BROWNING. Crown 8vo. cloth. 4s.

———————————— POETICAL WORKS.
By ELIZABETH BARRETT BROWNING. Fourth Edition, with Corrections and Additions. Three vols. fcap. cloth. 18s.

———————————— AURORA LEIGH; A POEM.
IN NINE BOOKS. By ELIZABETH BARRETT BROWNING. Fifth Edition, with
Portrait of Mrs. Browning. One vol. fcap. cloth. 7s.

BROWNING (ROBERT) — POETICAL WORKS.
By ROBERT BROWNING. A New Edition, with numerous Alterations and Additions.
Two vols. fcap. cloth. 16s.

———————————— CHRISTMAS EVE AND
EASTER DAY. A POEM. By ROBERT BROWNING. Fcap. 8vo. cloth. 6s.

———————————— MEN AND WOMEN.
BY ROBERT BROWNING. In two vols. fcap. 8vo. cloth. 12s.

BURCHETT — LINEAR PERSPECTIVE.
For the Use of Schools of Art. By R. BURCHETT, Head Master of the Training Schools
for Art Masters of the Science and Art Department. Fifth Edition. Post 8vo. cloth, with
Illustrations. 7s.

———————————— PRACTICAL GEOMETRY.
THE COURSE OF CONSTRUCTION OF PLANE GEOMETRICAL FIGURES. By
R. BURCHETT. With 137 Diagrams. Fourth Edition. Post 8vo. cloth. 5s.

———————————— DEFINITIONS OF GEOMETRY.
32mo. sewed. 5d.

BUTT — THE HISTORY OF ITALY FROM THE
ABDICATION OF NAPOLEON I. With Introductory References to that of Earlier
Times. Two vols. 8vo. cloth. 36s.

CECILIA METELLA;
Or, ROME ENSLAVED. Post 8vo. cloth. 10s. 6d.

COLERIDGE — SEVEN LECTURES ON SHAKE-
SPEARE AND MILTON. By the late S. T. COLERIDGE. A list of all the MS. Emen-
dations in Mr. COLLIER'S Folio, 1632; and an Introductory Preface by J. PAYNE
COLLIER, Esq. Demy 8vo. cloth. 12s.

COLLINS — A NEW SENTIMENTAL JOURNEY.
By CHARLES ALLSTON COLLINS. With Two Illustrations by the Author. Post 8vo.
cloth. 3s.

MR. THOMAS CARLYLE'S WORKS.

UNIFORM EDITION.

Handsomely printed in Crown Octavo, price Six Shillings per Volume.

THE FRENCH REVOLUTION: A HISTORY. In 2 Volumes. 12s.

OLIVER CROMWELL'S LETTERS AND SPEECHES. With Eluci-
dations and Connecting Narrative. In 3 Volumes. 18s.

LIFE OF JOHN STERLING. }
LIFE OF SCHILLER. } One Vol. 6s.

CRITICAL AND MISCELLANEOUS ESSAYS. In 4 Volumes. 24s.

SARTOR RESARTUS. }
HERO WORSHIP. } One Volume. 6s.

LATTER-DAY PAMPHLETS. One Volume. 6s.

CHARTISM. }
PAST AND PRESENT. } One Volume. 6s.

TRANSLATIONS OF GERMAN ROMANCE. One Volume. 6s.

WILHELM MEISTER. By GÖTHE. A Translation. In 2 Volumes. 12s.

CARLYLE—HISTORY OF FRIEDRICH THE SECOND,
called FREDERICK THE GREAT. By THOMAS CARLYLE. With Portraits and Maps.
Third Edition. Vols. I. and II., demy 8vo., cloth. 40s. Vols. III. and IV. in the Press.

—————— PASSAGES SELECTED FROM THE
WRITINGS of THOMAS CARLYLE, with a Biographical Memoir by T. BALLANTYNE.
Post 8vo., cloth. 7s.

COOPER—THE PURGATORY OF SUICIDES.
By THOMAS COOPER. A New Edition. Fcap. cloth. 7s. 6d.

CRAIK—THE ENGLISH OF SHAKESPEARE;
Illustrated in a Philological Commentary on his Tragedy of 'Julius Cæsar.' By GEORGE
LILLIE CRAIK, Professor of History and of English Literature in Queen's College,
Belfast. Second Edition. Post 8vo., cloth. 5s.

—————— OUTLINES OF THE HISTORY OF THE
ENGLISH LANGUAGE. For the Use of the Junior Classes in Colleges, and the Higher
Classes in Schools. By GEORGE L. CRAIK. Fourth Edition, revised and improved. Post
8vo., cloth. 2s. 6d.

A 3

CHAPMAN AND HALL'S
SELECT LIBRARY OF FICTION.
PRICE TWO SHILLINGS EACH NOVEL.

MARY BARTON: a Tale of Manchester Life.

RUTH. A Novel. By the Author of 'Mary Barton.'

CRANFORD. By the Author of 'Mary Barton.'

LIZZIE LEIGH; and other Tales. By the Author of ' Barton.'

THE HEAD OF THE FAMILY. A Novel.

AGATHA'S HUSBAND. By the Author of ' John Halifax Gentleman.'

OLIVE. A Novel. By the Author of ' The Head of the Family.

THE OGILVIES. A Novel. By the Author of ' The Head o the Family.'

ALTON LOCKE : Tailor and Poet. By the Rev. CHAR KINGSLEY. With a new Preface, addressed to the Working Men of Great Britain.

THE FALCON FAMILY; or, Young Ireland. A Satirical Novel By M. W. SAVAGE.

THE BACHELOR OF THE ALBANY. By M. W. SAVAGE.

MY UNCLE THE CURATE. A Novel. By M. W. SAVAGE.

THE HALF SISTERS. A Tale. By Miss JEWSBURY.

THE WHITEBOY: A Story of Ireland in 1822. By Mrs S. C. HALL.

EUSTACE CONYERS. By JAMES HANNAY.

MARETIMO : A Story of Adventure. By BAYLE ST. JOHN.

MELINCOURT. By the Author of 'Headlong Hall.'

THE BLITHEDALE ROMANCE. By NATHANIEL HAWTHORNE.

₊ *Other Popular Novels will be issued in this Series.*

Notices of the Press.

'The Fictions published by this Firm in their "Select Library" have all been of a high character.'—*Press.*

' Who would be satisfied with the much-thumbed "Library Book," when he can procure, in one handsome volume, a celebrated Work of Fiction now offered by Messrs. Chapman and Hall at the low price of Two Shillings?'—*Britannia.*

'Capital Novels, well worth the price asked for them.'—*Guardian.*

CHAPMAN AND HALL'S
STANDARD EDITIONS OF POPULAR AUTHORS.

SS ANNA DRURY'S MISREPRESENTATION. Second Edition. 5s.

ILBURY NOGO. By the Author of 'Digby Grand.' 5s.

ANTHONY TROLLOPE'S CASTLE RICHMOND. A Novel. New Edition. 5s.

THONY TROLLOPE'S DOCTOR THORNE. A Novel. Sixth Edition. 5s.

NTHONY TROLLOPE'S THE BERTRAMS. A Novel. Fifth Edition. 5s.

ANTHONY TROLLOPE'S THE KELLYS and THE O'KELLYS. Fourth Edition. 5s.

NTHONY TROLLOPE'S MACDERMOTS OF BALLYCLORAN. Third Edition. 5s.

. M. THACKERAY'S IRISH SKETCH-BOOK. With Illustrations by the Author. Third Edition. Crown 8vo. 5s.

BERT SMITH'S WILD OATS AND DEAD LEAVES. Second Edition. Crown 8vo. 5s.

IRS. GASKELL'S NORTH AND SOUTH. Fourth Edition. 5s.

. A. SALA'S GASLIGHT AND DAYLIGHT; with some London Scenes they Shine upon. Second Edition. 5s.

. H. WILLS' OLD LEAVES GATHERED FROM 'HOUSEHOLD WORDS.' 5s.

OBERT HOUDIN'S MEMOIRS : Ambassador, Author, and Conjuror. Written by HIMSELF. Third Edition. 5s.

ISS MULOCH'S HEAD OF THE FAMILY. Sixth Edition. 5s.

ENRY MORLEY'S GOSSIP. Second Edition. 5s.

A 4

WORKS BY MR. CHARLES DICKENS.

ORIGINAL EDITIONS.

THE PICKWICK PAPERS. With Forty-three Illustra
tions by Seymour and 'Phiz.' 8vo. 1l. 1s.

NICHOLAS NICKLEBY. With Forty Illustrations b
'Phiz.' 8vo. 1l. 1s.

SKETCHES BY 'BOZ.' A New Edition, with F
Illustrations by George Cruikshank. 8vo. 1l. 1s.

MARTIN CHUZZLEWIT. With Forty Illustrations b
'Phiz.' 8vo. 1l. 1s.

THE OLD CURIOSITY SHOP. With Seventy-five Ill
trations by George Cattermole and H. K. Browne. Imperial 8vo. 13s.

BARNABY RUDGE: A Tale of the Riots of 'Eight
With Seventy-eight Illustrations by G. Cattermole and H. K. Browne. Imperial 8vo.

AMERICAN NOTES, for General Circulation. F
Edition. 2 vols., post 8vo. 1l. 1s.

OLIVER TWIST ; or, the Parish-Boy's Progress. Ill
trated by George Cruikshank. Third Edition. 3 vols., post 8vo. 1l. 5s.

OLIVER TWIST. 1 vol. 8vo., cloth. Illustrated. 11s.

DOMBEY AND SON. With Forty Illustrations by 'Phiz.
8vo., cloth. 1l. 1s.

BLEAK HOUSE. With Forty Illustrations by 'Phiz.
8vo., cloth. 1l. 1s.

LITTLE DORRIT. With Forty Illustrations by 'Phiz.
8vo., cloth. 1l. 1s.

HARD TIMES. Small 8vo., cloth. 5s.

THE UNCOMMERCIAL TRAVELLER. Third Edition
Post 8vo., cloth. 6s.

A TALE OF TWO CITIES. With Sixteen Illustratio
by 'Phiz.' 8vo. 9s.

CHILD'S HISTORY OF ENGLAND. 3 vols., sq
cloth. 10s. 6d.

CHRISTMAS CAROL. With Illustrations. Fcap. 8vo.
cloth. 5s.

CRICKET ON THE HEARTH. With Illustrations. Fcap
8vo., cloth. 5s.

THE CHIMES. With Illustrations. Fcap. 8vo., cloth. 5s

THE BATTLE OF LIFE. With Illustrations. Fcap. 8vo
cloth. 5s.

THE HAUNTED MAN AND THE GHOST'S BARGAIN
With Illustrations. Fcap. 8vo., cloth. 5s.

WORKS BY MR. CHARLES DICKENS.

THE ILLUSTRATED LIBRARY EDITION,

Beautifully printed in Post Octavo, and carefully revised by the Author. With the Original Illustrations. Now issuing in Monthly Volumes, price 7s. 6d. each.

Already Published.

PICKWICK PAPERS	2 vols.	15s.
NICHOLAS NICKLEBY	2 vols.	15s.
MARTIN CHUZZLEWIT	2 vols.	15s.
OLD CURIOSITY SHOP	2 vols.	15s.

To be followed by

BARNABY RUDGE	2 vols.
SKETCHES BY BOZ	1 vol.
OLIVER TWIST	1 vol.
DOMBEY AND SON	2 vols.
DAVID COPPERFIELD	2 vols.
PICTURES FROM ITALY, and AMERICAN NOTES	1 vol.
BLEAK HOUSE	2 vols.
LITTLE DORRIT	2 vols.
CHRISTMAS BOOKS	1 vol.

CHEAP AND UNIFORM EDITION.

Handsomely printed in Crown Octavo, cloth, with Frontispieces.

	s.	d.
THE PICKWICK PAPERS	5	0
NICHOLAS NICKLEBY	5	0
MARTIN CHUZZLEWIT	5	0
BARNABY RUDGE	4	0
OLD CURIOSITY SHOP	4	0
OLIVER TWIST	3	6
SKETCHES BY BOZ	3	6
CHRISTMAS BOOKS	3	6
AMERICAN NOTES	2	6
DOMBEY AND SON	5	0
DAVID COPPERFIELD	5	0
BLEAK HOUSE	5	0

MR. DICKENS' READINGS. Fcap. 8vo.

A CHRISTMAS CAROL IN PROSE	1	0
THE CRICKET ON THE HEARTH	1	0
THE CHIMES	1	0
THE STORY OF LITTLE DOMBEY	1	0
THE POOR TRAVELLER, BOOTS AT THE HOLLY-TREE INN, AND MRS. GAMP	1	0

DANTE'S DIVINE COMEDY, THE 'INFERNO.
A Literal Prose Translation, with the Text of the Original Collated with the best Editions, and Explanatory Notes. By JOHN A. CARLYLE, M.D. Post 8vo., with a Portrait, cloth. 14s.

DANTE'S DIVINE COMEDY;
Or, THE INFERNO, PURGATORY, AND PARADISE. Rendered into English Metre, by FREDERICK POLLOCK. With Fifty Illustrations, drawn by GEORGE SCHARF, Jun. Post 8vo., cloth. 14s.

DAVIDSON—DRAWING FOR ELEMENTARY SCHOOLS.
By ELLIS A. DAVIDSON, Head-Master of the Chester School of Art. Published under the sanction of the Science and Art Department of the Committee of Council on Education. Post 8vo., cloth. 3s.

DE PONTÈS—POETS AND POETRY OF GERMANY.
BIOGRAPHICAL AND CRITICAL NOTICES. By Madame L. DAVESIES DE PONTÈS. Two volumes, post 8vo. cloth. 18s.

DIETRICH—RUSSIAN POPULAR TALES.
Translated from the German version of ANTON DIETRICH. With an introduction by JACOB GRIMM. Post 8vo. cloth. 5s.

DIREY—GRAMMAIRE FRANÇAISE.
Par L. DIREY. 12mo. cloth. 3s.

———— LATIN GRAMMAR.
By L. DIREY. 12mo. cloth. 4s.

———— AND FOGGO'S ENGLISH GRAMMAR.
12mo. cloth. 3s.

DIXON—ROBERT BLAKE, ADMIRAL AND GENE-
RAL AT SEA. Based on Family and State Papers. By HEPWORTH DIXON, Author of 'Life of William Penn.' Cheap edition, post 8vo. boards. 2s. Post 8vo. cloth, with portrait. 3s. 6d.

———— WILLIAM PENN.
AN HISTORICAL BIOGRAPHY. By WILLIAM HEPWORTH DIXON, Author of 'Life of Howard.' With a portrait. Second edition, fcap. 8vo. cloth. 7s.

DRAYSON — PRACTICAL MILITARY SURVEYING
AND SKETCHING. By Captain DRAYSON, R.A. With illustrations. Post 8vo. cloth. 4s. 6d.

DYCE'S ELEMENTARY OUTLINES OF ORNAMENT.
Fifty selected plates. Folio, sewed. 5s.

EDINBURGH TALES.
In one thick volume, imperial 8vo. full gilt back. 8s. 6d.

ELEMENTARY DRAWING BOOK.
Directions for introducing the First Steps of Elementary Drawing in Schools, and among Workmen. With Lists of Materials, Objects, and Models. Prepared and published at the request of the Council of the Society of Arts. Small 4to. cloth. 4s. 6d.

ESQUIROS—THE ENGLISH AT HOME.
By ALPHONSE ESQUIROS. Translated by LASCELLES WRAXALL. 2 vols. post 8vo. cloth. 18s.

FAIRHOLT—COSTUME IN ENGLAND.
A History of Dress, from the Earliest Period until the close of the Eighteenth Century; with a Glossary of Terms for all Articles of Use or Ornament worn about the Person. By F. W. FAIRHOLT, F.S.A. With nearly 700 Engravings, drawn on Wood by the Author. Second edition, crown 8vo. cloth. 16s.

————————TOBACCO: ITS HISTORY AND ASSO-
CIATIONS. Including an account of the Plant and its Manufacture, with its Mode of Use in all Ages and Countries. By F. W. FAIRHOLT, F.S.A. With 100 Illustrations by the Author. Post 8vo. cloth. 9s.

————————THE HOME OF SHAKESPEARE,
ILLUSTRATED AND DESCRIBED. By F. W. FAIRHOLT, F.S.A., Author of 'Costume in England,' &c. With 33 Engravings. Small 8vo., sewed. 2s. 6d.

FINLAISON — NEW GOVERNMENT SUCCESSION-
DUTY TABLES. For the Use of Successors to Property, their Solicitors and Agents, and others concerned in the Payment of the Duties Levied on all Successions, under Authority of the present Statute, 16 & 17 Victoria, cap. 51. By ALEXANDER GLEN FINLAISON. Post 8vo. cloth. 5s.

FOSTER—HISTORY OF ENGLAND FOR SCHOOLS
AND FAMILIES. By A. F. FOSTER. With numerous Illustrations. Post 8vo. cloth. 6s.

FROM HAY-TIME TO HOPPING.
By the Author of 'Our Farm of Four Acres.' Second edition, small 8vo. cloth. 5s.

GALLENGA—THE HISTORY OF PIEDMONT.
By ANTONIO GALLENGA, Member of the Sardinian Parliament, &c. In 3 vols. crown 8vo. cloth. 24s.

GARDEN THAT PAID THE RENT (THE).
Fourth edition, post 8vo. boards. 2s.

GASKELL.—CRANFORD—MARY BARTON—RUTH—
LIZZIE LEIGH. By Mrs. GASKELL. Post 8vo. boards. Price 2s. each.

GASKELL—NORTH AND SOUTH.
Fourth and cheaper edition. Crown 8vo. cloth. 5s.

—————————MOORLAND COTTAGE.
With Illustrations by BIRKET FOSTER. Fcap. 8vo. cloth. 2s. 6d.

GERMAN LOVE.
FROM THE PAPERS OF AN ALIEN. Translated by SUSANNA WINKWO
with the sanction of the Author. Fcap. cloth. 4s. 6d.

HAND (THE) PHRENOLOGICALLY CONSIDERED.
Being a Glimpse at the Relation of the Mind with the Organization of the Body.
8vo. with Four Plates, cloth. 4s. 6d.

HAWKINS — A COMPARATIVE VIEW OF
ANIMAL AND HUMAN FRAME. By B. WATERHOUSE HAWKINS, F.L.S., F.G
with Ten Illustrations from Nature by the Author. Folio, cloth. 12s.

HAXTHAUSEN—THE RUSSIAN EMPIRE.
ITS PEOPLE, INSTITUTIONS, AND RESOURCES. By Baron VON HAXTHAUS
Author of 'Transcaucasia,' &c. Translated and issued under the immediate sanction
the Author. In 2 vols. 8vo. cloth. 28s.

——————————TRANSCAUCASIA.
Sketches of the Nations and Races between the Black Sea and the Caspian. By
VON HAXTHAUSEN. With Eight Coloured Illustrations by GRAEB. 8vo. cloth. 18

——————————THE TRIBES OF THE CAUCASUS
WITH AN ACCOUNT OF SCHAMYL AND THE MURIDS. By BARON VO
HAXTHAUSEN. Post 8vo., cloth. 5s.

HEATON—THE THRESHOLD OF CHEMISTRY;
An Experimental Introduction to the Science. By CHARLES HEATON. With numer
ous Illustrations. Post 8vo., cloth. 4s.

HEINRICH HEINE'S BOOK OF SONGS.
A Translation. By JOHN E. WALLIS. Crown 8vo., cloth. 9s.

HENSLOW—ILLUSTRATIONS TO BE EMPLOYE
IN THE PRACTICAL LESSONS ON BOTANY. Adapted to all classes. Prepared f
the South Kensington Museum. By the Rev. PROFESSOR HENSLOW. With Illustra
tions. Post 8vo. 6d.

HOUSEHOLD WORDS (THE).
Conducted by CHARLES DICKENS. 19 vols., royal 8vo, cloth. 5s. 6d. each. (All th
back Numbers and Parts may now be had.)

HOUSEHOLD WORDS (THE)—CHRISTMAS STORIES
FROM. Royal 8vo., cloth. 2s. 6d.

INDUSTRIAL AND SOCIAL POSITION OF WOMEN,
IN THE MIDDLE AND LOWER RANKS. Post 8vo., cloth. 10s. 6d.

JERVIS—THE RIFLE-MUSKET.
A Practical Treatise on the Enfield-Prichett Rifle, recently adopted in the British Service. By CAPTAIN JERVIS WHITE JERVIS, M.P., Royal Artillery, Author of the 'Manual of Field Operations.' Second and Cheaper Edition, with Additions. Post 8vo., cloth. 2s.

————OUR ENGINES OF WAR, AND HOW WE
GOT TO MAKE THEM. By CAPTAIN JERVIS WHITE JERVIS, M.P., Royal Artillery. With many Illustrations. Post 8vo., cloth. 6s.

JEWSBURY—THE HALF-SISTERS.
A Novel. By GERALDINE E. JEWSBURY. Cheap Edition. Post 8vo, boards. 2s.

JOHNSON—A WINTER'S SKETCHES IN THE SOUTH
OF FRANCE AND THE PYRENEES. With Remarks upon the Use of the Climate and Mineral Waters in the Cure of Disease. By FREDERICK H. JOHNSON, M.R.C.S. ENG., L.A.C., formerly President of the Hunterian Society of Edinburgh. Crown 8vo., cloth. 8s. 6d.

KEIGHTLEY—THE LIFE, OPINIONS, AND WRIT-
INGS OF JOHN MILTON. With an Introduction to 'Paradise Lost.' By THOMAS KEIGHTLEY. Second Edition. Demy 8vo., cloth. 10s. 6d.

————THE POEMS OF JOHN MILTON.
WITH NOTES by THOMAS KEIGHTLEY. 2 vols., 8vo., cloth. 21s.

KELLY—LIFE IN VICTORIA IN 1853 AND IN 1858.
By THOMAS KELLY. 2 vols., post 8vo., cloth. 21s.

KINGSLEY—ALTON LOCKE; TAILOR AND POET.
An Autobiography. By the Rev. CHARLES KINGSLEY. Cheap Edition. Post 8vo., boards. 2s.

KOHL—KITCHI-GAMI:
WANDERINGS ROUND LAKE SUPERIOR. By J. G. KOHL. With Woodcuts. 8vo. cloth. 13s.

LEAVES FROM THE DIARY OF AN OFFICER OF
THE GUARDS DURING THE PENINSULAR WAR. By LIEUT.-COL. STEPNEY COWELL STEPNEY, K.H., late Coldstream Guards. Fcap., cloth. 5s.

LENNARD—TALES FROM MOLIÈRE'S PLAYS.
By DACRE BARRETT LENNARD. Post 8vo., cloth. 10s. 6d.

LEWIS—CHESS FOR BEGINNERS;
In a Series of Progressive Lessons. With Twenty-four Diagrams printed in Colours. By WILLIAM LEWIS. Third Edition. Small 4to., cloth. 2s. 6d.

MR. CHARLES LEVER'S WORKS.
LIBRARY EDITION. =
IN DEMY OCTAVO, ILLUSTRATED BY PHIZ.

ONE OF THEM. Demy 8vo., cloth. With 30 Illustrations
16s.

DAVENPORT DUNN; A Man of Our Day. 1 Thick Vol.
demy 8vo., cloth. With 44 Illustrations. 23s.

THE MARTINS OF CRO' MARTIN. 2 Vols. With 40 Ill
trations. 14s.

HARRY LORREQUER. 1 Vol. With 22 Illustrations. 7s.

CHARLES O'MALLEY, THE IRISH DRAGOON. 2 Vo
With 44 Illustrations. 14s.

JACK HINTON, THE GUARDSMAN. 1 Vol. With 2
Illustrations. 7s.

TOM BURKE OF 'OURS.' 2 Vols. With 44 Illustrations
14s.

THE O'DONOGHUE: A TALE OF IRELAND FIFTY YEARS AGO
1 Vol. With 26 Illustrations. 7s.

THE KNIGHT OF GWYNNE. 2 Vols. With 40 Illustra
tions. 14s.

ROLAND CASHEL. 2 Vols. With 40 Illustrations. 14s.

THE DALTONS; OR, THREE ROADS IN LIFE. 2 Vols. Wi
44 Illustrations. 14s.

THE DODD FAMILY ABROAD. 2 Vols. With 40 Ill
tions. 14s.

CHEAP· AND UNIFORM EDITION,
WITH ILLUSTRATIONS BY H. K. BROWNE.
This Edition is handsomely printed in Crown Octavo. Each Volume contains
EIGHT ENGRAVINGS BY H. K. BROWNE.
Bound in Cloth. Price 4s.

JACK HINTON. 4s.

TOM BURKE OF 'OURS.' In 2 Vols. 8s.

HARRY LORREQUER. 4s.

CHARLES O'MALLEY, THE IRISH DRAGOON. In
Vols. 8s.

THE O'DONOGHUE. 4s.

THE KNIGHT OF GWYNNE. In 2 Vols. 8s.

ROLAND CASHEL. In 2 Vols. 8s.

THE DALTONS. In 2 Vols. 8s.

THE DODD FAMILY ABROAD. In 2 Vols. 8s.

OWRY'S ATLAS.

With a Copious Index.   100 Coloured Maps.   Large 4to., half-bound.   12s.

A New Series of Maps, in large 4to., price One Penny each Map plain, and Two Pence with the Boundaries coloured, completed in 100 Maps, any of which can be purchased separately, plain 1d., coloured 2d.

LIST OF THE MAPS.

Sheet.		Sheet	
1, 2.	World in Hemispheres—2 Maps.	54, 55.	Turkey in Asia and Western Persia —2 Maps.
3, 4.	World on Mercator's Projection—2 Maps.	56.	Eastern Persia.
5.	Europe.	57, 58.	Syria and Arabia Petræa—2 Maps.
6.	British Isles.	59, 60.	China and Indian Seas—2 Maps.
7, 8.	England and Wales—2 Maps.	61.	Australia and New Zealand—General Map.
9.	Scotland—General.		
10.	Ireland—General.	62, 63.	Australia—2 Maps.
11.	France, in Provinces.	64 to 66.	New South Wales—3 Maps.
12 to 15.	France in Departments—4 Maps.	67.	Victoria or Port Philip District.
16.	Holland and Belgium.	68.	New Zealand.
17.	Spain and Portugal—General.	69, 70.	Polynesia—2 Maps.
18 to 21.	Spain and Portugal—4 Maps.	71, 72.	Africa—2 Maps.
22.	Italy—General.	73 to 75.	Egypt, Nubia, Abyssinia, and Red Sea—3 Maps.
23 to 26.	Italy—4 Maps.		
27.	Prussia and German States.	76, 77.	North Africa—comprising Morocco, Algiers, and Tunis—2 Maps.
28 to 31.	Germany and Switzerland—4 Maps.		
32.	Austrian Empire.	78 to 80.	West Africa—comprising Senegambia, Liberia, Soudan, and Guinea —3 Maps.
33, 34.	Hungary and Transylvania — 2 Maps.		
35.	Turkey in Europe and Greece.	81, 82.	Southern Africa—2 Maps.
36.	Bosphorus and Dardanelles.	83.	British North America.
37.	Greece and the Ionian Islands.	84.	Arctic Regions.
38, 39.	Sweden and Norway—2 Maps.	85, 86.	Canada, New Brunswick, and Nova Scotia—2 Maps.
40.	Denmark.		
41.	Russia in Europe.	87.	North America—General.
42.	Asia, North.	88, 89.	United States—2 Maps—General.
43, 44.	Asia, South, and Indian Seas—2 Maps.	90 to 93.	United States—4 Maps.
		94.	Mexico.
45.	India—General.	95.	West Indies and Central America.
46 to 52.	India—7 Maps.	96.	South America—General.
53.	Persia and Tartary.	97 to 100.	South America—4 Maps.

YTTON—MONEY.

A Comedy, in Five Acts.   By Sir EDWARD BULWER LYTTON.   8vo. sewed.   2s. 6d.

NOT SO BAD AS WE SEEM;

OR, MANY SIDES TO A CHARACTER.   A Comedy, in Five Acts.   By Sir EDWARD BULWER LYTTON.   8vo. sewed.   2s. 6d.

RICHELIEU; OR, THE CONSPIRACY.

Five Acts.   By Sir EDWARD BULWER LYTTON.   8vo. sewed.   2s. 6d.

THE LADY OF LYONS;

OR, LOVE AND PRIDE.   A Play, in Five Acts.   By Sir EDWARD BULWER LYTTON.   8vo. sewed.   2s. 6d.

'CULLAGH — INDUSTRIAL HISTORY OF FREE

NATIONS.   Considered in Relation to their Domestic Institutions and External Policy.   By W. TORRENS M'CULLAGH.   2 vols. 8vo. cloth.   24s.

M'CULLAGH—USE AND STUDY OF HISTORY.
Being the Substance of a Course of Lectures delivered in Dublin. By W. TORREN
M'CULLAGH. Second edition, 8vo. cloth. 10s. 6d.

MACKNIGHT—HISTORY OF THE LIFE AND
OF EDMUND BURKE. By THOMAS MACKNIGHT, Author of 'The Right Hoi
Disraeli, M.P., a Literary and Political Biography;' and 'Thirty Years of Foreign Po
a History of the Secretaryships of the Earl of Aberdeen and Viscount Palmerston.' 3 vo
demy 8vo. cloth, price 56s.

MACREADY—LEAVES FROM THE OLIVE MOUNT.
Poems. By CATHERINE FRANCES B. MACREADY. Fcap. 8vo. cloth. 5s.

MARIOTTI—ITALY IN 1848.
By L. MARIOTTI. 8vo. cloth. 12s.

MARKET HARBOROUGH;
OR, HOW MR. SAWYER WENT TO THE SHIRES. Third edition, post 8vo. cloth.

MAYHEW—PAVED WITH GOLD.
OR, THE ROMANCE AND REALITY OF THE LONDON STREETS. An Unfashionabl
Novel. By AUGUSTUS MAYHEW (one of the Brothers Mayhew). With Twenty-
Illustrations by Phiz. Demy 8vo. cloth. 14s.

MELINCOURT;
OR, SIR ORAN HAUT-TON. By the Author of 'Headlong Hall,' &c. Cheap Edi
Post 8vo. boards. 2s.

MEMOIRS OF ROBERT HOUDIN,
Ambassador, Author, and Conjuror. Written by Himself. Third and cheaper Edition,
crown 8vo. cloth. 5s.

MEMOIRS OF A STOMACH.
Edited by a Minister of the Interior. Ninth edition, fcap. sewed. 1s.

MENZIES—EARLY ANCIENT HISTORY;
Or, The Ante-Greek Period as it appears to us since the most recent Discoveries in Egypt
and Assyria. With References to Wilkinson, Layard, and other authorities. Intended for
popular use. By HENRY MENZIES. 1 vol. post 8vo. 4s. 6d.

MEREDITH (L. A.)—OVER THE STRAITS.
By LOUISA ANNE MEREDITH. With Illustrations. Post 8vo. cloth. 9s.

MEREDITH (OWEN)—LUCILE. A POEM.
By OWEN MEREDITH. Crown 8vo. cloth. 12s.

MEREDITH (OWEN)—SERBSKI PESME;
OR, NATIONAL SONGS OF SERVIA. By OWEN MEREDITH. Fcap. cloth. 4s.

——————————————— THE WANDERER.
A Poem. By the Author of 'Clytemnestra,' &c. Second edition, foolscap 8vo. cloth. 9s. 6d.

MEREDITH (GEORGE)—THE SHAVING OF SHAG-
PAT. An Arabian Entertainment. By GEORGE MEREDITH. Post 8vo. cloth. 10s. 6d.

——————————————— THE ORDEAL OF RICHARD
FEVEREL. By GEORGE MEREDITH. 3 vols. post 8vo. cloth. 31s. 6d.

MICHIELS—SECRET HISTORY OF THE AUSTRIAN
GOVERNMENT, AND OF ITS SYSTEMATIC PERSECUTIONS OF PROTESTANTS.
Compiled from official documents. By ALFRED MICHIELS. Post 8vo. cloth. 10s. 6d.

MILLINGTON—HERALDRY;
IN HISTORY, POETRY, AND ROMANCE. With numerous Illustrations. Post
8vo. 9s.

MISCELLANEA GRAPHICA:
Representations of Ancient, Medieval, and Renaissance Remains, in the possession of Lord
Londesborough. Drawn, Engraved, and Described by FREDERICK W. FAIRHOLT,
F.S.A., Honorary Member of the Society of Antiquaries of Normandy, Picardy, and Poictiers.
The Historical Introduction by THOMAS WRIGHT, M.A., F.S.A., &c., Corresponding
Member of the Institute of France. In one volume, imperial 4to. cloth, price 3l. 16s., with
Forty-six Plates, some of them printed in colour, and numerous Engravings on wood.

MONEY — TWELVE MONTHS WITH THE BASHI-
BAZOUKS. By EDWARD MONEY. With Coloured Illustrations. Post 8vo. cloth. 7s.

MORGAN—THE MIND OF SHAKSPERE, AS EX-
HIBITED IN HIS WORKS. By the Rev. A. A. MORGAN, M.A. Second edition,
foolscap 8vo. cloth. 6s.

MORLEY—OBERON'S HORN;
A BOOK OF FAIRY TALES. By HENRY MORLEY. Illustrated by C. H. Bennett.
Crown 8vo. cloth. 5s.

——————————————— FABLES AND FAIRY TALES.
By HENRY MORLEY. With Thirty Illustrations by Charles Bennett. Post 8vo. cloth. 5s.

MORLEY—MEMOIRS OF BARTHOLOMEW FAIR.

By HENRY MORLEY. With Eighty Illustrations. Demy 8vo. cloth. 21s.

————————THE LIFE OF HENRY CORNELIU

AGRIPPA VON NETTESHEIM, Doctor and Knight, commonly known as a Magician By HENRY MORLEY. In 2 vols. post 8vo. cloth. 18s. ;

—————————JEROME CARDAN.

A BIOGRAPHY. By HENRY MORLEY. Two vols. post 8vo cloth. 18s.

—————————THE LIFE OF BERNARD PALISSY, OF

SAINTES. His Labours and Discoveries in Arts and Science. By HENRY MORLEY. Post 8vo. cloth. Price 12s. Second and cheaper Edition.

—————————HOW TO MAKE HOME UNHEALTHY.

By HENRY MORLEY. Reprinted from the 'Examiner.' Second edition, small 8vo. stiff wrapper. 1s.

—————————GOSSIP.

By HENRY MORLEY. Reprinted from the 'Household Words.' Second and cheaper edition. Crown 8vo. cloth. 5s.

————————— A DEFENCE OF IGNORANCE.

By HENRY MORLEY. Small 8vo. cloth. s.

MULOCH—THE HEAD OF THE FAMILY.

By Miss MULOCH. Sixth edition, crown 8vo. cloth, 5s. Cheap edition, post 8vo. boards. 2s

—————————OLIVE; A NOVEL.

By Miss MULOCH. Cheap edition, post 8vo. boards. 2s.

—————————THE OGILVIES; A NOVEL.

By Miss MULOCH. Cheap edition, post 8vo. boards. 2s.

—————————AGATHA'S HUSBAND.

By Miss MULOCH. Cheap edition, post 8vo. boards. 2s.

MUSHET—BOOK OF SYMBOLS.

A Series of Seventy-five Short Essays on Morals, Religion, and Philosophy. Each Essay Illustrating an Ancient Symbol or Modern Precept. By ROBERT MUSHET. Second edition, post 8vo. cloth. 6s.

NORTON—CHILD OF THE ISLANDS; A POEM.

By the Hon. Mrs. NORTON. Second edition, square 8vo. cloth. 6s.

NUTS AND NUTCRACKERS.

With upwards of 50 Illustrations by PHIZ. Third edition, fcap. boards. 2s.

OUR FARM OF FOUR ACRES, AND THE MONEY

WE MADE BY IT. Seventeenth edition, small post 8vo. boards. 2s.

RAMBLES AND RECOLLECTIONS OF A FLY-

FISHER. Illustrated. With an Appendix, containing ample Instructions to the Novice, inclusive of Fly-making, and a List of really useful Flies. By CLERICUS. With Eight Illustrations. Post 8vo. cloth. 7s.

REDGRAVE—A MANUAL AND CATECHISM ON

COLOUR. By RICHARD REDGRAVE, R.A. 24mo. cloth. 9d.

READING FOR TRAVELLERS.

A NEW LIBRARY OF RAILWAY LITERATURE. Printed in a clear legible Type, expressly adapted to the convenience of Railway Travellers.

OLD ROADS AND NEW ROADS. Fcap. sewed. 1s.

MAGIC AND WITCHCRAFT. Fcap. sewed. 1s.

FRANKLIN'S FOOTSTEPS. By C. R. MARKHAM. Fcap. sewed. 1s. 6d.

THE VILLAGE DOCTOR. Translated by Lady DUFF GORDON. Fcap. sewed. 1s.

MONTENEGRO AND THE SLAVONIANS OF TURKEY. By Count VALERIAN KRASINSKI. Fcap. sewed. 1s. 6d.

CHARACTER AND ANECDOTES OF CHARLES II. By the late CHARLES BARKER, M.A. Fcap. sewed. 1s.

SAMUEL JOHNSON. By THOMAS CARLYLE. Fcap. 1s.

FLORIAN AND CRESCENZ. By BER. AUERBACH. Fcap. sewed. 1s.

THE HUNGARIAN EMIGRATION INTO TURKEY. By a HONVED. Fcap. sewed. 1s.

READING FOR TRAVELLERS—*continued.*

SIR PHILIP SIDNEY AND THE ARCADIA. By JAMES C
Fcap. sewed. 1s.

A VISIT TO BELGRADE. Fcap. sewed. 1s.

BURNS. By THOMAS CARLYLE. Fcap. sewed. 1s.

PICTURES FROM THE EAST. By JOHN CAPPER. Fcap. sewed. 1s.

A VISIT TO THE SEAT OF WAR IN THE NORTH. Fca
sewed. 1s.

CARDINAL WOLSEY ; HIS RISE AND FALL, AS RELATE
BY CAVENDISH. Fcap. sewed. 1s.

ALFIERI ; HIS LIFE, ADVENTURES, AND WORKS. A Sk
by CHARLES MITCHELL CHARLES. Fcap. sewed. 1s.

RIDGE—HEALTH AND DISEASE, THEIR LAWS;
WITH PLAIN PRACTICAL PRESCRIPTIONS FOR THE PEOPLE. By BENJAMIN
RIDGE, M.D., F.R.C.S. Second Edition. Post 8vo., cloth. 12s.

ROBERT MORNAY.
By MAX FERRER. Post 8vo., cloth. 9s.

RODENBERG—THE ISLAND OF THE SAINTS, A
PILGRIMAGE THROUGH IRELAND. By JULIUS RODENBERG. Translated by
LASCELLES WRAXALL. Post 8vo., cloth. 9s.

ROMAN CANDLES.
Post 8vo., cloth. 8s.

ROSCOE—POEMS, TRAGEDIES, AND ESSAYS.
By WILLIAM CALDWELL ROSCOE. Edited, with a Prefatory Memoir, by his
brother-in-law, RICHARD HOLT HUTTON. Two vols. crown 8vo., cloth. 21s.

ROYAL NURSERY A B C BOOK.
With Five Hundred Woodcuts, and Eight Coloured Pages. Crown 8vo., sewed. 1s.

SALA—GASLIGHT AND DAYLIGHT, WITH SOME
LONDON SCENES THEY SHINE UPON. By GEORGE AUGUSTUS SALA. Crown
8vo., cloth. Second Edition. 5s.

ST. JOHN, BAYLE—THE SUBALPINE KINGDOM;
Or, EXPERIENCES AND STUDIES IN SAVOY, PIEDMONT, AND GENOA. By
BAYLE ST. JOHN. 2 vols. Post 8vo., cloth. 21s.

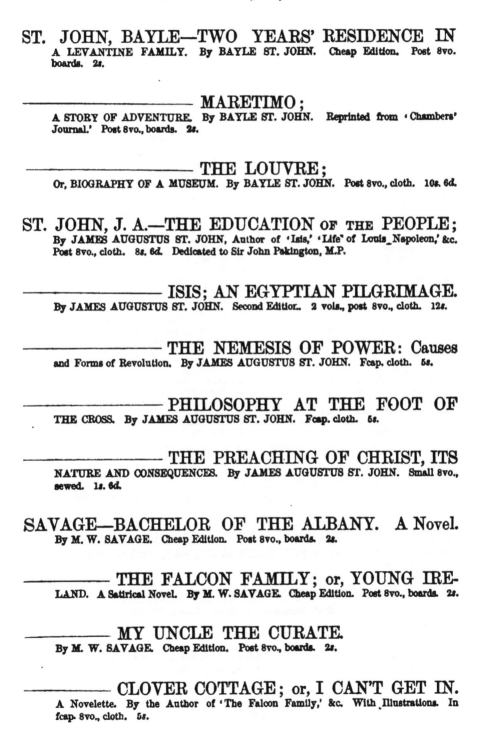

ST. JOHN, BAYLE—TWO YEARS' RESIDENCE IN
A LEVANTINE FAMILY. By BAYLE ST. JOHN. Cheap Edition. Post 8vo.
boards. 2s.

———————————— MARETIMO;
A STORY OF ADVENTURE. By BAYLE ST. JOHN. Reprinted from 'Chambers'
Journal.' Post 8vo., boards. 2s.

———————————— THE LOUVRE;
Or, BIOGRAPHY OF A MUSEUM. By BAYLE ST. JOHN. Post 8vo., cloth. 10s. 6d.

ST. JOHN, J. A.—THE EDUCATION OF THE PEOPLE;
By JAMES AUGUSTUS ST. JOHN, Author of 'Isis,' 'Life' of Louis Napoleon,' &c.
Post 8vo., cloth. 8s. 6d. Dedicated to Sir John Pakington, M.P.

———————————— ISIS; AN EGYPTIAN PILGRIMAGE.
By JAMES AUGUSTUS ST. JOHN. Second Edition. 2 vols., post 8vo., cloth. 12s.

———————————— THE NEMESIS OF POWER: Causes
and Forms of Revolution. By JAMES AUGUSTUS ST. JOHN. Fcap. cloth. 5s.

———————————— PHILOSOPHY AT THE FOOT OF
THE CROSS. By JAMES AUGUSTUS ST. JOHN. Fcap. cloth. 5s.

———————————— THE PREACHING OF CHRIST, ITS
NATURE AND CONSEQUENCES. By JAMES AUGUSTUS ST. JOHN. Small 8vo.,
sewed. 1s. 6d.

SAVAGE—BACHELOR OF THE ALBANY. A Novel.
By M. W. SAVAGE. Cheap Edition. Post 8vo., boards. 2s.

———————————— THE FALCON FAMILY; or, YOUNG IRE-
LAND. A Satirical Novel. By M. W. SAVAGE. Cheap Edition. Post 8vo., boards. 2s.

———————————— MY UNCLE THE CURATE.
By M. W. SAVAGE. Cheap Edition. Post 8vo., boards. 2s.

———————————— CLOVER COTTAGE; or, I CAN'T GET IN.
A Novelette. By the Author of 'The Falcon Family,' &c. With Illustrations. In
fcap. 8vo., cloth. 5s.

SHARPE'S ATLAS:

Comprising Fifty-four Maps, constructed upon a System of Scale and Proportion the most recent Authorities, and Engraved on Steel, by J. WILSON LOWRY. V a Copious Consulting Index. In a large folio volume. Half morocco, gilt back. edges, plain, 36s.; or with the maps coloured, 42s.

CONTENTS.

1. The World—Western Hemisphere.
2. The World—Eastern Hemisphere.
3. The World—Mercator's Projection.
4. Europe, with the Mediterranean.
5. Great Britain and Ireland.
6. England and Wales—Railway Map, North.
7. England and Wales—Railway Map, South.
8. Scotland.
9. Ireland.
10. France—Belgium—Switzerland.
11. Belgium and Holland.
12. Prussia, Holland, and German States.
13. Switzerland.
14. Austrian Empire.
15. Turkey and Greece.
16. Greece.
17. Italy.
18. Spain and Portugal.
19. Northern Sweden, and Frontier of Russia.
20. Denmark, Sweden, and Russia on the Baltic.
21. Western Russia, from the Baltic to the Euxine.
22. Russia on the Euxine.
23. Russia on the Caucasus,
24. Russia in Europe.
25. Northern Asia—Asiatic Russia.
26. South-West. Asia—Overland to India.
27. South-Eastern Asia — Birmah, China, and Japan.

28. Australia and New Zealand.
29. Egypt and Arabia Petræa.
30. Nubia and Abyssinia to Babel Mande Strait.
31. Asia Minor.
32. Syria and the Turkish Provinces on th Persian Gulf.
33. Western Persia.
34. Eastern Persia.
35. Affghanistan and the Punjab.
36. Beloochistan and Scinde.
37. Central India.
38. The Carnatic.
39. Bengal, &c.
40. India—General Map.
41. North Africa.
42. South Africa.
43. British North America.
44. Central America.
45. United States—General Map.
46. United States—North-East.
47. United States—South-East.
48. United States—South-West.
49. Jamaica, and Leeward and Windw Islands.
50. Mexico and Guatemala.
51. South America.
52. Columbian and Peruvian Republics, Western Brazil.
53. La Plata, Chili, and Southern Brazil.
54. Eastern Brazil.

The above Maps are sold Separately. Each Map, Plain, 4d.; Coloured, 6d.

SHARPE—STUDENT'S ATLAS.

With a Copious Index. 26 Coloured Maps, selected from the preceding. Folio, bound. 21s.

SLACK — THE PHILOSOPHY OF PROGRESS

HUMAN AFFAIRS. By HENRY JAMES SLACK, F.G.S., Barrister-at-Law. 8vo., cloth. 6s.

SMITH (ARTHUR)—THE THAMES ANGLER.

By ARTHUR SMITH. With Numerous Woodcuts. Second Edition. Small post 8v sewed. 1s.

———— (ALBERT)—WILD OATS AND DEAD LEAVE

By ALBERT SMITH. Second Edition. Crown 8vo, cloth. 5s.

——————————TO CHINA AND BACK:

BEING A DIARY KEPT OUT AND HOME. By ALBERT SMITH. 8vo. sewed. 1

MITH (REV. JAMES)—THE DIVINE DRAMA OF
HISTORY AND CIVILISATION. By the Rev. JAMES SMITH. 8vo., cloth. 12s.

(MRS.) — PRACTICAL AND ECONOMICAL
COOKERY, with a Series of Bills of Fare; also, Directions on Carving, Trussing, &c.
By Mrs. SMITH, many years professed Cook to most of the leading families in the
Metropolis. Post 8vo., cloth. 5s. 6d.

TIGANT—A VISION OF BARBAROSSA, AND OTHER
POEMS. By WILLIAM STIGANT. Fcap. 8vo., cloth. 7s.

AYLOR—PHILIP VAN ARTEVELDE. By HENRY
TAYLOR. Sixth edition. Fcap. 8vo. cloth. 3s. 6d.

EDWIN THE FAIR; ISAAC COMMENUS;
THE EVE OF THE CONQUEST, AND OTHER POEMS. By HENRY TAYLOR.
Third edition. Fcap. 8vo. cloth. 3s. 6d.

ALES OF THE TRAINS:
Being some CHAPTERS OF RAILROAD ROMANCE. By TILBURY TRAMP.
With Numerous Illustrations by 'PHIZ.' Fcap. boards. New Edition. 1s. 6d.

CKERAY—THE IRISH SKETCH-BOOK.
y M. A. TITMARSH. Third Edition, Uniform with Thackeray's 'Miscellaneous
ssays.' In crown 8vo., cloth, with Illustrations. 5s.

NOTES OF A JOURNEY FROM CORN-
HILL TO GRAND CAIRO, BY WAY OF LISBON, ATHENS, CONSTANTINOPLE,
AND JERUSALEM. By W. M. THACKERAY. With a Coloured Frontispiece.
Second Edition. Small 8vo., cloth. 6s.

CHRISTMAS BOOKS:
Containing 'MRS. PERKINS' BALL,' 'DR. BIRCH,' 'OUR STREET.' Cheap Edition.
In one square volume, cloth, with all the original Illustrations. 7s. 6d.

HURSTAN—THE PASSIONATE PILGRIM;
Or, EROS AND ANTEROS. By HENRY J. THURSTAN. Crown 8vo., cloth. 8s. 6d.

ILBURY NOGO;
Or, PASSAGES IN THE LIFE OF AN UNSUCCESSFUL MAN. By the Author of
'Digby Grand.' 2 vols. post 8vo., cloth. 21s. And New Edition, 1 vol. crown
8vo. 5s.

OWNSHEND — DESCRIPTIVE TOUR IN SCOT-
LAND. By CHAUNCY HARE TOWNSHEND. With twelve Illustrations. 8vo.
cloth. 9s.

SERMONS IN SONNETS:
WITH A TEXT ON THE NEW YEAR: and other Poems. By CHAUNCY HARE
TOWNSHEND. Small 8vo. cloth. 7s. 6d.

TOWNSHEND—THE THREE GATES.
IN VERSE. By CHAUNCY HARE TOWNSHEND. Second Edition, with additions and Portrait. Post 8vo. cloth. 10s. 6d.

TROLLOPE (ANTHONY)—THE MACDERMOTS OF
BALLYCLORAN. By ANTHONY TROLLOPE. New and Cheaper Edition. Crown 8vo. cloth. 5s.

——————————— **CASTLE RICHMOND.** A
Novel. By ANTHONY TROLLOPE. Three vols. post 8vo. cloth. 31s. 6d.
Also, A NEW AND CHEAPER EDITION. Crown 8vo. cloth. 5s.

——————————— **THE KELLYS AND THE**
O'KELLYS. By ANTHONY TROLLOPE. Fourth Edition. Post 8vo. cloth. 5s.

——————————— **THE WEST INDIES AND**
THE SPANISH MAIN. By ANTHONY TROLLOPE. Fourth Edition, with Map. Post 8vo. cloth. 9s.

——————————— **DOCTOR THORNE.**
A Novel. By ANTHONY TROLLOPE. Sixth Edition. Crown 8vo. cloth. 5s.

——————————— **THE BERTRAMS.**
A Novel. By ANTHONY TROLLOPE. Second Edition. 3 vols. post 8vo. cloth. 31s.
Also, Fifth Edition. Crown 8vo. cloth. 5s.

TROLLOPE (T. A.)—PAUL THE POPE AND PAUL
THE FRIAR. A STORY OF AN INTERDICT. By THOMAS ADOLPHUS TROLLOPE. With a Portrait. Post 8vo. cloth. 12s.

——————————— **FILIPPO STROZZI.** A Biography.
By THOMAS ADOLPHUS TROLLOPE. Post 8vo. cloth. 12s.

——————————— **THE GIRLHOOD OF CA**
RINE DE MEDICI. By T. ADOLPHUS TROLLOPE. In 1 vol. post 8vo. cloth. 10s.

——————————— **A DECADE OF ITALIAN**
WOMEN. By THOMAS ADOLPHUS TROLLOPE. With Portraits. 2 vols. post 8vo. cloth. 21s.

——————————— **TUSCANY** in 1849 and in 1859.
By THOMAS ADOLPHUS TROLLOPE. Post 8vo. cloth. 10s. 6d.

TROLLOPE (THEODOSIA) — SOCIAL ASPECTS OF
REVOLUTION, IN A SERIES OF LETTERS FROM FLORENCE. Reprinted from the 'Athenæum.' With a Sketch of Subsequent Events up to the Present Time. By THEODOSIA TROLLOPE. Post 8vo. cloth. 8s. 6d.

TWILIGHT THOUGHTS. By M. S. C.,
Author of 'Little Poems for Little People.' Second Edition, with a Frontispiece. Fcap. cloth. 1s. 6d.

TWINING — THE ELEMENTS OF PICTURESQUE
SCENERY; or, STUDIES OF NATURE MADE IN TRAVEL, with a View to Improvement in Landscape Painting. By HENRY TWINING. Vol. II. Imp. 8vo. cloth. 8s.

WALMSLEY — SKETCHES OF ALGERIA DURING
THE KABYLE WAR. By HUGH MULLENEUX WALMSLEY. Post 8vo. cloth. 10s. 6d.

WAYFARING SKETCHES AMONG THE GREEKS
AND TURKS, AND ON THE SHORES OF THE DANUBE. By a Seven Years' Resident in Greece. Second Edition. Post 8vo. cloth. 9s.

WHIST-PLAYER (THE).
THE LAWS AND PRACTICE OF SHORT WHIST. EXPLAINED AND ILLUSTRATED BY COLONEL BLYTH. With numerous Diagrams printed in Colours. Imp. 16mo. Second Edition. 5s.

WHITE — ALL ROUND THE WREKIN.
By WALTER WHITE. Second Edition, post 8vo. cloth. 9s.

———— NORTHUMBERLAND AND THE BORDER.
By WALTER WHITE. Second Edition. With a Map. Post 8vo. cloth. 10s. 6d.

———— A MONTH IN YORKSHIRE.
By WALTER WHITE. Fourth Edition. With a Map. Post 8vo. cloth. 4s.

———— A LONDONER'S WALK TO THE LAND'S
END, AND A TRIP TO THE SCILLY ISLES. Second Edition. Post 8vo. cloth. With four Maps. 4s.

———— A JULY HOLIDAY IN SAXONY, BOHE-
MIA, AND SILESIA. By WALTER WHITE. Post 8vo. cloth. 9s.

WHITE—ON FOOT THROUGH TYROL;
IN THE SUMMER OF 1855. By WALTER WHITE. Post 8vo. cloth. 9s.

WILKINSON — THE HUMAN BODY AND ITS CON-
NEXION WITH MAN. Illustrated by the principal Organs. By JAMES JOHN GARTH WILKINSON. Post 8vo. cloth. 5s.

—————————— THE REVIVAL IN ITS PHYSICAL,
PSYCHICAL, AND RELIGIOUS ASPECTS. By W. M. WILKINSON. Second Edition. Small 8vo. cloth. 3s. 6d.

WILLIAMS — HINTS ON THE CULTIVATION OF
BRITISH AND EXOTIC FERNS AND LYCOPODIUMS; with Descriptions of One Hundred and Fifty Species and Varieties. By BENJAMIN SAMUEL WILLIAMS. 8vo. cloth. 3s. 6d.

—————————— THE ORCHID-GROWER'S MANUAL;
Containing a Brief Description of upwards of Two Hundred and Sixty Orchidaceous Plants, together with Notices of their times of Flowering, and most approved Modes of Treatmen By BENJAMIN SAMUEL WILLIAMS. With a Coloured Frontispiece. 8vo. cloth. 5s

WILLS — OLD LEAVES GATHERED FROM 'HOUSE-
HOLD WORDS.' By W. HENRY WILLS. Post 8vo. cloth. 5s.

WORNUM — THE CHARACTERISTICS OF STYLES;
An Introduction to the Study of the History of Ornamental Art. By RALPH N. WORNUM. In royal 8vo. cloth, with very many Illustrations. Second Edition. 8s.

YONGE — THE LIFE OF FIELD-MARSHAL ARTHUR,
DUKE OF WELLINGTON. By CHARLES DUKE YONGE. With Portrait, Plans, and Maps. 2 vols. 8vo. cloth. 40s.

—————————— PARALLEL LIVES OF ANCIENT AND
MODERN HEROES, OF EPAMINONDAS, PHILIP OF MACEDON, GUSTAVUS ADOLPHUS, AND FREDERICK THE GREAT. By CHARLES DUKE YONGE, Author of 'A History of England,' &c. Small 8vo. cloth. 4s. 6d.

ZSCHOKKE — AUTOBIOGRAPHY OF HEINRICH
ZSCHOKKE. 8vo. cloth. 6s.

THE NATIONAL REVIEW.

PUBLISHED QUARTERLY.

Price 6s.

THE NATIONAL REVIEW, in defining its distinctive position, may dispense with the language of promise, and appeal to the results of the last six years.

It leaves to the Magazines the office, which they so well discharge, of furnishing intellectual amusement, and holding the mirror up to life, with only incidental and variable moral purpose.

It leaves to the other Quarterlies the office of representing some constituted party in Church or State; whose political or ecclesiastical creed forms their fixed centre of gravity, and determines the direction and latitude of their critique on literature, art, manners, and philosophy.

Warring with no interest, and identified with none, it is free to approach every problem from the scientific side, to treat it with conscientious thoroughness, and seek for it a judicial solution. To learn the policy of a party or the doctrines of a sect, the reader must look elsewhere; but if he cares for the principles which underlie the conflicts of the hour, if he is eager rather for the opening truth of the future than the watchwords of the past, he will meet, in the NATIONAL REVIEW, the sympathy of men who have nothing to prop up and nothing to destroy, but are resolved to carry every discussion to the ultimate test of reality and right.

The break-up of old feuds and factions has made room for a journal conducted in this spirit. In every stratum of educated English society liberal men abound who can welcome trustworthy reports of the newer aspects of religious and philosophic thought, and are glad to seek light on their political duties in the atmosphere rather of the closet than of the clubs. On the quiet strength of this growing class the REVIEW has relied through occasional storms of partisan displeasure. At the same time, it has never, by any cosmopolitan professions (which are but another form of party narrowness) contradicted its name of 'National.' In times of foreign conflict, the Reviewers have not construed the relations of international justice to the invariable disparagement of their own country. In the discussion of internal reform, they have protested against the imitation of alien democracies, and traced a method truly historical for the adequate expansion of political franchise. In demanding free development for the religious thought and life of England, they have never treated the existing creeds and churches as effete, or despaired of their enlargement to the spiritual exigencies of the nation. The notices, though numerous, of foreign literature and history, only serve to make clearer the general tone of hearty reverence for the distinctive bases of English character, life, and institutions.

Of the literary workmanship of the REVIEW, the Conductors are perhaps less at liberty to speak than of its spirit and principles. They may, however, be permitted, in evidence of its quality, to refer to the volumes already republished from its pages.

In one respect the NATIONAL REVIEW enters, with the year 1861, upon a new stage. The publishers, with the experience of several years to guide them, are taking a considerable stake in the publication. Their direct interest in it, however, will in no way affect the literary management, except by disembarrassing it of business cares, and obtaining for it, as they hope the encouragement of an ample and growing success.

BOOKS FOR THE  USE OF SCHOOLS,

ISSUED UNDER THE

AUTHORITY OF THE

SCIENCE AND ART

DEPARTMENT,

SOUTH

KENSINGTON.

THE CHARACTERISTICS OF STYLES. An Introduction
to the Study of the History of Ornamental Art. By RALPH N. WORNUM. Seco
Edition. In royal 8vo., with very many Illustrations. 8s.

BURCHETT'S LINEAR PERSPECTIVE. By R. BURCHETT
Fifth Edition. Post 8vo. With Illustrations. 7s.

BURCHETT'S DEFINITIONS OF GEOMETRY. 24mo
sewed. Third Edition. Price 5d.

BURCHETT'S PRACTICAL GEOMETRY. Fourth Editio
8vo. cloth. Price 5s.

DYCE'S ELEMENTARY OUTLINES OF ORNAMENT.
Selected Plates, small folio, sewed. Price 5s.

TEXT TO DYCE'S DRAWING ROOM. Fcap. 8vo. Price

REDGRAVE'S MANUAL AND CATECHISM ON COLO
Second Edition. 24mo. sewed. Price 9d.

REDGRAVE ON THE NECESSITY OF PRINCIPLES
TEACHING DESIGN. Fcap. sewed. Price 6d.

A DIAGRAM TO ILLUSTRATE THE HARMONIOUS RE
LATIONS OF COLOUR. Small folio. Price 9d.

PRINCIPLES OF DECORATIVE ART. Folio, sewed. Price 1s

LINDLEY'S SYMMETRY OF VEGETATION. 8vo. sew
Price 1s.

ROBINSON'S LECTURES ON THE MUSEUM. Fcap. sewed
Price 6d.

AN ALPHABET OF COLOUR. Reduced from the works
Field, Hay, Chevreuil. 4to. sewed. Price 3s.

DIRECTIONS FOR INTRODUCING ELEMENTAR
DRAWING IN SCHOOLS AND AMONG WORKMEN. Published at the request
the Society of Arts. Small 4to. cloth. Price 4s. 6d.

ILLUSTRATIONS TO BE EMPLOYED IN THE PRA
TICAL LESSONS ON BOTANY. Adapted to all classes. Prepared for the South K
sington Museum. By the REV. PROF. HENSLOW. With Illustrations. Post 8
Price 6d.

DRAWING FOR ELEMENTARY SCHOOLS: Being a Man
of the Method of Teaching Drawing, specially adapted for the Use of Masters of N
and Parochial Schools. By ELLIS A. DAVIDSON, Head Master of the Chester Schoo
of Art. Published under the sanction of the Science and Art Department of the Com
mittee of Council of Education. Post 8vo. cloth. 3s.

Lightning Source UK Ltd.
Milton Keynes UK
UKHW020039080119
335173UK00009B/1086/P